D1376126

Tashi Delek,

*To Diane — the most beautiful
Bush in the world.*

*For my parents, who have both given me
a lifetime of love and support.*

YOU ARE A BRAVE MAN

A KIWI ODYSSEY IN THE HIMALAYAS

Elizabeth Harding

RANDOM
HOUSE
NEW ZEALAND LTD

Random House New Zealand Ltd
(An imprint of the Random House Group)

18 Poland Road
Glenfield
Auckland 10
NEW ZEALAND

Sydney   New York   Toronto
London   Auckland   Johannesburg
and agencies throughout the world

First published 1996

© 1996 Elizabeth Harding
The moral rights of the author have been asserted.

Printed in New Zealand
ISBN 1 86941 302 4

CONTENTS

INTRODUCTION

Khunde Hospital is situated in the Nepal Himalayas at 3840 metres (12,595 feet), just off the main trekking routes to Everest Base Camp and Gokyo. The hospital was built in 1966 by Sir Edmund Hillary, and is funded mainly by the New Zealand Himalayan Trust and Canadian International Development Association. Over the 28 years it has been operating, doctors from New Zealand, Canada and the United States of America have volunteered to run it for a two-year posting.

The hospital is responsible for the 6000 Sherpas and Nepalis living in the Khumbu, and the 10,000 trekkers who visit the area each year. There is an airfield at Lukla, one day's walk away, and a twice-weekly helicopter service from Shyangboche, only 20 minutes' walk from the hospital. The nearest road is at Jiri, about five days' walk away.

The hospital is open from nine to five, six days a week. There is always a member of staff available for emergencies. Local patients are charged Rs 10 ($NZ0.40) for a consultation, and Rs 35 ($NZ1.40) as a flat rate for hospital admission. Foreigners pay Rs 1000 ($NZ40) plus medication costs for consultations, and considerably more for housecalls or admissions.

The acute/short-stay ward has three beds. There is also an eight-bed long-stay ward mainly used by patients with tuberculosis or frostbite, who often need to stay for a couple of months. As with other Nepali hospitals, the family also needs to stay to prepare meals and provide much of the patient's nursing care.

From 1993–95 the hospital was staffed by two New Zealanders, myself, a 34-year-old general practitioner, and Diane Bush, a 38-year-old nurse. Two Sherpa health workers, Kami Temba (aged 37) and Mingma Temba (aged 32), who have both worked there for 15 years, interpret for the doctors, can treat people in the clinic on their own, accompany the doctor to village clinics and house/tent calls, and prepare the meals. Neither have had formal medical training, but have excellent practical skills, and are fine clinicians.

The hospital employs a mail runner who spends his life catching the bus from the Trust office in Kathmandu to Jiri, walking up to Khunde, and then travelling back again, doing the round trip every 13 days. This ensures a reliable mail service for the hospital.

The hospital supervises six village health clinics, which are visited about every two months. The closest health clinic is in Phortse, two or three hours' walk away, and our furthest (visited far less frequently) is Bung, four long days' walk from the hospital. Each village health worker is selected from that village, having variable education and skills, and is trained for two weeks at the hospital before starting work. The clinics are open for two hours a day, six days a week, charge Rs 5 (NZ 20c), and provide a simple level of treatment, such as antibiotics for skin infections,

THE TWO VILLAGES OF KHUNDE AND KHUMJUNG.

or the contraceptive Depo Provera. The health workers refer more complicated cases on to the hospital.

Khunde is a small village with about 300 inhabitants, but is within one hour's walk of the main trekking town of Namche (700 inhabitants), and 20 minutes from Khumjung village (900 inhabitants). During the beginning of our stay, there was no electric power available in the village, but the hospital used solar power, generators, and kerosene heaters and stoves to make life comfortable.

The hospital has an X-ray machine, mostly used for chest X-rays to detect tuberculosis and for limb fractures. Until power was connected the computer ran off a generator. It is used for correspondence, accounts and record keeping. The small laboratory allows staff to look for acid-fast bacilli in tuberculosis, and do a few routine blood tests. There are equipment and facilities to perform, for example, an emergency Caesarean section.

However, most surgical interventions are on a much more minor scale.

From February 1993 to January 1994, staff saw 6250 outpatients, either at the hospital, at home or in the village health clinics. This equates to an average of 20 per working day. 25 per cent were under 18 years of age.

Of the 529 outpatients seen outside the hospital, 435 were seen at village health clinics, and 94 were house calls.

KHUNDE HOSPITAL OUTPATIENT SURGERY AND OPERATING THEATRE.

The most common problems seen were respiratory tract infections, falls and injuries, skin infections, gastroenteritis, gastritis/gastric ulcer, contraception, eye problems, especially bacterial and allergic conjunctivitis, and cataracts. Glasses are very popular.

A total of 100 patients were admitted to the hospital over the same year. Fifty-five per cent of admissions were adults (18 years and over), and 58 per cent were male.

Most common reasons for admission were: abdominal pathology, for example, gastric ulcer, gastro-enteritis, pancreatitis, hepatitis; frostbite; obstetric/deliveries; serious infections, for example, meningitis, pneumonia, typhoid; accidents, for example, fractures; and tuberculosis.

Operations are performed under ketamine (an LSD derivative that allows patients to keep breathing on their own while unconscious). Most operations are minor, involving reduction of fractures or debridement and/or amputation of frost-bitten fingers or toes.

In addition, a number of radial and hand fractures were reduced using a Bier (local) block. A symphisiotomy and Kielland forceps delivery was perfomed under local anaesthetic.

Foreigners comprise 3.4 per cent of total patient numbers. Most present with respiratory tract infections, gastro-intestinal infections and altitude-related symptoms.

The running of the hospital depends entirely on donations. Many trekking groups and expeditions will drop off their leftover medicines on their way home, which is of great benefit.

Some very generous donations of medical equipment have unfortunately been of little use to the hospital, and have had to be handed on to more sophisticated hospitals elsewhere in Nepal. If people wish to donate items, it is much more helpful to write first and ask what is needed:

Khunde Hospital,
C/- Himalayan Trust,
P.O. Box 224,
Kathmandu,
Nepal.
Fax: 9771 411 4750

The postal service is not always reliable. It is better to bring items of value personally to the Kathmandu office, or, even better, directly to the hospital.

Dr Elizabeth Harding
Khunde Doctor 1993–1995

ACKNOWLEDGEMENTS

Respect and gratitude to Kami and Mingma for their patient friendship and competence.

Thanks to the Himalayan Trust, and especially to Mike Gill, for giving us a go.

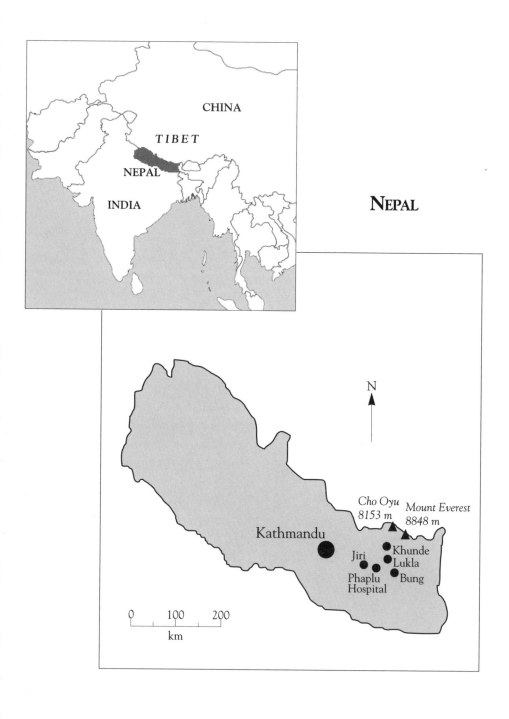

NEPAL

THE KHUMBU

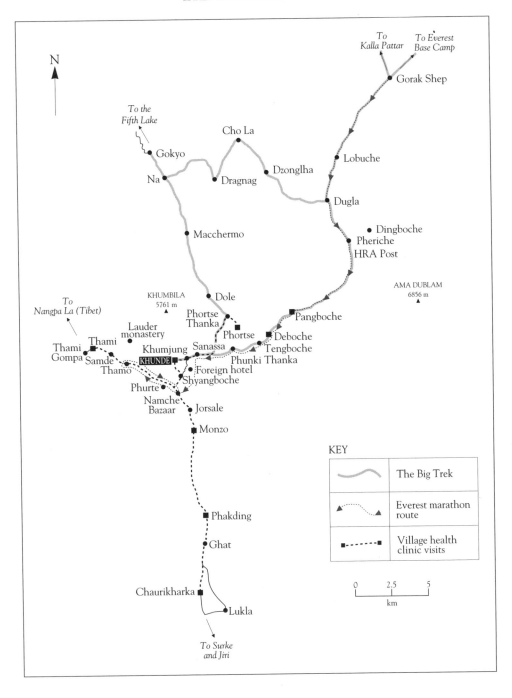

N

To
Kalla Pattar

To Everest
Base Camp

Gorak Shep

To the
Fifth Lake

Cho La

Lobuche

Gokyo

Dzonglha

Na

Dragnag

Dugla

Maccchermo

Dingboche

Pheriche
HRA Post

KHUMBILA
5761 m

AMA DUBLAM
6856 m

To
Nangpa La (Tibet)

Dole

Phortse
Thanka

Pangboche

Lauder
monastery

Phortse

Thami

Deboche

Thami
Gompa

Khumjung

Sanassa

Tengboche

Samde

KHUNDE

Phunki Thanka

Thamo

Foreign hotel

Phurte

Shyangboche

Namche
Bazaar

Jorsale

Monzo

KEY

Phakding

Ghat

Chaurikharka

Lukla

To Surke
and Jiri

| The Big Trek |
| Everest marathon route |
| Village health clinic visits |

0   2.5   5

km

THE TREK FROM JIRI TO KHUNDE

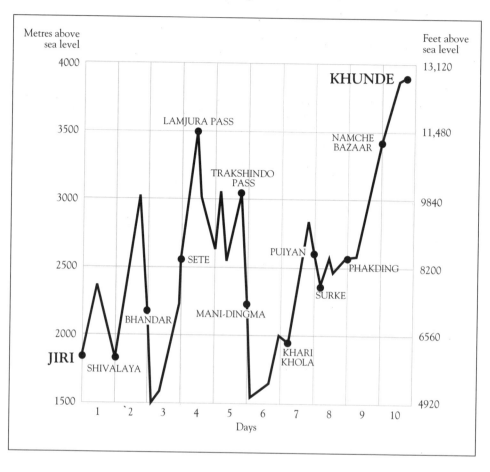

Altitudes

Local:
Khunde	3840 m
Khumjung	3790 m
Shyangboche	3720 m
Foreign hotel	3870 m

Pharak:
Namche	3441 m
Namche Bridge	2843 m
Jorsale	2774 m
Monzo	2835 m
Phakding	2652 m
Chaurikharka	2674 m
Lukla	2850 m

Base Camp Trail:
Sanassa	600 m
Tashinga	3480 m
Phunki Thanka	3250 m
Tengboche	3867 m
Deboche	3750 m
Pangboche	3985 m
Dingboche	4358 m
Pheriche	4272 m
Dugla	4595 m
Lobuche	4928 m
Gorak Shep	5184 m
Kalla Pattar	5549 m
Everest Base Camp	5357 m

Gokyo Valley:
Phortse Thanka	3420 m
Phortse	3840 m
Dole	4084 m
Macchermo	4410 m
Na	4400 m
Gokyo	4750 m
Gokyo Peak	5483 m
Dragnag	4690 m
Cho La	5420 m

Thami Valley:
Phurte	3475 m
Thamo	3444 m
Lauder Monastery	3850 m
Thami	3800 m
Thami Gompa	3980 m
Nangpa La	5716 m

Bung:
Surke	2293 m
Puiyan	2780 m
Pangkoma	2846 m
Pangkoma La	3173 m
Bung	1680 m

"Solo doctor post for two years working in Nepal. Beautiful views. Minimal pay."

The advertisement on one of the laboratory forms jumped out at me. I sat and gazed out the window for a while, dreaming of snowy peaks, saving lives, doing something really worthwhile; then I sighed and tossed it in the bin. Next week the same advertisement appeared. I looked a little longingly at it, then again threw it away. That afternoon, I discovered it uncrumpled and placed back on my desk with a note scribbled by my practice nurse, "This would be perfect for you, Liz." And I thought it would be too. I'd done my elective in the Solomon Islands about five years previously, and had loved it so much I hadn't wanted to come home.

In the tea room, some of the other practice nurses had also heard of the job, and encouraged me to apply for it. "What about Diane?" was my feeble excuse for inaction, but they wouldn't hear of it. "She's a nurse, why wouldn't she want to go with you. Ask her!" So I phoned her at work and said casually, "Oh, by the way, how would you like to live in Nepal for two years?" I was shocked by the instant reply of, "Sure, if you want." I really had to take it more seriously after that, and we talked it through that night. Next morning I rang up about the job, not expecting to get very far.

The contact was a pathologist, Mike Gill, who I'd heard of in connection with writing books about his mountaineering adventures. He was not available and had to call me back. Mike, of course, phoned when I had a room full of patients, but I could hardly ask them to leave, so I just talked to him, eagerly listened to by the whole family.

Once we'd established a few details about the job and my qualifications, he asked, "Are you married?"

"Um, sort of."

"Oh, so you're living with someone. We don't mind that. We insist on a couple. We've sent single people before, but they get too lonely and it's too hard for them. So, what does your boyfriend do?"

Now, I thought, Be brave, you want this job, so just go for it.

"Well-actually-my-partner-is-a-woman-but-I-guess-that-wouldn't-really-matter-would-it-and-she's-a-nurse," I gabbled out rapidly, going bright red.

My family of patients all looked a little stunned, but no one ran screaming from the room.

There was a brief pause at the end of the phone — a very long 10 seconds, as I waited for the polite brush-off, or even the click of a hang-up. What followed was a slightly strained, "No, I don't think that would matter. It might work out quite well to have two women working there."

I felt a mixture of relief and trepidation as we organised to meet and discuss things further. What had I got us into?

The meeting with Mike and his wife went well, and soon we were off to have drinks with Sir Edmund Hillary and his wife, June. Ed (as we were told to call him) had always been a childhood hero of mine, and I remember the excitement of shaking his hand and feeling that even if we didn't get the job at least we'd met the man in person. Diane was so overcome when she met him that her practised "How do you do, Sir Ed" dissolved into an odd croaking sound, and she seemed to be quite incapable of speech for the next few minutes.

June managed to carry the conversation while we sorted ourselves out, and they made things as easy as possible for us. Ed was not much of a conversationalist, and the only thing we remember him saying was "Now who's the bossy one?", meaning which of us was the nurse. June irritated us slightly by telling us "what lucky girls" we were to be considered for the job, but, as patronising as that sounded, it probably wasn't far off the mark.

The interview process continued, with us staying the weekend with other members of the selection committee. This was followed by two, more formal interviews with a panel of about eight people, each lasting several hours. It included us separately "having a good chat with this nice lady we'd like you to meet" about how Diane and I met and how we got on together. It was only later that we were told that she was a psychologist from Volunteer Services Abroad, assessing our stability as individuals and as a couple! Fortunately we got on very well, and she commented that if we didn't get the job here she was sure that VSA would be delighted to take us on.

The interviews were hard-going at times, and seemed to focus very much on our relationship. Many questions very sensibly tried to determine its stability. "What sort of things do you fight about?" "What do you mean you don't fight? Do you think that's quite healthy?" "Who makes the final decision if you buy something or not?"

At times we felt that their enquiries went too far, and that we were just objects of curiosity. One woman seemed obsessed with the fact that we might buy a double sleeping bag (something we didn't even know existed). She had many questions about our personal living set-up, and when Di, in exasperation, explained that we were just as much a couple as she and her husband were, and that if we could have the privilege of getting married we would, she anxiously debated whether we should wear back aprons with our ingis. (Usually married Sherpa women wear a warm apron around the back of their traditional dresses, as well as the front.)

One of the other doctors voiced the hope that we wouldn't be having friends visit us, because they didn't want a whole lot of funny-looking people around the hospital. Fortunately, all I could do was grin and think of the unlikely scenario of our friends Stuart and Keith bouncing down the hill towards the hospital, hand in hand, dressed in pink tutus and high heels, shrieking, "Here we are, darlings!" Di very coolly replied that most of our friends were very like us, and none of them were "funny looking". It wasn't until later that it dawned on me that this really was a very ignorant and insulting comment.

KHUNDE VILLAGE

In many ways it was refreshing to verbalise our feelings and philosophies. We learnt a lot about each other. We were also aware that we were talking to a rather conservative group of people, who very possibly didn't know any lesbian or gay people, and some obviously believed many of the sensationalised media stereotypes that exist about our very diverse culture. We had recently been in Auckland's first "coming out" parade, line dancing in cowboy gear on the back of a truck. The parade was an exciting, fun time, with floats representing the gay and lesbian churches, parents and family supporters, choir, and running, swimming and ten-pin bowling groups, as well as the night-clubs and other more flamboyant exhibits. Although many thousands of people turned up to watch and support the parade, the local papers printed almost nothing about it, and television news showed about 30 seconds of a posturing outrageous drag queen and bare-breasted women on stilts. It is not surprising that the average person has such an unusual idea of how we live.

We tried to be understanding of their misconceptions and felt that, even if we didn't get the job, it was an opportunity to give them some realistic insight into our often misunderstood lifestyle. It in some ways became a matter of gay pride. Anyway, we wanted the job and were prepared to put up with a lot.

By the end of the interview process we were well sick of the whole thing. We were tired of having to justify our very existence and felt quite harangued. The other short-listed couple were to be interviewed that afternoon, and we would be phoned that night with the committee's decision. As far as we knew, that was the other couple's only interview compared to the two months of grilling we'd received. We'd heard that the other doctor was a keen climber, and was friends with someone on the selection committee. Our friends assured us that the straight couple would undoubtedly win.

By the time the phone call arrived, we'd already rationalised the whole situation and thought of all the reasons why we didn't want their stupid job after all. The doctor who we felt had particularly disliked us made the call. I heard his voice and my heart sank.

"Well, Liz, I've just rung to congratulate you and Diane on your successful selection as the new Khunde doctors."

"Oh, OK, thanks for ringing, bye now." It wasn't until I'd hung up that I realised that we'd made it and got the job.

We spent the rest of the night yahooing and ringing our friends to tell them it was all going to happen.

The doctor who rang us was understandably quite confused. In the end he got Mike to phone the next morning to check that we still wanted the job. We were out bragging, but he worked it out when he listened to our answer-phone message.

"Yeehaa lil' dawgies. Weez a goin' to Neeepawl. Don't you go makin' any big plans for the next couple of years, coz we ain't gonna be here. YEEE-HAAA!"

We arrived in Kathmandu and were greeted by the rather stern Trust administrator. Two of her servants piled our luggage on to the back of a minivan, while we were driven to the flat. It was a festival day, and the place looked as if it had gone mad. The streets were full of eager young Nepali men covered in and throwing red and yellow dye at each other. We were excited by all the activity, but our companion frowned on such frivolity and warned us not to leave the Trust compound since it was not safe. She wouldn't explain where the danger lay.

We moved into the austere flat and sat bored and frustrated that we couldn't have a look around the place. Our bedroom has two single beds and adjoins the main Trust office. Servants and Trust workers walk around the flat all day, wandering into our room at odd times.

It is strange having servants. I still can't really bring myself to call them that and feel more comfortable with "staff". The cook is a pleasant, ex-army guy who cheerfully smokes all day, dropping his ash into the dreadful limited concoctions that he produces. He makes our beds each morning, washes and irons our clothes, makes us cups of tea and basically will do anything we want him to. He likes us very much because we go out a lot for our meals. Despite this he is extremely eager to please, and we have to be careful not to show any unintentional displeasure, or he will fall about himself trying to make it right.

We are trying to make friends with some of our neighbours. The gateman lives in a small room at the entrance to the compound with his wife, two children and their dog. They seem to spend most of their time sitting and glaring at us.

There is a boy, I guess about 10 years old, who is staying with his mother in a shed out the back of the Trust flat. He lives about 10 days' walk from Kathmandu and was working in the family fields when caught in a landslide. He fell from a great height suffering a nasty multiple compound fracture of his right leg. His father decided that his leg would never be any good and left him to die. His mother, however, was furious at her husband, disobeyed him and organised other family members to pick the boy up and carry him to the nearby hospital. It was monsoon, so the five-day walk involved fighting through muddy, slippery tracks. The Sherpa doctor at Phaplu (another Trust hospital) could not do much more than splint the leg and prevent infection. He organised for the Trust to pay for the boy to be flown to Kathmandu, but due to bad weather the boy was unable to get down here for two months. He has required a number of operations to try to repair his leg. It is a lot shorter than the other one and quite painful, and he is waiting in Kathmandu until he is well enough to walk back to his village. Neither he nor his mother speak any English, and they are very shy. However, Diane already has them sitting on our front porch, and has taught the boy to play solitaire. He is very good — better than me.

The first morning, I got up at sunrise and went for a walk to explore the area. I was a bit frightened, since already the streets were filling up, and people looked so different and austere. We were staying in Dilli Bazar, a local people's area, quite a distance from the tourist spots, and many people stared at me. At first I tried smiling back, but they seemed to stare more sternly, so I just got on with walking about. I was amazed by the exotic beauty of the city. The old-style buildings and cobble-brick pavements were so unlike anything I had seen before. As I turned the corner on to the main street I gasped with delight to see an incredible large orange ball, which seemed to fill the horizon. The sunrise was magnificent. I wanted to stop people and shake them to make them enjoy the sight. Everyone just pushed past me and continued on to their destination. People looked so different. It was as if I was on a busy movie set, with everyone costumed, carrying odd and heavy loads, with the perfect backdrop.

I had promised Diane that I would only walk to the corner, since she too had some concern about either of us venturing too far, but I couldn't stop myself. All about me were new and exciting things. Meat shops opened, and the shop owners would casually carry out lumps of meat and then stick the beast's head up on a hook, as we would an advertising poster. I was shocked to almost trip over a couple of children, who looked about six, huddled up together in a sack, having obviously slept the night there.

Rubbish was piled high at each street corner, and I watched in sick fascination as children appeared and sifted through the debris for something to eat. One family was huddled around some cardboard they had found and set alight to keep warm. Cows roamed freely through the traffic and people, feeding on the street debris, even chomping away at the cardboard boxes.

People began setting out offerings and blessings on the pavement and starting their morning prayers. I got caught behind a group walking through a temple. Each person would stop and ring the bell, say a short prayer, dab red powder on the forehead, ring another bell and then move on. I was very embarrassed to be caught up in this, but it seemed rude to push past and interrupt them. No one seemed to care, and appeared to ignore me with contempt. Obviously another ignorant foreigner.

I turned into another street and, to my enormous excitement, saw a great temple floating in the middle of a large area of water. The orange sun was set behind it, and I was overcome with my good fortune to be able to see the Ganges that I'd heard so much about. This was really something. I'd seen the Grand Canyon a few years ago, and now here was another wonder of the world. I'd heard that the Hindu people place their loved ones' bodies into the Ganges, and I waited a long time in anticipation, waiting to see a dead body float by. None were to be seen, but I delighted in the grandeur of the beautiful palace and imagined this great river starting way up in the Himalayas (probably at Mount Everest) and moving on down through to India. And here I was standing on its banks. It was a truly significant moment for me.

An hour had passed and I felt I'd better hurry back to the flat, where Diane would be worried about me. I passed the same two children, who had now woken up and were burning the sack, holding their hands over it to keep warm. Where would they sleep tonight? How would they keep warm? Yes, this was what I'd done medicine for. Here I was in this amazing, exotic city with such need, and I could do my bit to save the world.

I arrived back at the flat full of excitement, raving about what I'd seen and the wonder of it all. Diane wasn't sure, but she didn't think that the Ganges went through Kathmandu. We found a map and worked out that I'd been looking at the local reservoir. I think I prefer the romanticism of ignorance!

It's spring, coming on for summer, here in Kathmandu, but it still gets quite cold at times, ranging from 1°C to 24°C in one day. Just now we have hit

A VIEW OF
KATHMANDU. a very cold rainy spell and are living in Polartek jackets and hats. It doesn't bode well for going up into the mountains, but I guess if we dress like Michelin men we'll eventually adjust. They told us it would be hot in Kathmandu! Despite the occasional coldness, we are settling well into life here.

There is a water and power shortage in Kathmandu. We try to conserve water by having infrequent showers and only flushing the loo when necessary. The power goes off every second evening.

We are being kept busy, in fact too busy, with five hours of Nepali lessons a day, two hours of computer lessons at night, and quite a number of hospital and clinic visits.

Our Nepali lessons are going well, although it's interesting how the struggle to learn shakes off the cobwebs from long-forgotten languages stored in the back-blocks of my brain. When I am really stuck for words I tend to come out with some combination of pidgin English, Roviana (from the Solomon Islands), schoolgirl Latin and Franglaise-Nepali; this certainly baffles our tutor, not trained in this newspeak. We've only been at it for two weeks, but we manage to go shopping, get places by taxi, order food, and have rather inane conversations with the staff and neighbours. The problem is that I'll sit down and work out my question in Nepali, then ask it. People are so inconsiderate as to answer me in very rapid Nepali, which I can't compute quickly enough and have to go away and think about. It's a bit of a conversation killer really.

There appear to be no Nepali words for "please", "sorry" and "thankyou". "Excuse me" is used rarely. Our cook giggles about the place saying, "You foreigners, always, please, please thankyou, thankyou, I'm sorry, I'm sorry . . . what for you say this all the time?" We find it very hard to get used to people not using these terms. When walking through crowds we can't help but bump into others, and they just walk on. If we say "excuse me" in Nepali, they just look at us strangely. I have given a few of our neighbours portrait photos that I've taken. They just grab them, with no "thankyou", nor any sign that they've even liked the gift, yet we see them race off and excitedly show their friends. Apparently they are not being rude, it's just the way it is here. But it'll sure take some getting used to.

This week we have also been learning to insert and remove Norplant. This is a contraceptive device consisting of six silastic capsules, which are placed under the skin and prevent pregnancy for five years. It can be removed any time, and fertility resumes immediately. At first I was very wary of it. I'd never heard of the device, and it is primarily used in Third World countries and in prisons and mental institutions in the West. However, it does seem to have a number of advantages for use in the Himalayas.

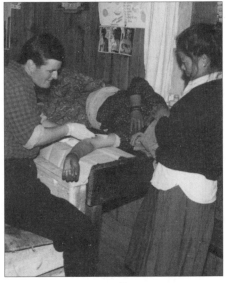

INSERTING A NORPLANT.

The government insists that all doctors who insert Norplant be officially trained and duly certificated. The Trust had written to the official Norplant trainers months ago, but when we checked it out, we found they'd filled their next two training courses without us. This caused some concern, since we are due to leave for Khunde in six weeks and will not be able to provide Norplant without the certificate. Our administrator was not surprised, saying that "most Nepalis don't think ahead, and tend to wait until the actual time, and then they don't do anything anyway". We were rather shocked when she suggested that we offer a fee (i.e., bribe) to get us into the free course. We went to see the doctor, "offering" in hand. He had no spaces free, but when he heard our situation, said he would immediately start training just for us. He would not consider a fee at all. He said that the government pays him a salary and that is enough. The Trust staff say he is a very good man and we are lucky to find him.

The government has ruled that hospital doctors must be 100 per cent public, or leave. They pay a very small salary, so almost all of the good or ambitious doctors have left the public system and set up in private. Most doctors working in the public system are those whose training is so poor (such as having been trained locally and unemployable anywhere else) that they are stuck there.

Our Norplant tutor appeared to be one of the few well-trained and dedicated doctors committed to providing public health care to the poor. He did as much as he could with the funding and equipment available. Surgical hygiene is a bit lacking when we insert the Norplant devices. Occasionally a mask is worn, if available. There are no gowns. The gloves are difficult to put on. They have obviously been washed and resterilised many, many times over. We poured talcum powder into them to help get them on to our hands. The needles and scalpels were all sterile but very blunt from overuse. I had to push very hard to get them through the skin. One day we had to postpone theatre for about half an hour because they had run out of soap and we couldn't scrub up. The patients seem to be very stoical, probably having had a much harder life than any New Zealander I know of. Three-quarters of the women who attend the Norplant Clinic have had no formal education at all.

Going to the doctor is very expensive, beyond a lot of people's means. In a country where the average annual income is $NZ350, the doctor charges $NZ3 every visit. Medicines are not subsidised. They are produced very cheaply locally, but in relative terms are still costly. Most people just go straight to the chemist, and can buy some horrifyingly toxic and also some useless medications, with probably little understanding of appropriate doses.

When we heard that we would be trekking for about two weeks up to the hospital, I imagined one of us falling down a bank and being left with a fractured limb for several days before rescue. I thought it might be helpful to have some injectable morphine for pain relief. I went to the local chemist to ask how I would go about getting hold of some, and even before I could tell him I was a doctor and show him proof of that, he just handed over several ampoules, for only a few rupees!

If you need to go to a public hospital, the cheapest bed, in a six-bed dormitory, is $NZ40 per week. Private rooms are available for $NZ140 per week. Any operation or procedure is more on top of that. For example, a cholecystectomy (gallbladder removal) costs the patient about $NZ48. Similarly, all medications, syringes and dressings involve an extra charge. Food can be bought from the hospital if your family chooses not to feed you, but they are responsible for all nursing care beyond giving out medicines, checking drips and taking vital signs. No family, no money — no treatment. The Nepalis say that "if you have money, you have life". Certainly if you are poor and get sick, no one will help you.

Our welfare system in New Zealand is certainly problematic and at times abused, but there is amazing security in knowing that if we get acutely unwell the government will provide health care for us. However, sometimes it seems as if New Zealand's health and education systems are moving towards the Nepali way, where the rich stay rich and healthy and the poor just struggle on without many breaks in life. We told our staff that in our country if you can't find a job, the government pays you a little money just to live. They just laughed and didn't believe us. "No one would work then," they would say.

It has been quite an eye-opener seeing the very simple conditions that exist in the hospitals. Unfortunately, our helper tends to get us all organised for our various hospital visits, only to find that he hasn't bothered to make an appointment with important and often very busy people. We find that we are just "dropping in", which is embarrassing and sometimes quite unsatisfactory. Often tours are given by "unimportant" people who know very little about what goes on. In some places basic needs were not even met. People lay in pain on soiled sheets or bare mattresses. Fly-covered containers of faeces or urine sat under or near the bed, waiting for some relative to empty them. At the other extreme, we saw enormous wastage. The main laboratory was filled with expensive equipment for measuring things like cholesterol ratios (hardly a priority I would have thought). The pathologist who showed us around casually pointed to most of the machines and said that such and such organisation had donated this, but it had broken down and no one knew how to fix it, or they didn't know how it worked so it had never been used.

Indeed, every doctor I come across seems to be a specialist. When I've been able to check their qualifications, they usually have a medical degree from somewhere in India (the gold standard around here) and a three-to six-month diploma, obtained preferably in the UK or America, in their specialty.

If I get seriously ill, please fly me out of the country to a Western hospital. Whatever happens, don't ever put me in a public hospital here.

There are many beautiful things about Kathmandu with its old architecture, temples and shrines. However, the pollution and traffic problems are incredible. I remember studying air and noise pollution at school and not thinking too much about it, but it's an entirely different thing to live amongst it.

There are very few road rules here — just keep to the left, stop at a traffic light (if a policeman is on duty there) and give way to anything bigger than you. Cycles can go up the wrong way on one-way streets. Pedestrian crossings are just driven through. The only advantage to the pedestrian is that people tend to congregate at a crossing and there is possibly safety in numbers. I try to walk in the middle of a group, so that if we are hit, the other bodies may cushion the impact. Cows are sacred, and wander happily and in complete safety through the busy streets.

Cars are registered, but have no warrant-of-fitness testing. Most of the three-wheeled motorbike taxis are really clapped out and billow black fumes. After a run, even as early as 6 am, I return with streaming eyes and an unpleasant cough bringing up black gunge. Some way to get fit. Di and I have succumbed to logic and now wear facemasks when we go out. We look forward to the clean air in Khunde.

And its peace and quiet. The noise level is constant and very stressful. People honk their horns frequently, some apparently constantly, as they weave in and out. No one, including pedestrians, seems to take any notice — except when the trucks blast their horns, then everyone scatters. We've become very good at identifying the type of vehicle coming from behind by the sound of its horn.

The Trust hired a pair of pushbikes for us to get around on. Diane amazes me by her fatalistic attitude to it all. She just puts her head down and goes for it. I spend most of my time in blind terror, expecting that every honk implies that I am doing something wrong, or am about to end my life under the front wheels of a passing truck. I get off at every intersection and fight my way through with the pedestrians, while Di sails on through and then has to wait patiently for me, laughing at my caution. To have a mountain bike is really something, and whenever we go out on them we hear admiring comments of "Americani" and "mountain bike" as we ride by.

My preferred mode of transport is on the back of the Trust's green mini ute. The staff insist that the memsahib be comfortable, and seat me on an armchair facing backwards. It is actually very comfortable. Once you get over the pointing fingers and laughter (including, I must mention, considerable delight from Diane, who gets the inside passenger seat) it is a marvellous way to sightsee. Sometimes I do wonder whether the staff are having their own little joke with me, but they assure me that this is how the BaaDasahib (big boss, Ed Hillary) travels himself when he comes to Kathmandu.

Diane is pretty hot stuff over here. The Nepali men find her larger build and long fair hair very appealing. I only have to leave her for a minute and she is surrounded by admiring young men. I reckon we could have her married off in a flash. She enjoys this attention considerably less than I do, and I must admit to chortling away from a distance. Of course I can't blame them. With my short hair, or whatever it is, none of the men seem the slightest bit interested in me.

The Trust gives us an allowance each week for our personal use. It seems ironic that for the past two or three years we've been trying so hard to be careful with our money, then we come to do voluntary work in one of the poorest countries in the world and we are expected to go out for dinner every night. Meals are inexpensive, and it is easier for the staff not to have to stay around to look after us in the evening. With the power cuts, meal preparation is also a problem.

The city looks even more exotic with the shops and restaurants lit by candles and fires. We are given soft drinks and catch taxis when we feel like it. Generally we are doing a lot of things we've been denying ourselves for years. Still, we'll make the most of it. Things won't be as luxurious at Khunde. A good meal for the two of us costs $NZ12 — two weeks' income for the average Nepali family. Everything is relative.

Diane and I walked to the centre of the city last Friday. It was lunchtime and we came across hundreds and hundreds of Muslims all bowed down praying to Mecca. They were lined up along roof-tops and in any free space they could find. Even the Hindu Nepalis, who seem to ignore most things and get on with their own business, stopped to watch this rather impressive sight.

The Pakistanis don't work on Fridays. Saturday is the main

A DEMONSTRATION BY COMMUNISTS IN KATHMANDU.

holiday for Nepalis, and Sunday is just a normal working day. We don't have Nepali or computer lessons on a Sunday, so it's a day off for us.

Our first day off, and unfortunately we were advised not to go out at all. So frustrating. We wanted to see more of Kathmandu than just early morning and night time. The Communists have made it a protest day against the government, and have asked all Nepalis to strike. The staff say that probably no one will open their shops, not especially because they support the Communists, but because they will be too scared to. Last time there was a Communist strike, people who did not comply had stones thrown at them and their shops wrecked. Seven people were killed during the protest.

We stayed in most of the morning watching the protesters marching past our compound. It didn't seem too dangerous, and we were seriously bored, so we decided to just wander down to the corner. There were lots

of policemen and soldiers with guns, but they all looked pretty relaxed. They smiled and waved at us and even posed for our photos, so we just wandered on. After half an hour we arrived at the main tourist centre. I usually hate the commercialism of this area with its persistent touters and beggars, but that day it was pleasant and quiet. We found a restaurant that was open and enjoyed a leisurely afternoon tea. We chatted to the waiter who suddenly got very excited and

SOLDIERS WAITING FOR SOMETHING TO HAPPEN DURING DEMONSTRATIONS.

warned us that our flat was in one of the most politically active and dangerous areas and we must not go back there. We experienced some trepidation walking back, but things seemed fine. We wandered past the central park and stopped to listen to a political rally. A politician ranted in Nepali on the main podium, but generally the crowd seemed subdued and peaceful. By the time we were near our flat it was early evening and we could feel a bit more tension in the air. Someone had set fire to a tyre in the middle of the intersection, and was rolling it through the traffic. The soldiers and policemen were looking grim and holding their guns at the ready. We could hear chanting coming from the direction of the rally and decided that we might settle back into the flat for the night.

We found out later that there had been an argument at one of the boys' colleges. Democracy versus Communism. One boy had died of head injuries. Since then there's been a lot of fuss about the upcoming student elections, with Communist and Democratic banners and flags all over the place. Last night Di decided she would like to have one of the flags. So she went up to a group of students at the college and asked for one. I felt that this was fool-hardy and stood away in the background, imagining at best a negative response, and at worst a bloody, violent battle. Very soon Di was surrounded by eager excited young men all trying to get their point of view across. They were extremely eager to give her their flags. When she was given the Communist one, the Democratic representative raced off to give her one of his. They were all very friendly and enthusiastic.

Walking home, about a quarter of a mile away, two very intense young men caught up with us wanting to know why we wanted the flags, and particularly why both. One, with the ardent madness of a devotee, wanted to know which side we agreed with and would not accept that both had merits. It was a little unnerving, since neither would tell us which side they were on. Di excelled in diplomacy, and finally said, "You know we come from a democratic country," to which they both beamed from ear to ear and wrung our hands enthusiastically. They told us that there was going to be a big fight at the college between the Communists and the Democrats. When we said, "Don't you mean talking?" he said, "No, fighting," showing us his fists. He then said that this was going to happen all over the country and would bring Nepal to a standstill. So I guess there's going to be a bit more trouble.

3

We've spent almost seven weeks in Kathmandu, which is certainly enough. We have visited some interesting places, met some good people (and some not so good), can speak reasonable halting Nepali, and can find our way around our 286 computer. So it's been a productive time, but feels very much a transition, and we look forward to settling somewhere for a while where we can put up our posters and photos and call it home. There is no radio or cassette player at the flat, so line dancing is a bit limited, and we really must extend our card-playing repertoire beyond "500" and "Last Card". Most of our gear, including our books, was flown up to Khunde about a month ago, when Ed Hillary and crowd went up by helicopter, so the highlight of the evening tends to be reading through the latest *British Medical Journal*. It has, in fact, some very good articles and makes for excellent reading, but wouldn't be my first choice of leisure activity and is rather indicative of the quiet — well, actually, boring — time we are having.

Our Nepali is coming along well and we can understand and talk to the staff here, who are very patient and speak slowly, clearly and simply to us, with a good deal of body language. It's entirely a different matter when they speak at a normal pace to each other, but I guess it'll come with practise. I have been trying to learn Sanskrit, the written Nepali language. It's frustratingly slow picking out the individual words in newspapers, signs or graffiti only to find that I have no idea what those words mean in English. Still, my vocabulary is expanding each day. Di also finds my Sanskrit practice frustrating, as she says I suddenly focus on a sign in the street, stop dead in my tracks, and visibly mouth each letter with a puzzled expression on my face, then shake my head and wander on, oblivious to the rest of the world, including those who have bumped into her behind me.

Getting our unaccompanied luggage turned out to be a real hassle. It took 25 days of red tape, letters to be written, taken and signed by the British Embassy, the Ministry of Foreign Affairs, and the New Zealand Consulate, plus payments for storage and to customs (I think that's called a bribe). We then spent two-and-a-half hours showing passports and signing forms in Sanskrit that I didn't understand, each accompanied by a "back-pocket fee", before we could finally pick up the bags once everything had been given the final OK. Then our bags were all opened in front of everyone, and quite a crowd collected to see what we had brought over. We thought it was a nightmare. The Trust worker said he was impressed that everything had gone so smoothly, and that it was unusual to get all of your bags in the same lot!

There have been some social highlights to break some of the monotony.

We were invited to a cocktail party to welcome the new New Zealand High Commissioner for India and Nepal. This was a bit of a surprise, and unfortunately we'd been told not to bring any good clothes to Kathmandu. We had spent our whole time there very casually dressed and had found many of the ex-patriot people we'd met a bit snooty, leaving us feeling very left out. I was not looking forward to it, and even considered feigning a stomach bug as Di and I mixed and matched our least-tatty clothes into some kind of respectable ensemble. We decided that if I sat with my feet under the chair, people might not notice our only clean pair of shoes — those I had borrowed from Di — her orange, red and white runners that she planned to use on the trek. These clashed less with Di's brightly coloured pink-and-black shirt and my black trousers, which I was wearing. Di wore our cleanest, least-stained polo shirt, my black-and-white Velcro trousers, and her very smart line-dancing cowboy shoes.

We arrived in our tempo (a three-wheeled motorbike taxi), amongst chauffeur-driven diplomatic vehicles, and walked in, heads held high, to a room filled with smartly tailored suits and best cocktail dresses, half expecting to be dragged out a side door by one of the staff.

We lined up to be greeted by the New Zealand ambassador and his wife, but before we could be formally introduced the ambassador's wife burst out with, "Ah, at last, some New Zealanders!" with a delighted beam on her face. I guess responding to our typical New Zealand costume?

Anyway, that certainly broke the tension for us. We found them very likeable and down to earth. We met quite a few other New Zealanders, Australians and Brits and had a great time, realising how much we'd missed just talking and laughing with people of our own age and culture.

It was a good night, topped off with a very late night rickshaw ride through the silent streets of Kathmandu. The compound security gates had been locked, and we were caught climbing over them when the gateman ran out in his shorty pyjamas. Half-sozzled and giggly, we thought we might be in for some trouble, but he just seemed most perturbed that we hadn't shouted out to wake him up to let us in. After all, that was his job. Since then, he and his family have been smiling and friendly to us.

Ed, June and Zeke O'Connor (President of the Sir Edmund Hillary Foundation of Canada and ex-football player in the Canadian League) arrived last week. We were invited at the last minute to join them upstairs for dinner and, although we both felt seedy with a stomach bug, thought we'd better make the effort. A number of journalists and film crew travelling with the party were also there. The whole evening seemed to be made up of enormous egos bouncing off each other, all trying desperately to impress Ed. On a couple of occasions I was left in mid-sentence, as attention was immediately turned to Ed if he so much as took a breath or looked as if he was about to speak. After a while I just shut up and felt uncomfortably like yet another hanger-on. Ed, in contrast, was easy company, and is to be much admired for retaining his simpleness and not letting his fame go to his head. He seems like a good average Kiwi bloke who's had some real adventures and done good things to help people but can't quite see what all the fuss is about.

The next evening was the Sherpa celebration of Ed's 40th anniversary of climbing Mount Everest. We were asked at the last minute. This did not surprise us. The Sherpa organiser had been very busy organising things for the BaDaasahib and we had been very much forgotten. At his best he made it obvious that we were pretty unimportant, and had left us to organise most things on our own. We came to realise that Sherpas and Nepalis certainly ooze charm when you are seen as important, but waste no effort on diplomacy if deemed not.

Diane was still too unwell to come, but I was so desperately bored and lonely I thought I'd give the party a go. We all went together and were told that Ed would be up on the stage with Lord John Hunt, and we would all be seated at a front table, where we would be served dinner. The rest of the people would have a buffet-style meal.

I wandered up with Ed, June and others in the party and we were bombarded with flashbulbs, about 10 television cameras and 50 photographers, who blasted away at Ed. It was all a bit overwhelming, and I dropped back into the crowd. I don't know how Ed can stand it.

June called me up to the table with them and said we should all look for our named places. It was quite embarrassing to have to walk around the whole area in front of a large seated crowd and cameras, to find that I was the only one in the group with no name place. Oh yes, the now-hated Sherpa organiser had decided that "we girls could just find a seat with the ordinary people", and had removed our names from the front table.

Since everyone had seated themselves early before the BaDaasahib arrived, there were only seats way at the back of the hall. I sat there for a while, too far back to see any of the Sherpa dancing, muttering away to myself, "Why are all the ancillary film crew sitting at the front table and not me. If I'd known I'd be sitting on my own, I wouldn't have come to their damned stupid do anyway . . ." The front nine rows were reserved for press, and were mostly free since they were all up the front using up film after film, so I thought, "Damn this for a joke, I'm not staying here." I pulled out my camera and confidently strutted up to the front row, flashing off a photo every few minutes. I glared at the Sherpa organiser, as if to say, "Just come and try to move me. Make my day, boy!"

From then on the evening improved a bit. I introduced myself to the man sitting next to me, who was very pleasant, and we chatted away about Ed's achievement of climbing Everest.

"Actually," he said, "this celebration is sort of about me to."

"Oh yes," I said very dubiously.

"About 15 years ago I climbed Everest without oxygen."

"Oh right, hmm, that must have been pretty neat for you," and then I went on to tell him about what I was going to do up in Khunde. I was a little bemused that this man thought his feat was such a big deal. After all, it's only a mountain, and climbing it first 40 years ago is a whole lot more important than wandering up it 25 years later. I was also rather annoyed that maybe he was trying to insult Ed by implying that he might have used oxygen when he summitted in 1952. I mean that would be cheating wouldn't it. What's the point of climbing to high altitude if you're going to supplement your oxygen? Anyway, he seemed a nice bloke so I forgave his attempt to steal Ed's thunder.

Later I was telling Diane about the do and she said, "What was that man's name again?"

A YOUNG MAN CARRYING A HEAVY LOAD UP DILLI BAZAR.

"Oh, Rupert something I think."

"You don't think it might have been Reinholt Messner, dear?"

"Yeah, that sounds like it. How do you know that?"

"Um, he's kind of famous. I was reading about him the other day. He was the first to summit Everest without oxygen, and apparently that's quite a big deal, so the celebration probably was something to do with him too."

Sorry Mr Messner. No offence intended.

Zeke stayed downstairs with us, and we came to like him very much. He finally admitted to being strongly opposed to the Trust associating itself with two homosexuals, and had conveyed that clearly to the selection committee before our final interview. Meeting us and realising that we were "nice girls after all" had made him rethink the whole issue. I am happy with who I am and who I love, but am still shocked and hurt to realise that some people hate me because of one aspect of my life, without taking the time to get to know the whole of me first. I believe that I was born a lesbian. If it was a matter of choice, I would certainly not have chosen to be a member of a much-hated and undervalued minority group. The choice I made was to be honest about who I am, and live with integrity and pride in myself.

We had thought that we'd been treated pretty well by the staff, but it was fascinating to see them become even more attentive to Zeke-sahib. One night when I was in the bathroom, a rather large rat wandered past. I told the cook that we had a rat in the house, and he cheerfully agreed. When I said that I didn't want the rat in the house, he smiled, shrugged his shoulders and walked off. The rat remained, and one morning I asked the cook if he could kill the rat for us. He was very shocked and said that he couldn't do that, so we continued to live with the rat. One night during the regular power cuts, Zeke came home with us after dinner. He went inside ahead of us, and we heard a shriek and then a crash. We ran in and tripped over him, the three of us grovelling around waving the torch about with Zeke saying that he'd stood on the Trust administrator's dog, and had he killed it? I managed to tell him that it wasn't a dog he had stood on. All of a sudden Zeke-sahib was demanding that the rat be killed, and the staff were all running about with great enthusiasm. Nothing actually was ever achieved, and when all the big-wigs had gone we asked the cook once more whether he was going to kill the rat. He shrugged his shoulders and said he'd been unable to find his revolver so how could he kill the rat. We were quite relieved and felt we could continue to live with the rat if an excited Nepali running around the flat with a loaded gun was the alternative.

It is difficult sometimes to live in a culture where it is universally accepted that men and boys are always more valuable than women and girls. Within that structure there is a very definite hierarchy, where some people, through birthright or wealth, matter more, and people at the bottom of the ladder really don't matter at all. There is a woman here, with a toddler permanently tied to her back, who sweeps the driveway and cleans up around the flat. She has worked here for about three years. We were never introduced to her, since she is "just the cleaner", and when we asked her name, we were told it wasn't important. We found out that our cook didn't even know her name, since he'd never bothered to find out. When we did eventually start talking to her in Nepali, the other staff initially tried to shuffle us off, saying it didn't look good for us to be seen talking with the cleaner.

Everything in Nepal has a respectful and disrespectful form, a bit like the polite and familiar forms of "you" in French. So, whenever you speak to anyone, you must be careful to assess and fit each other into the correct hierarchical level. I am happy enough to use the disrespectful terms for children and animals (though that can be debated too), but cannot feel comfortable classifying the worth of adults. I have, however, referred to some of the taxi drivers who have ripped us off as "u" rather than the respectful "wahaa". We finally managed to stop one suicidal, drug-crazed maniac after a few minutes of torture driving us through the streets on the wrong side of the road. I was very pleased with myself as I waved my finger in his face and shouted in Nepali, "You are a very bad driver!" to which he smirked and drove off. Later, as we walked along, Diane pointed out that what I'd actually said was, "I am a very bad car." Ah, the frustrations of speaking in another language.

21

It is also a bit hard not to feel offended when somebody speaks to me in the disrespectful form, because I am a woman, or younger than them, or a European (whom some Nepalis look down on as immoral and depraved).

As our tutor explained, "A husband never respects his wife, and must always use the disrespectful form with her. He must never do anything to help his wife. She must do everything for him. He only provides the food for her to cook. She must do anything he wants her to. The man can go where he wants, when he wants, and answers to no one. A woman cannot leave the house without permission from her husband, father or older brother. No woman is allowed to speak to any man who is not in her immediate family or her husband. If I saw my wife talking to another man, I would throw her out of the house. We never divorce, but I could take another wife, though it would not be approved of. Husbands and wives don't fight and divorce, like in your culture, because the wife always agrees with and obeys her husband, so no fights. It works very well." Nepali men aren't very keen on women's liberation, and disdainfully compare it to evil spirits. Can't blame them really, they've certainly got the good end of the deal.

We have bought some great paintings from the Janakpur Women's Art Project, where some aid workers in the Terai saw the paintings that the women drew on their houses. They provided skills in making home-made paper and encouraged the women to sell their art. It took some persuasion, because the women couldn't believe anyone would pay money for their "doodlings", which are a bit like Picasso's flat profiles of faces. They are great and are very popular with the tourists. One indicator of how well they are doing is that the men of the village got jealous and, rather than wallowing in the reflected glory and added income, put considerable effort into trying to close the women's operation down.

A TYPICAL PAINTING FROM THE JANAKPUR WOMEN'S DEVELOPMENT CENTRE.

Things should be a little more comfortable in Khunde, where, because many of the men of the village are off trekking, the women have a lot more responsibility for doing "worthwhile" jobs, such as running teahouses and looking after the farming and crops (as well as the unacknowledged tasks of keeping house and bringing up the children), and have higher status than other women in Nepal. Still, at parties the men sit on cushioned benches next to the fire, while the women sit on the floor near the door. I guess we'll have to get used to sitting cross-legged too.

If a first-born is a girl, she is named after the day of the week, with "Phutti" on the end, which means "bring a boy next time". A second daughter is called "Tsumje" — "no more boys". And yes, a third daughter may be called "Tsumje Phutti". Interesting welcome to the world.

Nepal is one of only three countries in the world where a woman's life expectancy is lower than the man's. The average man dies at 58, while the average woman only reaches 51 years. This is attributed to the extremely hard life they lead, death during childbirth, and the fact that families are far less likely to take a woman or girl for medical treatment if they get sick.

A HOUSE ON DILLI BAZAR.

These are just a few facts of life of living here, and are unlikely to change during our stay. Hopefully we will be able to find an acceptable space where we can stay true to ourselves but accept and live within their culture.

It is interesting to see the co-operation and tolerance between the Hindu and Buddhist religions (though if you get people talking, they will always explain how the other side has not quite got it right), who share temples, religious festivals and even gods. They have a Living Goddess, who lives in a room in Durbar Square, in central Kathmandu. She is chosen at the age of five from the goldmakers class of a Buddhist family, and must never have bled, i.e., been scratched, cut or bruised. She is taken from the family by the Hindus, who keep her in a room, dress her in ornate clothing and

A HINDU LAMA.

make-up, and worship her. Nobody is ever allowed to talk to her, and she is the only person the King bows down to. She lives in this room until she reaches menarche (has her first period), and then is freed to live a "normal" life, and another five-year-old girl is chosen. It is considered a great honour, but I think if I was a Buddhist, goldmaker, Nepali girl, I'd be out there getting as many bumps and bruises as I could before they caught me.

There are a lot of good and enviable things about the Buddhist and Hindu religions and their fatalistic attitude to life. However, a consequence of this can be a general indifference to the well-being of others. One day, after a very long, hot walk home, I slipped and fell into a small ditch just outside the flat, where people have seen us around for about six weeks. The contents of my bag, including various cameras lenses, fell out on to the busy road, but I found it hard to retrieve them, since I'd hurt my leg quite badly and couldn't put any weight on it. So I grovelled about, tearfully crawling amongst the traffic, trying to retrieve my belongings and, with difficulty, managed to get upright and hop to the compound gate. Many familiar faces just sat and watched me.

When I told our Nepali tutor, he seemed to feel that it was fairly typical. It was probably my lowest point since we had arrived, and I couldn't think of many good reasons not to pack my bags and go home. But my leg settled down very quickly — just a strain — and pretty soon I was excited about being here and looking forward to working in Khunde.

We start our trek up into the mountains in a few days. We seem to have got used to the background noise level, and I have lost my terror of the roads, ambling across them with an almost confident, fatalistic nonchalance. We still find the indiscriminate, near-constant honking of horns and the air pollution from the black smoke emanating from the tempos and trucks a bit much, and are looking forward to the quiet and clean air in Khunde.

W e arrived in Namche and stayed the night with Lynley Cook and David Murdoch, the previous Khunde doctors, who had come down to meet us. The next morning we wandered up the hill to Khunde. Unfortunately it was quite misty, and we couldn't really see where we were going. It gave us quite an eerie, unreal feeling to arrive at a place for which we had planned for over a year. The air seemed to burst with emotion as we came over the ridge and recognised, from photos, the place that was to be our home for the next two years. Soon the clouds cleared, and we were delighted by the panorama of ice-capped mountains surrounding us. I wondered whether, if I climbed back over the green hills and reached out, I would actually touch a magnificent two-dimensional movie-set. It all seemed a bit too marvellous to be real, especially since the scenery "hadn't been there" as we'd walked up.

Having now seen some other parts of Nepal, I can't imagine why anyone who didn't have to would ever live in Kathmandu. Our initial enthusiasm waned considerably towards the end of our stay there. There are certainly interesting places to visit and people to see, but we will never miss the air pollution, traffic and noise there. The wonderful quiet, interrupted only by the tinkle of yak bells, and the clean, fresh air is just so good.

The trek from Jiri went very well. We were greatly relieved to have had a comfortable private van for the drive from Kathmandu to Jiri. The road was terrible, very steep, with more pot-holes than flat road for a lot of the trip. There was only enough room for one vehicle at a time, with very steep cliffs at the roadside. We would quite often screech to a halt as another vehicle appeared around the corner. There would then follow a 25 long process of backing up to find a flat bit of land to get off the road so the other vehicle could get through. We saw a number of the local buses, and can see why our friends in Kathmandu refer to them as the "vomit comets". They fit three people to a two-person seat and are jam-packed, those without seats having to stand sardined together. The roof is also packed with people. An average trip from Kathmandu to Jiri takes 13 hours, and there is one fatal public bus crash a week.

We had about 90 kg of gear with us, but our guide insisted that his friend could porter it all alone. For this we would pay him the double rate of $NZ10 a day. The guide only carried his day pack and received $NZ8 a day plus food.

Diane found the first hill out of Jiri very hard work. Being the fitter one, I started off as the honourable trekker, walking behind her. However, after she had stopped for a breather 10 times within a half-hour period (I am not exaggerating) I decided that the day was about to end in divorce, or, more likely, Di would be found at the bottom of the Jiri hill with a walking pole through her back. Considering these options, I felt it was more sensible to leave Di with our very patient guide and go on ahead. Di also felt much

DI ON THE TREK FROM JIRI.

more comfortable not having to listen to my very controlled and increasingly more obviously insincere mutterings of, "It doesn't matter at all," "I'm sure you're doing your best," and "It's not a race." I really enjoyed the solitude of walking on my own and would stop every hour or so and sight-see while the rest caught up. The weather was mostly fine and the rhododendrons were out, so I had some magnificent views. I was fascinated to walk along a trail and come across a Hindu offering to the gods for a safe journey. It could be mistaken for a pile of rubbish in the middle of the trail. On closer inspection, there was the head of a baby goat, money, uncooked rice, paper with writing on it, blood spread around, vegetables, and leaves.

Di improved each day, and coped very well. There is no doubt that she suffered at times, but remained continually cheerful and uncomplaining.

The first night we stayed in Shivalaya, a small village by a river. I was intrigued to see a toddler wandering about playing with a soft toy that had a string attached to it. The child would occasionally cuddle and pet the toy, throw it in the air, or just walk around dragging it behind. I'd not seen Nepali children with toys and was relieved to see that kids here do get to have them after all. I wandered closer to the child and beamed at the mother working nearby. The "toy" turned out to be a large dead rat! Mum seemed quite happy for her child to continue his play.

We would spend up to a day climbing a great long hill, only to find that we would have to go down into a long valley and up the side of another enormous hill. When I complained to the guide that we didn't seem to be getting anywhere, he said, "Oh yes, memsahib, much up-coming and down-going."

I found that I really enjoyed the uphills, and became quite euphoric with the endorphin rush — my heart racing and sweat pouring. Downhill I found to be a real drag, and all my forgotten sports injuries came back to haunt me. Di was the opposite. Her cardiovascular system let her down a bit going uphill, but she could motor down, and as the days went on, I would struggle to keep up on the downhill stretches.

The only real mishap was when I went over on my ankle on the sixth day, coming down from the highest mountain pass. The top and sides of my foot went black with bruising and looked very impressive, fortunately appearing much worse than it felt. I fancied myself giving the impression of the great brave hero as I limped on for the next day or so, but apart from a few sympathetic noises from Diane (in considerable pain herself), the guide and porter thought nothing of it.

SHIVALAYA.

MEAT VENDORS AT SALLERI MARKET (NEAR PHAPLU HOSPITAL).

27

Jiri to Lukla is a main portering route, since it is usually cheaper to pay a porter to carry a load than to use air freight. The legal load for a porter is 35 kg, but they are paid per kilogram carried, so understandably take on as

much as they possibly can. We saw some amazingly heavy loads. One group of men carried a thick coil of steel wiring for a suspension bridge. Each would wrap the coil several times across his body, then hand it on to his friend. In this way, four men were tied together and walked for about five days in unison, up and down the steep trails. Others in the gang had thick three-metre-long pipes. These were carried in pairs parallel to the ground. The trails are quite narrow, so these men would have to walk the distance sideways most of the way, edging their difficult loads around tight corners.

The handover with the previous doctors went very well. They've obviously done a very good job up here, and I hope to follow in their fashion. Over their last few days, many villagers came up to the hospital to say goodbye, with tea, chang (rice wine), and khaarta (white silk scarves given as a farewell gift). Sherpas are definitely hospitable to a fault. We delighted at the antics of people offering food and drink. It is considered a bit rude to accept the first time something is offered, so there develops an entertaining game, where the giver says "shey, shey" (eat/drink) and the recipient covers his/her cup or plate, looks away with a moan and says "no, no, no, no, no". At the same time, the giver joins in with "shey, shey, shey, shey, shey". Then the recipient (who wanted the stuff in the first place) gives another moan and reluctantly holds out his/her hand, plate or cup to be filled. After a sip or mouthful, there's some more "shey, shey, shey", and "no, no, no", and the receptacle is filled again. People who are really good at it put on a great show, hiding their plate or cup behind their backs, and almost have the giver chasing them about the room. And just when you think they really don't want any more, at the very last second, they'll thrust their cup or plate out for some more. It's really very impressive, but not so much fun when it's your turn to drink chang at eight o'clock in the morning. People are, in general, a lot softer on us, realising that we're a bit green to the dynamics of play, but I always seem to have more than I intended to before "no" means no. Di decided from the start to be a teetotaller, which has made life a lot easier for her.

The "coming-going" party was very enjoyable, though few people spoke English, or Nepali, and they tended to smile shyly and catch only glimpses of the two new doctors. Yes, Diane is a doctor here too. When she tries very hard to explain that I'm the doctor and she's the nurse, the locals just smile and say "same, same".

DIANE, LYNLEY AND THE AUTHOR IN THEIR BEST INGIS FOR THE "COMING-GOING" PARTY.

All of the parties run to pretty much the same protocol. All the men sit on one side of the room, near the fire, and all the women sit on the other side, on the floor, unless there are spare seats. We are the first Khunde couple to be able to sit together at parties. Everyone is given either chang or sweet milk tea. Then comes a meal, usually rice, dhal bhaat (a thick legume soup), and stew, served to each person individually. Seconds are handed out, more tea or chang is served, and when everyone is tanked up and relaxed enough the men start singing, joined later by the women. Then the dancing starts. The men make up one side of a circle and the women the other. Everyone wraps their arms around their neighbour's waist and conducts repetitive footwork patterns. There is no external music and everyone sings along in melodious haunting tones. We were very soon enveloped into the circle. Sherpa dancing is harder than it looks, but although we were more often out of step than in, we felt warmly accepted. It was very enjoyable, and felt like a coming together/bonding ritual. We danced on for about three hours, while people walked around the middle of the circle persuading us to drink chang from the one cup.

With all the Everest expeditions coming home, we've already had some interesting people dropping into the hospital. We were especially

pleased and excited by Jan Arnold's successful summit. We met Jan and her husband Rob Hall in Kathmandu and liked them very much. They are good friends of the previous doctors. They dropped in with Gary Ball on their way down, and we found them good company. We'll look forward to seeing them next year. Jan was delighted to have summitted.

I'd never thought much of people climbing mountains, but Jan's harrowing descriptions of climbing up the last few metres in 50-knot winds sounded incredibly frightening. I was fascinated to realise that you don't just start at Base Camp and climb to the top of Everest. In order to acclimatise, you go up to Camp One first day, and then back down again. Then you climb to Camp Two and down again. And continue on like that, up and down, until you've acclimatised to the altitude. So actually you climb a lot more than the mountain itself. It's quite an involved process, and expeditions spend two or three months at Base Camp in preparation. It certainly is a bigger deal than I'd imagined.

We also heard the sad tale of Passang Lhamu, who was the first Nepali woman to get to the top of Everest but died on the way down. She has now been made a national hero. She was a 32-year-old Sherpani who had made several unsuccessful attempts to summit over the years. She was determined to be the first Nepali woman to summit, and was strongly supported by her husband, who sounds as if he was rather obsessed with the idea. Another woman in the Indo-Nepali team was also keen to be the first, and there had been a number of verbal public fights in Kathmandu about who would get to the top first.

At Base Camp, although the weather conditions were poor and they had no radio backup, Passang Lhamu headed up, determined to beat the other woman, who was about to make her move. She was accompanied by an extremely good Sherpa mountaineer, who was unwell with tuberculosis. The local people say that he'd been told that he would lose his job if he didn't get Passang Lhamu to the top. He was seen to be coughing up blood at South Cole on the way up.

They made very slow progress. All climbers know that if you haven't got to a certain point on the mountain by a particular time, then you must turn back, or else you won't have time to safely get back down again.

Passang Lhamu arrived at the south summit at about 2 pm, and must have known that she would not have time to return safely. She and her companion summitted anyway, and only got down to the south summit again before having to bivouac. The weather was very bad, and no one could get close to rescue them. They both died on the mountain.

The local people say that she must have known she'd never make it down again. Basically she committed suicide for the posthumous glory of being the first Nepali woman to summit Everest. I wonder what consolation that is to her three small children who are left behind. There is a lot of local bitterness about the man who died with her. The Nepali government insisted that her body be retrieved from the mountain for a grand state funeral. Many people risked their lives to do this. Usually bodies remain on the mountain that killed them. It is really sad that with a little more planning and patience she may well have survived a successful summit. In the end, the other woman from the Indo-Nepali team had to turn back anyway.

People living in this area do talk a lot about climbing. With 37 summitting Everest a couple of weeks ago, and another 15 a few days later, it's hard not to get caught up in it all. I'm very pleased for the people who are successful, and it doesn't matter how many people do it, it is still a great achievement, but I'm very happy just to look at the mountains from a distance.

I am beginning to understand the fascination of mountains. Their appearance changes with the light, weather and time of day. There is something very special about sitting surrounded by ice-capped peaks. Parts of the mountain disappear behind clouds, and then suddenly burst out through a window in the cloud, looking as if they are hanging in mid-air. I feel that I am developing a relationship with them. My favourite mountain is Khumbila, just behind the hospital. It is a sacred mountain, unable to be climbed, and is considered to be the god of this region. Maybe it's the altitude getting to me, but I certainly sense that it's more than a lump of rock.

In the early hours one morning, I was woken to deliver a baby. The Sherpanis are certainly a stoical lot. The three women I've delivered so far have made very little fuss about the whole business — quite different to the shrieks and cries of many of the deliveries I've been involved in in New Zealand. It's apparently very rare for the women to require pain relief at all during labour. I'm quite sure that if I have a baby I'll need all the pain relief I can get.

The delivery went well. A healthy baby and mum always leaves me buzzing and feeling good about the world. I hope I never lose that specialness and wonder at a new life. I wandered back to the flat at about 5 am, just as the sun was beginning to rise behind Tamserku, a beautiful mountain that faces the hospital. It was snowing lightly and the ground was covered in what looked like icing sugar. I'd never seen it snow before and, caught up in the moment, danced around the front area of the hospital trying to catch the snowflakes on my hands and face. I spun around to see a very puzzled expression on our health worker's face. He must think he's got a mad woman to stay.

One night during the handover a small girl was carried up, unconscious after falling from a bank. She continued to worsen and the weather was too bad to fly her down to Kathmandu. At one stage we were seriously considering doing burr holes (drilling a hole in the skull to let the growing blood clot out), but fortunately she improved spontaneously, and is now home fit and well. It made me realise that I will at times be trying procedures that will be well beyond my training or abilities. The challenge

of this is certainly one of the reasons I came here, but it doesn't stop me going weak at the knees thinking of all the possibilities. I find it hard to get to sleep at night realising that I am the only doctor in the entire area, and that anything could happen any time and I'll just have to have a go.

We have inherited a group of Tibetan boys (aged 5 to 18 years old) who were brought over from Lhasa in Tibet to go to school at Dharamsala in India. The guides lied to their parents telling them it was an easy few days' walk. One father paid double rates for his seven-year-old son to be carried the whole way. After 20 days of fighting through the snow, the group turned up at the hospital. The boys' parents had sewn money into their clothing, and the guides took that money saying that they would organise a plane to fly them to Dharamsala. Needless to say they disappeared and haven't been seen since. The boys were exhausted, many with frostbite and pneumonia. They were shocked and very frightened. One 18-year-old boy died a few days after arriving, despite heroic attempts at resuscitation by the previous doctors. The boy whose father had paid double rates had the worst frost-bitten feet.

There was no way we could get them to Kathmandu because, as illegal refugees, they wouldn't be allowed on the airplane, and we couldn't find anyone who would risk carrying them to Jiri. So the boys have been living in the long-stay ward.

Kami Temba, one of our health workers, has befriended them, and gradually the true story of their journey is coming out. The boys say that their guides beat them with sticks when they were too exhausted to go on. Two boys collapsed on the way, and when the guides couldn't get them up, they left them on the trail to die. Kami says that the guides will go back to Lhasa with tales of how all the boys are doing so well at school in Dharamsala, and it will be many years before the boys' parents find out about their misfortune.

A 60-year-old woman came in yesterday after walking five days to see me. She complained of tiredness and an ache in her upper abdomen. She looked very

KAMI TEMBA.

anaemic and her skin was baggy from significant weight loss. Her liver was enlarged with a hard mass the size of an apple in it. It was heart-breaking to explain to her that there wasn't anything I could do and that soon she would be dead. She took it very stoically. I gave her some iron tablets and paracetamol, and she wandered off back home with her husband, to die slowly and painfully away from any medical help.

We are very well supported by our two health workers, who have both been at the hospital for over 15 years. Kami lives at the hospital with us, and goes home for four days every fortnight. His wife and daughter live in Thami, (two to three hours' walk away). His son is at school in Kathmandu. When he was a child he used to walk from Thami to Khumjung School (just past our village) and back every day. His father died when he was five, and he and his mother and three sisters struggled to survive. Kami came top of the high school and was granted a

scholarship from the Trust to train to be doctor at a Kathmandu University. Unfortunately, after only one semester, his mother died, and he was required to return home to look after his two unmarried sisters. He speaks fluent English, Nepali, Sherpa and Tibetan, and is an excellent clinician.

Mingma, the other health worker, lives with his wife and three daughters in the village. He left Class Eight to work at the hospital. They are both remarkably warm and easy-going yet hard-working. We feel extremely lucky to have them around. I'm sure that we will become very good friends.

We also have a hospital dog and cat. Longin (beggar) is a fat, sweet-natured corgi-type who lives for eating riggis (potatoes). Pus is a slightly schizophrenic grey cat with a piercing Siamese-style meow. Our flat is strewn with photos of family and friends and is beginning to feel like home. It feels right to be here, but we feel homesick at times, and are sure to be ready to come home in two years' time. It's very easy to fall into the role of the nameless doctor memsahib — here today, replaced by another tomorrow. The locals are friendly, but they know we're only here for a finite time.

We've been at Khunde for a month now. Things seem to be running very smoothly and we are very happy. The monsoon has already started, with plenty of rain for the riggis. Our veges in the greenhouses are doing very well, so it looks as if we'll have a good varied diet for a while. Thanks to the previous doctors for planting so well. The garden in front of the flat is also flourishing. On the way back from a house call, Kami and I came across the O-Sho procession to bless the crops for the year. Mingma had the job of blowing the shell horn, and they all insisted that we join them. It was great fun as we circumnavigated Khumjung and Khunde in a clockwise direction accompanied by large flags, three little girls dressed up as godesses, a lama bashing his cymbals, with an enthusiastic friend beating a large drum, and many laughing and excited local children marching cheerfully through the villages. We all stopped at the small hill above the chorten, where we burnt juniper and had a puja, accompanied by chang handed around to each person. I seemed to reluctantly get much more than everyone else, much to the delight of the people around me. Mingma finally came to my rescue, but I still haven't worked out a "no" that means no. The village looked quite remarkable with small juniper branches burning on most people's stone fences. Kami and I stopped off at the hospital, but the procession continued on, getting merrier and merrier for the next few hours. We had a good hard rain the next day, which is a sign that the crops are going to do very well this year, so everyone is happy.

The last of this season's Everest expeditions seem to have gone through, and some have been very generous in donating their leftover medical supplies.

Some supplies have not been so useful. We were visited by the Korean Womens' Everest Expedition, who donated a large quantity of medicines,

O-SHO AT KHUNDE.

unfortunately mainly vitamins and heat rubs. Fortunately they stayed around to translate the Korean names, so that I could understand what to use them for. It felt as if they shot off about 10 rolls of film recording this momentous occasion. I had voiced concern to Kami that they had seemed particularly unprepared for problems at altitude, since we didn't see any acetazolamide, nifedipine or steroids. I think he was amused at my naïvity as he explained that they sell the "good" drugs down in Kathmandu and tend to unload on us things that are not worth carrying down. He said that this is the first time the Koreans have ever donated anything to the hospital, so I guess it's a good start. Anyway, we were effusive in our thanks, and they seemed very happy when they left.

The Indo-Nepali Womens Everest Expedition sent a message up from Namche saying that they had a large load of very valuable medicines for us and would I come down immediately to meet the expedition doctor and pick them up. It was almost dark and we had a very sick two-year-old boy with bronchopneumonia and possible meningitis, and a drunk, stroppy head-injured man (whom the same expedition doctor had just sent up to us on a stretcher with the note!) to deal with at the time, so we sent Tsumje (our housekeeper) down with a note. Tsumje was very happy to carry the 26-kg load — a load that I couldn't even lift off the ground! — up the steep ridge to the hospital for about $NZ3. It may sound a bit ungrateful, but we were disappointed to discover the contents of the bag: about 150 packets of glucose powder enriched with Vitamin D, hundreds of bottles of homeopathic doses of Vitamins A or B combined with frighteningly high doses of Vitamin D, and about 100 bottles of Vitamin E capsules. (I wouldn't have thought sexual prowess was a big issue when summitting, or is there something you mountaineers haven't told us?) Anyway, we very graciously sent off a thank-you letter to their sponsors, but I have no idea what we're going to do with the vitamins. The glucose has come in handy, since we gave our frost-bitten Tibetan boys a packet to share each day to supplement their diet, which brought happy smiles all around.

We were all set to head off to Thami to combine a clinic with the Mani-Rhimbdu festival, last week. However, we decided to change one of the boy's dressings before we left. This seven-year-old boy's frostbite is so bad that he requires ketamine anaesthetic each dressing change. His feet have looked dreadful for a while now, and the frost-bitten area did in fact "fall off" that morning. I ended up having to debride away most of his forefoot. We decided to postpone the Thami visit for a day, just to be sure that the poor wee boy had adequate pain relief, and to explain what had happened to him. He took the news tearfully but stoically, and had most of us shedding a tear with him.

Just after that a German trekker raced in moaning and groaning, having decided he was dying of cerebral oedema. To help matters a friendly trekker had given him three 40-mg frusemide tablets on the trail, to "save his life". This would have only dehydrated him further. He was experiencing his first migraine, which certainly can be frightening, and I gave him some injectable pain relief and anti-nausea medication and put him in a corner of the short-stay ward to sleep it off. He was certain that I was an incompetent fool who was about to mismanage him to his death, and carried on for quite a while until he went off to sleep.

He was utterly horrified that I was scheduled to be in Thami at that time and could "just leave anyone to die" while I was out of the area. He was not prepared to believe that Mingma is a very competent medical assistant and was generally insulting to everyone. Advising him to descend became a tempting option, but he was perfectly well in the morning and turned up at Mani-Rhimbdu the next day.

However, we were very pleased we had stayed the extra day. Just as it was getting dark, about 50 people arrived carrying a man on a stretcher. It turned out to be one of the Trust's senior carpenters. He had been cutting a tree, which had snapped and he had fallen about four metres on to his upper back. He had not been knocked out but was unable to move any of his limbs. A friend had carried him on his back for half an hour to find a stretcher and two hours later he reached us. He did in fact have a quadriplegia, with some vague gross movements of his arms, and pinprick sensation only above the upper chest. We managed to put on a hard collar under traction and stabilised him overnight, with long and involved explanations of how important it was for his back and neck not to be moved about. He had quite a difficult time, and we were up for most of the night. In the early morning he jumped when I gave him an injection, which gave me the hope that the spinal cord was "bruised" rather than severed. That morning was the very last scheduled flight from Shayngboche airfield, and was the only fine day we'd had in many, so some luck must have been going his way. We gave the carpenter instructions about not moving his back and neck and wrote a letter to the airline people reiterating its importance in capital letters. The carpenter's friends carried him down, while I checked on another patient, and I arrived at Shyangboche just in time to see the plane taking off. The carpenter's friends cheerfully announced that "his legs were moving a little bit when they lifted him into his seat". They didn't seem to notice my face go white, and I saw no point in making a fuss after the fact. I rationalised that if he had a thoracic fracture that could survive being carried on someone's back for half an hour, then sitting in a plane seat couldn't be much worse. We are waiting to hear news of him. I can't imagine how a quadriplegic gets on in Nepal.

Mani-Rhimbdu is a religious festival held at the monastery each year. We stayed with Kami and his family.

Kami, his wife Da Doma and I climbed the steep hill up to the monastery on the first afternoon and attended the blessing. I had expected

HERALDING THE START OF MANI-RHIMBDU.

it to be a solemn event, but it was a real push-and-shove fight to get up to the lamas. People pushed in and fell all over each other. Finally we reached the front and held ferociously to each other in line. Then came the fun. For crowd control, so that not too many people came to the Rimpoche (the reincarnate lama) at a time, the monks had a large wooden stick, which they would at intervals slam in between the line's legs, blocking further movement. Sometimes they missed the gaps, and there would be a yelp from the crowd. The part of the line that was left behind would then need to bunch up even further (which had seemed impossible), and we would all cling to each other in an effort not to fall off the platform. Others standing in the "queue" on the ground saw the disruption as another opportunity to push in, and would leap up, clinging on to various body parts until we were obliged to squeeze them in or be dragged off the platform on to the floor with them. Finally the stick would be pulled out and there would be a mad dash to get past it before it was replaced. The first monk poured some tea into my cupped hand, and I drank a little, then poured the rest over my head as I'd seen the others ahead of me do. The next monk, dressed in a Santa Claus hat and dark glasses (only I seemed to be amused by this), patted me on the head with a rainbow-coloured staff. Then came the Rimpoche. I laid my khaarta beside him and placed my donation on the table in front of him. He in turn gave me a handful of small nuts, which I rapidly swallowed, and I moved on to the next monk. He gave me some sampa balls (like uncooked biscuit mix), which I also gobbled. The last monk poured some chang into my cupped hand, some of which I drank and the rest I poured over my head. Beside him, another monk enthusiastically banged his drum. Then I moved off the platform and had to fight out of the way of those who were still queuing. It was quite a wrestle, but I had been officially blessed by the Rimpoche, which pleased Kami and Da Doma considerably.

THE CYMBAL DANCE OF MANI-RHIMBDU.

The blessing went on for about two hours, then friends suggested a beer at the nearest teahouse. I still haven't sorted out this "shey, shey, shey" business, and into my second bottle of San Miguel was feeling very happy with the world. An old Sherpa man across the room kept holding out his glass of beer and talking away fervently. A trekker friend explained that he was talking to me, and it was a sign of respect that he was offering me his beer and I must go over and drink it. Not wanting to seem rude, I confidently strode over and took his beer. Fortunately, before I drank it, Kami quickly let me know that he'd been offering it to the Sherpani beside me. So I ceremoniously, and I hope with some dignity, took it over to her, blushing to my roots. She then held it up and made a speech to him, and the game continued as the glass went from one to the other, each trying to out-respect the other! Fortunately, they hadn't taken much notice of me; I was just another idiot tourist to them. The steep walk down the hill was hard work, with the ground very dry, dusty and slippery, and if Di hadn't been waiting at Kami's house I'd have been tempted to stay up there until the morning.

The next morning, we did our 7.30 am clinic at 8.15 am when the health worker arrived with the key. We saw three people. No one wants to get sick at Mani-Rhimbdu. We all wandered up the hill and watched some magnificent dancing for many hours. The monks, dressed up in different

costumes with elaborate masks, leapt about with enthusiasm and great skill.

The favourite item for the locals was called the Hermit, where two men put on a slap-stick kind of pantomime. No one could hear what they were saying, so it didn't matter to us that it was in Sherpa. The crowd just loved it, and were a delight to watch. They seemed genuinely frightened in the scary bits, and fell about in laughter at other times. There was basically the straight man and the funny man, and they would produce screams of delight with such antics as shaking up a beer bottle and spraying it into the crowd. There were take-offs of the Sherpa culture and Buddhism, such as walking around blessing various crowd members with a covered object, only to reveal it as a wooden cup. Unfortunately for us, they were too popular, and the up-until-now very restrained crowd pushed in closer and closer to see what was happening. Di and I were sitting in the front and at times found ourselves doubled over with the crush of boney knees in our backs and various arms slung over us by people behind trying to get a better view. The effects of the free-flowing chang were becoming apparent as the man to our right vomited into the crowd (at least clearing some space for us), and one to our left fell down unconscious. We decided we'd probably seen enough and fought our way out of the monastery to negotiate the steep path home.

On the way down we came across a man slumped against one of the mani (prayer) walls. We checked that he was alive and, as he was already in a modified recovery position, left him where he was. We noticed that other Sherpas didn't even take any notice of him as they walked down. When I mentioned him to Kami, he said that Mani-Rhimbdu was always like that. Lots of people drink chang until they drop. Certainly alcohol is a big part of society. Most people don't let it take over their lives, but there are a few permanently drunk people living in Khunde. People often drink chang to help them work better! Especially carpenters, who fall off building sites with frightening regularity. Chang is also called the "Sherpa taxi" — it makes walking easier because you're there before you know it.

The monks are an interesting lot. Apart from not being allowed to marry, they seem to have a cushy number. Certainly they live a much more comfortable lifestyle than the average Nepali or Sherpa. They are paid well and charge a lot of money to do the pujas. On top of this it is very auspicious to feed your monks well, and they are the only fat people I've seen in Nepal. We see the monks quite often not because they get sick, but because it is the fashion for them to wear glasses. The more variety the better, so they come and feign short-sightedness, being unable to read their prayer books. They also seem to "lose" their glasses at an alarming rate. At the Mani-Rhimbdu I was fascinated to see the row of monks in front of us change their glasses throughout the day. I discovered why the dark glasses seemed to be particularly popular that day when I happened to go around the side where they were sitting, and counted six of the eight sound asleep during one of the more drawn-out dances. I don't know how they managed to stay sitting cross-legged for the whole day, which lasted about 10 hours, but then I guess they get a lot of practice.

The Rimpoche is in fact married with two children, which dropped his popularity for a while. Monks usually make a vow of celibacy, but since he is the reincarnate lama they couldn't really toss him out. Quite a few monks marry, and have to leave the monastery. It creates a bit of a scandal for a while, then people forget about it, but they can never be monks again. The Rimpoche became popular again when he insisted on the Mani-Rhimbdu staying on the same date in May. The Rimpoche from the Tengboche changed the date of their Mani-Rhimbdu to September to suit the trekkers so the Tengboche Monastery would make more money. He also removed the Hermit item because the tourists find it boring. It sounds as if the re-opening of the Tengboche Monastery will be a real circus, but since the Trust has paid so much money towards it we'll have to turn up. It seems that the Tengboche Monastery has become just a tourist asset and has lost its religious viability.

THAMI RIMPOCHE (LEFT) RETURNING FROM A PUJA.

Nuns are a dying breed. They are not as respected as the monks and are very much a second choice to do the pujas. They are certainly not overfed and live almost completely on potatoes, which they beg from the villagers at harvest-time. Most need support from their families to survive, thus people are not usually thrilled if a family member wants to become a nun. Most of the nuns we have met are elderly, as young women, understandably, are rejecting it as a lifestyle.

Before we left Thami we had the misfortune of bumping into an odd, possibly psychotic woman called Gertrude (about whom the previous doctors had warned us). She invited herself into Kami's house for breakfast and stayed and stayed. She has an obsession that one of the local Sherpas, who owns a large trekking agency, is raping large numbers of his trekkers. She has made it her mission in life to hand out extremely libellous pamphlets about this issue to everyone she meets, stating the man's name and that he is spreading AIDS throughout the world. She has written many articles, one of which was unfortunately published in a popular overseas newspaper, thus heightening her enthusiasm. She is causing a lot of trouble around the place with other antics, such as refusing to pay when she's stayed in some teahouses, claiming she has no money. She is obviously a troubled woman, but one to be avoided, and we made it very clear that we were not the slightest bit interested in her story.

Di and I wandered back to an almost empty hospital. The Tibetan boys had gone. While we were in Thami, a group of Tibetans from Kathmandu had arrived with a letter from the United Nations, who had chartered a flight from Shyangboche to get the boys to Kathmandu. Mingma said they were so happy, with grins from ear to ear, and had flown out the morning we'd walked back from Thami. We are very happy for them because I'm sure things will run very smoothly for them now, but we were sad to have been unable to say goodbye, and will miss them around the hospital. Still, it is a very good outcome, and I know that the previous doctors will be relieved that all their hard work was worthwhile.

It seems that our Sherpani midwife has left us. About a week after the previous doctors left, she told us that her mother-in-law was sick in hospital in Kathmandu and asked for 10 days' leave to visit her. Of course that was fine. But the day after she left, the woman who runs the teahouse she had been staying in said that our midwife had gone for good and would we pick up the hospital gear she'd left behind. Other locals came to tell us the same story, and we came to realise that we were the only people in the village who didn't know that she had been planning her "escape" for quite a while. I am a bit saddened that she didn't feel that she could tell us she wasn't happy and wanted to go. We certainly wouldn't have tried to stop her. Anyway, I feel happy to cover the obstetric load without her, and we'll work at selecting a couple of local women to train in midwifery for the future.

As we get to know the local people better, it's fascinating how people's spiritual beliefs tie in with how they see their own health and future. Many people follow the Buddhist calendar, which is a bit like a horoscope, but is taken a lot more seriously. Each year a group of lamas do astrological readings and come up with the next year's readings. There are specifically bad days, where if you marry you will end up alone, and if you give food or money to anyone else you will end up poor. There are days where anything, especially a business enterprise, that is started on that day is doomed to fail. My favourite are the Buddha Days, about two every month, where every positive or negative action is multiplied by 100. That seems to fit in well with my own philosophy of good and bad karma. It gets even more exciting on one of the four Great Festival Days each year, where your deeds are multiplied by 100,000. And at a Solar Eclipse, make that 1,000,000,000,000 times!

FIXING THE KHUNDE CHORTEN.

Today is both a Buddha Day *and* a solar eclipse. People really do go around being especially nice to each other on these special days, including myself (I'm not taking any chances). The mani walls become crowded, particularly with elderly women wandering around them in a clockwise direction for hours, doing their prayers on such an auspicious day.

The villagers have wisely chosen today to start the annual renovations of the chorten. We went down to have a look and ended up helping break up the clay. The clay is carried up from a special river below Namche, three hours away, then is broken up to make a type of cement. This is layered over last year's cracking surface. It was great fun as we struggled through laughing conversations in our attempts at Sherpa-Nepali-English. Of course the chang flowed freely, and I tried to ignore one of the locals who started singing and dancing from the top of the steps of the stupa.

We tend to pay a lot of attention to the calendar in the running of the hospital. We always check before planning one of the clinic visits that it's not a bad day to start things. Similarly, people don't turn up for a Norplant insertion on such a day. If they are sick, they might put off coming to see us, if it is one of the bad days.

For a while I wondered why a lot of the babies who come to see us have a smudge of black soot on the end of their noses. Fortunately, I didn't follow my natural impulse to wipe it clean. The general belief is that when you're sick, your luck is down, and that's when you are most vulnerable to evil spirits. So if a young child is sick, and has to leave the safety of the house, the soot protects them. Sick people are especially susceptible to evil spirits at night, which explains why I'm not called out of my bed very often. (Though this can at times have disastrous consequences, mostly I'm quite pleased about these bad nocturnal spirits.)

Another interesting phenomenon is that it is very bad luck for a woman in labour to be seen by another woman. Terrible things can happen, such as a boy baby turning into a girl just before it is born. So women in labour will often sneak up to the hospital completely covered by blankets, and usually at night, so no one sees them. It is considered that a woman's menstrual period and especially a delivery are capable of contaminating people around her, particularly the mother or mother-in-law. Contaminated people will get sick and/or have their lives shortened. As a consequence, some women are left alone in the cow-shed to deliver. They must then clean up the mess and wash all their clothes themselves. There are no traditional birth attendants, and the husbands are usually the only ones present at the delivery. Fortunately, being a foreigner, I don't count and am able to help. Things are changing a little, and some women will have their mother or sister with them. I have been very impressed with the way the Sherpa men support and help their partners through labour. Lots of back rubbing, giving sips of fluids, very intent and with genuine caring. The Hindu men are quite a different group up here, and some have been known to hit their wives to quieten them down during labour. We tend to have them wait outside.

It is extremely rare for anyone to know their birthday. It just isn't an issue here. Except of course we still think they're important! Often people will have no idea how old they are, but will always know their "animal year", for example, I was born in the year of the pig, and Di is a sheep. These repeat every 12 years, so it is easy to work out someone's age, since it's pretty hard to be 12 years out. For example, a pig was born in 1947, 1959, 1971, or 1983, so I must be 46, 34, 22, or 10. The animal years, like the astrological calendar, are taken quite seriously, and people are supposed to have a personality consistent with their animal year. For example, a woman born in the year of the tiger is perceived as a pushy type who will try to dominate her husband, and often will not get the opportunity to

44

marry. A man born in the year of the tiger is, however, seen as ambitious and very desirable. Certain animal years are significant for different things. This is the year of the bird, where people are thought to die very quickly. Hence it is an important year for pilgrimage, and old people become even more devoted in their prayers and rituals. Next year is the year of the dog. This and the year of the pig are times when many women become pregnant, so I guess I'll be a bit busier obstetrically in '94 and '95, since these beliefs tend to be self-fulfilling, and the few women on contraception will often stop in these special years.

There are only about 50 Sherpa names, so many people share the same name. Already I know eight Mingma Tserings (which means born on Tuesday, long life). People use their race as their surname, so all Sherpas are Mr Sherpa or Mrs Sherpani, as are the Rais and Mangars, and some people even use Nepali as a last name. As you can see, it does not differentiate very well. So a person's full name is not usually enough, and we get into the habit of saying, "Oh I saw Mingma Tsering, married to Ang Dooli, from Khunde the other day." Each of the names have a meaning, which is again taken more seriously than our names. For example, everyone knows that Kami had an older brother die before he was born. The Kamis are one of the low-classes. If a family has a son who dies, the next boy is called one of the low-class names in order to appease the gods and make him seem so unimportant that he is not worth taking as well. In a very class-oriented society it is interesting that there is no stigma attached to having the low-class name, as long as you are from a higher class. There is no similar naming for girls; it's not so important if a girl dies.

Surprisingly, with so much importance being placed on being masculine, most names are used by both men and women, so people with the same name can be of either sex. It can make record keeping a little difficult at times. Many old people are called Gaga. This is in fact a term of respect, and one of our favourite people in the village is Gaga Doma. It still feels a little rude to call her this, but it would be quite offensive for me to leave off the Gaga. Young people are often called Ang, and at some time in their lives, usually after the age of 60, the Ang changes to Gaga.

What fascinates me as much as the differences are the similarities between different cultures. Children must be the same all over the world. I am amazed at the similarities of the games they play. Knucklebones and marbles are played with stones, skipping with plaited yak hair made into rope, hopscotch lines are scraped into the dirt, and even hackysack is played with a weighted sock.

*T*he monsoon has really set in, with the cloud so low at times that we cannot even see out of the window. The village is beautifully green with all the riggis and buck wheat growing well. The temperature ranges from 2-20°C, so it's quite comfortable. We have plenty of veges and dairy products to mix with our daily regime of riggis. Potato is a good nutritious food, but I may never want to look at another one when we get home.

A week ago we had Dumje, a festival practised for over 300 years, which celebrates the anniversary of the death of the patron saint Lama Sanga Dorji, and requests various gods to subdue demonic enemies of the village.

It lasts for five days and is basically just party, party, party. Ten families are chosen the year before to be sponsors, and this goes in about a 12-year cycle. It is an enormous expense for the families. Each have at least one party for the whole village, where they have to provide all the drinks and food. They also provide one mana (about two cups) of uncooked rice to everyone who attends the gompa (temple) on their appointed day. One of our friends, who was a Dumje sponsor about 15 years ago, said one mana of rice cost $NZ0.20 then, and this year cost him $NZ1.40. He's just a subsistence farmer, so his income hasn't really increased over that time. Trekking has certainly increased the cost of living up here.

Unfortunately, with a number of families in the Khumbu being extremely wealthy, people compete on a material level to look good. Some families will easily spend a year's income to keep up with the others. There are quite a number of poor families here, but also many rich ones who have family members who run trekking/climbing agencies and shops in Kathmandu. Rather than the number of fields or yaks a person owns, it is now income that determines someone's status. There is little incentive for people to train in any of the professions, since the government pays teachers, for example, $NZ120 per month, while an uneducated porter can start at $NZ8-12 per day and work up to an expedition job.

On the third day of Dumje, at the gompa, one of the richest men was calling out names and handing out khaarta and certificates to a number of the others there. I thought this was acknowledging good works, such as being on the hospital committee, or achievements over the year, and was upset to find that the list showed how much money each had donated to the gompa. Those who had given less than $NZ40 did not receive khaarta, and families who did not give anything were also named! I found out later that this man, who runs about 20 trekking agencies, had threatened his Sherpa workers that if they did not donate a certain amount they would lose their jobs! There was a lot of bitter feeling that Kathmandu Sherpas were taking over the power of the gompa because they could donate amounts such as $NZ1000 (probably only representing a few day's work), yet poorer families may have saved for many months to raise their $NZ40. One drunk man got very angry and started abusing one of the rich benefactors, but was soon quietened down. I didn't really understand what the fight was about at the time, and was impressed at the gentle way they dealt with him. His friends would come over and hug and humour him, tried to give him khaarta too, and did a very good defusing job. A lot of people get very drunk at Dumje, and they have designated local people to act as security guards for the week to stop any fights.

We were invited to five Dumje parties, and they really were fun. We'd arrive and find a seat — not as easy as you'd think. There is a definite hierarchy of seating. The men sit on one side of the room, and women on the other (often on the floor if there isn't enough seating). They sit in order of importance, usually the oldest at the head of the room, but rich people, and "sahibs" and "memsahibs" sit at the important end as well. The trick is always to aim for a place a few people below where you're supposed to sit (since it's considered rude to just go to the front), then there's great pushing and shoving as people move down and push you up to where you should be. It's quite embarrassing for us, because if there's no seating for the women they insist we sit with the men. One advantage is that more men than women speak English. No one likes to speak Nepali (so much for all our lessons in Kathmandu).

Once seated, the women are given chiyaa (tea), and the men chang. I think I've got the "shey, shey" routine worked out. It is apparently very bad luck to give someone only one serving of anything, but people are happy if you stop at two or three. *Except at Dumje!* Very soon everyone moved on to chang, and the serious drinking began. If the host or hostess thought you weren't drinking quickly enough they would grab your glass and literally pour it down your throat! Spluttering and spilling drink down your chin did nothing but spur them on to a repeat attack, since some had been wasted. I actually found it quite degrading and felt rather assaulted, but seemed able to stay in the merry atmosphere of it all.

Then came the enormous meal of rice and Sherpa stew (meat and vegetables), followed by more enforced drinking. Then people would start to sing, and finally the benches were taken away and we all danced. Again the hierarchy of position is important. Di and I are always put at the head of the line, next to the men, which is a great sign of respect. However, this doesn't work so well because it is better for us to have people who know what they're doing on either side. Most of the men are great, but as some of the less prestigious men get drunk, they push their way up to us. Being drunk, they often fall about the place, which makes it even harder for us to keep in step.

Interestingly, Di is usually shown more respect and put ahead of me. To be big is good, showing that you are rich and have servants to do heavy work for you. Di is in fact fading away, but when she proudly announces to our Sherpa friends that she's lost 16 kg, they all look worried and sad for her.

After a few dances the hosts come around with a large cup of chang, and each person takes three sips and is given a khaarta. Soon after that, everybody suddenly leaves *en masse*.

On the trail, we came across a group of monks on the way to the gompa. Amongst them was the Gen Lama (a Tibetan term of respect for older people, a bit like Gaga). We all touched foreheads with him and he blessed us.

As we wandered further along the trail, we passed a dog, just standing inside his property minding his own business. One of our Sherpa friends (who seemed a perfectly friendly and amiable man) walked over to the dog and kicked him hard in the head. The dog yelped and ran off. The group laughed and walked on. Di and I were horrified. We asked Kami later why it had happened. He explained that one of the worst things a person can be reincarnated as is a dog. So dogs are reincarnates of very bad people and deserve all the misery they get. Sounds like a self-fulfilling prophecy to me. We said that if dogs (like people) were treated with love and respect, they would be good animals, but Kami just agreed that Longin is a very lucky dog. Most dogs in Nepal are not. We wondered why people kept dogs if they thought so little of them. Kami explained that some keep them as guard dogs, but mostly they have them to clean up the baby's mess when they poo on their clothes or the floor!

We were then led to another party, but this was just a drinking one. We all sat around while young men enthusiastically belted out a hearty song to each of us and made us drink three large gulps of either chang or rum. (The song was actually a Buddhist hymn, though it sounded more like the crowd at an Eden Park rugby match.) They kept coming around and around until, fortunately, Mingma rescued us and took us up to the gompa.

Here the monks were doing their pujas, and the more influential people (not us this time) were being fed again. Then the uncooked rice was handed out to everyone. The locals had all brought plastic bags; we had to put it in our jacket pockets. They used to give cooked rice made into balls, but each day everyone would get two (one from each sponsoring family), so a household of eight could get 80 rice balls over the week. And because everyone is so well fed anyway, it all went to waste.

The week continued on like this. The third day was the worst, when we had been invited to two parties on the same day, and had to drink and eat twice as much! That afternoon, in the gompa, the monks were dancing in costumes and masks (like at Mani-Rimbdu), then they lit the butter fire. Butter is very important in all religious festivals. (Every time you are given a drink, a blob of butter or flour is placed on the rim of the glass for good luck.) Many people from the village added a knob of butter to the pile. The wood fire was started with kerosene, and the butter mountain put on top of a tray. It eventually melted, while the monks blew their instruments and did the puja. Then the dancers returned. While they were dancing, other monks would throw more kerosene or rum on the fire, and it would flare up to about 20 feet high. Some of the monks were drunk, and a bit clumsy, and I was very worried that they would fall into the fire. It was also very close to the cross-legged seated crowd, mainly children, and also near to Di, Mingma and Longin (the hospital dog, who was very frightened). It was so crowded that escape would have been difficult. Fortunately, nothing bad happened, and everyone was delighted by the show. When I voiced my concern to Mingma later, he said that a few years ago a drunk man had kicked the tray of melted butter into the crowd and about 30 people had been burned.

We are certainly "Dumjed-out", but have increased our popularity around the place. We held clinics in the morning before going to the parties, and were extremely lucky that no one got seriously ill during the evenings, when I was not at my best. However, my cries of needing to stay sober just in case I was needed at the hospital were literally drowned out with chang until I stopped worrying about it. Apparently, it has always been done like that. In the same way that carpenters drink to work better, it's felt that I'll perform more efficiently tanked up. I don't like it at all, but teetotal doctors have usually been quite unpopular. It is a very alcoholic society. At least these festivals occur only a few times a year.

I am still coming across differences, even opposites, in our cultures. Boys wear their hair in pigtails, so I am forever calling a him a her. The women wear ingis, but the men and children tend to wear Western sweatshirts and trousers. It is, however, easy to pick the sex of the younger children. Instead of toilet-training, the young ones have the crotch cut out of their trousers, and crouch wherever they are to do their business. Urine just soaks into the wooden floor, or the child's mother may wipe it up. The houses are so smokey from the cooking fire that I never notice any other unpleasant smells. Both Di and I have developed a near-permanent allergic rhinitis, which is in some ways a blessing. With no warm water available, body-washing is an uncommon event. I can't blame them — if we didn't have our solar-powered hot water we wouldn't be showering either. Also, cleanliness is not a social expectation here, and very soon we stopped noticing it too.

Babies are fed solids from birth here, and thrive on it. This rather blows away our theory of waiting three to five months. Virtually the moment the baby is born, yak butter is stuffed in his/her mouth, and they all take it quite happily. From then on the mother feeds the baby by chewing the food in her mouth then transferring it mouth-to-mouth. They also give the medicine syrups this way, which at first shocked me a little, but it certainly seems more efficient than struggling with a teaspoon or syringe, since they cover the babies mouths until they have swallowed, instead of letting them spit it over everything.

Mothers are also fed immediately after delivery, usually chang porridge. This is a truely disgusting brew. It is very bad luck if they don't eat this, and they are considered at risk of getting "pung", which seems to be a variation of post-natal depression where mothers lose all interest in caring for their babies and won't go out into the sunlight. It is a very serious condition, since if the family is not available or willing to take over the care of the child, she/he usually dies. Some very enthusiastic mothers and mothers-in-law will try to force-feed chang porridge into the delivering mother's mouth just as she is pushing the baby out!

Infant mortality is dropping, but I still see women who want their Norplant removed because their baby died recently. The majority have not sought medical help for the child. One of the very prominent women in the village has only three grown-up sons out of sixteen pregnancies.

When a person dies, his or her name is never mentioned again, and all photos of that person are taken down. It is even very bad form to say, "I'm sorry to hear that your father died." The most people do to acknowledge the death is to visit the family with chang or chiyaa and say "aachhu", which means sorrow or sadness. It is particularly bad to die on a Tuesday, when it is felt that seven more people will shortly follow that person. If someone dies on a Sunday, three others will die soon after. On the night after the body is cremated, the monks may do a puja in the house and bang their drums and cymbals loudly, while the family will bash pots and pans to frighten the deceased's ghost away from the family home. Recently one of my patients died on a Tuesday, which is bad enough, but the Gen Lama stated that this was also a very inauspicious day on which to die and that this man would bring very bad luck on Khunde. In the middle of the night after he was cremated, we were awoken by a row of monks marching around the village making a real racket to frighten his ghost from the area.

For a year after someone has died, the family must not dance and cannot get married. Tenzing Norgay's grandson, who lives in Australia and had planned to climb Mt Everest on the 40th anniversary of his grandfather and Ed Hillary's summit, had to cancel the expedition because his uncle was killed just below the summit earlier in the year.

Most Sherpas and Nepalis cremate their dead. If someone has died from smallpox (not really a problem now) or measles, they must be buried, since the belief is that the smoke from the body will spread the disease. Interestingly, there are no such restrictions for other infectious diseases such as tuberculosis and leprosy (much more common). What really fascinates me are the Tibetan funerals, where they neither bury nor cremate their dead, but feed them to the eagles. Everyone goes to one of the special funeral areas, the body is stripped, and each limb is tied to a rock — spread-eagled (sorry, a tasteless yet irresistible pun). The lamas blow their funeral horns, and a great flock of eagles appear. There are people whose full-time job is to prepare the bodies, and they proceed to hack the meat off the body with large knives. The eagles feed on the corpse until it's down to the bones, then the workers crush the bones with an axe on a special area of flat rock, fracture the skull and smear the brain over the bones. The eagles feed on that too. They are called sky burials.

We admitted a woman who lives about two hour's walk away and turned up at the hospital heavily pregnant with a breech baby. Her last baby was a footling breech, which means the baby comes one foot first rather than presenting its bottom. The previous doctor made an urgent visit to her last year and sadly delivered a dead baby. Footling breeches usually don't survive delivery. I convinced her to move into the short-stay ward until she delivers, hoping that I can help her have a better outcome.

I wasn't all that confident in my ability to deliver a breech baby, and looked through an old obstetric text that contained horrifying pictures of all the different things that can go wrong at a delivery. It mentioned the occasional necessity of performing a symphisiotomy, which involves cutting through the ligament between the front pubic bones to enlarge the outlet through which the baby can come. I knew next to nothing about this procedure, but found a "paint-by-numbers" guide in a tropical medicine journal.

In the meantime, the dental technician from Namche turned up in the middle of one night, in labour. It was her first baby and she is related to many important local people. We like her very much and were particularly concerned that all went well for her.

Her mother-in-law, Ang Doolie, insisted that she deliver in the classroom, rather than the surgery or short-stay ward, because she believes that ghosts live in those two rooms and the classroom is the only safe one. I attempted to argue that if anything went wrong we could do very little, but the family insisted. I examined her and things seemed to be moving along well, and I couldn't foresee any problems.

She became fully dilated and ready to push the baby out in good time, and we grovelled around on the floor using torches and candle-light, preparing for the delivery. After an hour of pushing, nothing much had happened, and I realised that the baby's head was caught in a deep transverse arrest. The head was too high up to pull out and was turned so that it was presenting its widest diameter to the pelvic outlet.

I put in a pudendal block (which previously I'd only observed and read about), where a needle is fed deep into each side of the vagina and local anaesthetic infiltrated to block the whole perineum. Once local anaesthesia was achieved I cut a very large episiotomy and attached a Ventouse extractor to the baby's head. This apparatus has a suction cup on the end, which grabs the baby's head and allows it to be gently pulled out. I had several tries at this, but the baby's head didn't move an inch. I then tried to pull the baby out with Kielland forceps, which look a little like large salad servers. I'd never used them before either, but had practised on mannequins many years ago.

By this time the poor dental technician had been pushing for three hours and was looking exhausted. I imagined that this was how women died in obstructed labour and felt quite desperate at our friend's plight.

I asked her husband and brother-in-law to carry her into the surgery, where we at least had an examination table and solar-powered lights. I couldn't hear a foetal heart beat, and felt sure that the baby was dead. I thought that the mother would also soon be dead if we didn't get the baby out. I had practised some Caesarean sections in New Zealand before I had left, but felt that I would be very slow, and would certainly put the dental technician's life even more at risk. I asked Diane to find the journal article on symphisiotomy, feeling it was the mother's best chance.

We had no stirrups, so the dental technician's husband had to stand with one of her knees over his shoulder. Diane balanced the other knee on hers and held the illustrated journal article up for me to follow. I catheterised the mother, then instilled more local anaesthetic. We tied a loose bandage around the mother's knees so that they would not spread too far apart and split the bone too far open. Diane read out from the book while I cut through the ligament, from the centre outwards in both directions. It bled quite a lot, which worried me since the article hadn't mentioned anything about that.

I waited for something to go "pop", to show that the outlet had widened, but nothing seemed to happen. I placed the forceps around the baby's head and pulled and strained, but nothing happened. I felt quite hysterical at the thought that I would not be able to get this baby out and that the mother might die. I remembered reading a ghastly part of the obstetric text that described how to extract a dead baby piece by piece from a live mother.

I just wanted to run away and pretend it wasn't happening.

I put the forceps on again and this time yanked and pulled and twisted, feeling that if the worst happened and I pulled the baby's head off, at least I could get the rest out and save the mother. Suddenly something moved and out came the baby's head.

I got such a shock when the baby let out a loud cry that I almost dropped everything. "Oh my God, Diane, it's alive, what do I do now?" I managed to calm myself down and bring the baby's body out. An enormous boy!

He looked a bit flat and I wanted to give him oxygen and resuscitate him a little, but Ang Doolie would have none of that. She and I wrestled with the baby for a few seconds, until she grabbed him from me and stuffed a glob of yak butter into his mouth. Then she covered the newly cut umbilical cord in soot and took him into the next room to show the rest of the family.

We weighed him later and he was a massive 5.2 kg. The average Nepali baby is born at 2.5 kg. As far as we could tell he seemed to be doing all the right things. I seem to have proved myself. One grandfather is boasting to all and sundry that he is the biggest baby ever born in the Khumbu. The other grandfather now beams from ear to ear whenever he sees me, "Good baby, good big boy." Ang Doolie came the next day and gave us both a back apron. "You and memsahib like man and wife," she said making a crude signal pushing one forefinger through a circle made by her other thumb and forefinger. "You wear over your ingi. Keep you warm in winter."

Mum recovered well and the next day went to stay with her mother-in-law in Khunde. She and her husband were delighted to hear that not all deliveries were like this one, and that now that her pelvis was wider she should have an easy time with the next baby. Though I did ask her to deliver in Kathmandu next time.

The journal article said that 12 per cent of women are permanently disabled after symphisiotomy, and we anxiously watched the dental technician's progress. For several days we made her wear a constricting bandage to keep her knees from moving too far apart. She very much wanted to go home to Namche, and we finally agreed that she could be carried down on a stretcher.

A couple of days later we were called down to see her as she was in considerable pain. Rather than have the embarrassment of being carried on a stretcher she had walked half the way herself and her husband had piggybacked her when they were out of sight. We explained that this was exactly the leg position we wanted her to avoid. However, things settled down after a few days of strong pain relief.

I went to the baby-naming ceremony in Namche. (Di was invited also, but unfortunately had woken up with yet another stomach-bug and couldn't trust herself to leave the flat.) It was very enjoyable, and even though I was seated between some of the Khunde women who do not speak any English we managed to get by with sign language and Nepali-

Sherpa. They fed us three times! No chance of me starving up here!

There has been an outbreak of gastro-enteritis in Phortse, fortunately very responsive to co-trimoxazole. Sadly two children have died. One six-year-old boy was dehydrated purposely, as is the local tradition. The other, an eight-year-old boy, became rapidly very ill on the day that the health worker ran out of medicines. He sent a runner and we sent some more medicines, which arrived the following morning, but by that time the boy had died.

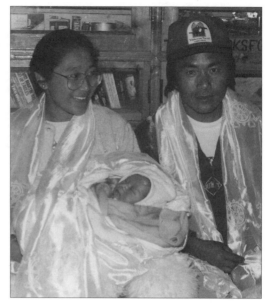

PROUD PARENTS AT THE NAMING CEREMONY.

We were also saddened and surprised to hear that our carpenter had died in Kathmandu. We couldn't find out any details. Kami says that he expected it. He suspects that the carpenter probably got pneumonia, and, because of his quadriplegia, the doctors chose not to treat him.

Kathmandu has been having more political troubles, with at least three people having been killed in the most recent Communist bandh (strike). Power lines have been cut down, and private vehicles and shops wrecked. There is a curfew on at present, and Kami, who was supposed to go down for computer lessons, has wisely decided to postpone this for a while.

The Communists have threatened that unless the Prime Minister resigns they will have a three-day transportation strike, followed by a three-day general bandh. If that does not achieve their goal, they plan to move 10 million protesters from around Nepal into Kathmandu to devastate the city!

The science teacher is building a lodge right in front of the hospital. Fortunately, it is only one storey, so our view won't be too obstructed. It is fascinating to watch the building progress. First the rocks are broken up from large ones outside the village, then carried in. The senior carpenter pegs out the boundaries with a rope, knotted every yard or so. The ditches for the foundations are still being dug. They have come across an enormous buried boulder, which they are patiently hacking away at, hoping to split into smaller ones so it can be removed. At times it becomes

The teacher's lodge being built.

the macho centre of the village, where many of the locals line up to have a bash in the hope that they will be the one to split it. The other men and young women stand and watch, "oohing" and "aahing" at their efforts.

Meanwhile, there is a line of seven or so men who sit patiently all day chipping away at the edges of the rocks to make flat sides for the outside of the house. These lads work very hard. They start at daylight and, apart from meal breaks, work until dark. No stopping for rain. They even work on a Saturday. The unions in New Zealand would have them blacklisted in a flash!

We are worried about Longin. She has been vomiting at least three times a day for the past two weeks and has periods of misery where she just lies about. There is no diarrhoea that we've seen, and her abdomen is soft, non-tender and has no obvious obstruction. Her appetite is mostly good, but I think she's a dog who eats whether she's hungry or not. We've tried resting her bowel, but she has so many alternate food sources that it's been pretty impossible. She's lost 25 per cent of her body weight over the last two weeks! She hasn't responded to a short trial of co-trimoxazole, and at present I'm trying norfloxacin and metronidazole (other antibiotics). Anti-nausea medication seems to give her temporary symptomatic relief. I don't know whether any of these drugs are safe or effective for dogs, and the veterinary books we have here are not very helpful. Poor baby, she's still as sweet tempered as ever, but her wagging tail does not compensate for her dull eyes and sad, pained expression. We're all hoping she gets better soon.

W e are thoroughly sick of the monsoon, living amongst the clouds and spending our "summer" in Polartek. Roll on trekking season. We want our mountain views back.

Three weeks ago, two friends, (the ones who had the 5.2 kg baby), had the final stage of their wedding. Sherpa marriages involve three separate ceremonies. First of all there is "sodane" (asking), where the parents of the boy visit the girl's family, drink lots of chang, and ask if they will agree to the match. (All unmarried women are called girls, and unmarried men boys, even into middle age. It grates a little, but we've got used to using their words because people get quite confused by terms such as "young woman".)

If the girl's parents agree, the boy can sleep with her at her parent's place. (This intrigues me since the entire family sleep together in one room. I haven't been brave enough to ask anyone about the logistics of love-making in a crowded room. And in front of your in-laws too!) It is preferable that they have a child (especially a boy) to prove fertility before the final ceremony. Once the girl becomes pregnant, the boy is committed and can get out of the arrangement only by paying a fine to her family. However, it is unusual for a couple to separate at this stage.

After a year or so comes the "dem-chang" (engagement party). Some people leave it at that, especially if the girl is poor and doesn't bring much dowry (or "dollary" as one of our health workers calls it). The final stage, the "zendi" (wedding) is very expensive, and its main purpose is to present the girl's dowry to the boy's family. Dowry is becoming a bit of a problem here. Again, with some families becoming very rich through expeditions and trekking, monetary expectations are rising. Family members are

expected to contribute to the dowry. This amount is recorded and must be reciprocated by the bride's family when their relatives' girls marry. With such inequalities in earning power, this can cause problems. It is also well known that women are killed for their dowries in India and Southern Nepal. Some families make a business out of it, with their sons marrying and murdering a long succession of brides, keeping the dowry each time. I can't see it happening amongst the Sherpas, but certainly people are asking for higher and higher dowries from the families. At least in Sherpa society, if the couple divorce, the wife takes her dowry with her. In fact, the more modern Sherpas refer to the dowry as marriage insurance.

Our friends both come from extremely rich families, so their zendi was quite a spectacle. With a healthy son delivered about a month ago, everything was going right for them. The zendi lasts for about three days. First of all, the groom (who lives in Khunde), went down to Namche (about one and a half hours' walk) to the bride's family. We sat with the other villagers at the chorten and watched the procession. The groom and his father were on horseback, while the other 30 relatives walked behind. At the chorten, juniper branches were burnt, chang drunk, and the lama gave a puja. The groom's outfit was superb. He was dressed in an ornate ankle-length embroidered brocade robe and a magnificent hat. The men wore the traditional black wrap-around robe and Stetson cowboy hats. The women wore their best ingis, adorned with all of their turquoise, zee and coral jewellery, and their fur, embroidered hats.

They attended eight parties over the next two days in Namche, all put on by the bride's relatives, then everyone came back up to Khunde to bring the bride to her husband's family home. The bride is supposed to look unhappy during the wedding parties because she is leaving her family. It is considered bad luck for the marriage if she does not cry at least once during the ceremony. Apparently, as they left Namche, about 50 members of her family stood howling their eyes out. In Khunde there was an enormous crowd waiting with us, since everyone wants to see the new bride who is to live in their village and, even more so, they like to see how much dowry she's brought with her.

Five of the men and the bride rode on horseback, followed by the remaining men and then the women, singing their hearts out and really whooping it up. The bride did a very good job of looking as miserable as she could. She had promised me she would ride the horse side-saddle because of her healing symphisiotomy, but she rode astride the horse, and I wondered how much of the misery was actually pain. I was really annoyed with her, imagining her hobbling around for the rest of her life, but later she explained it away by saying it wouldn't have looked good. Following the close relatives came more family, doing elaborate dances with sheathed "khukuri" (machete-type knives) and pom-poms made out of yak hair. Then came about 20 people and 15 mules carrying the many rugs and copper pots that made up the dowry. All $NZ128,000 of it! It's the richest zendi Khunde's ever seen.

Then there were six more parties in Khunde. Di and I were invited to some of them (which was quite an honour, since it's very much a family affair). Di went to two of the parties and had a great time. I was unfortunately a bit seedy that day and stayed at home. The next day, the bride's parents and some more relatives came up to the village, so more parties followed.

Most couples live with the husband's family for a number of years before they can afford to "separate" and live in their own house. Many never leave. However, the groom's father has already built him a house in Khunde, and they moved there for a week. Because the husband needed to get back to work (in a completely different area of Nepal) and the wife runs her dental business in Namche, she has moved back down to live with her parents there. Our friends probably won't see much of each other. Although they get on well, this doesn't seem to worry them at all. Many couples in Nepal have arranged marriages and spend a lot of time apart because of work availability. No one seems to think anything of it.

Our friend's younger brother also had his zendi two weeks ago. His bride's family, not to be out-done, came up with $NZ144,000. It has been a really busy time for the family. There are lots of weddings in the monsoon. It's a quieter time for most of the villagers, with the riggis planted, the yaks grazing up-valley, and few nosy trekkers.

Di and I will celebrate our third anniversary next week. Working and living together seems to suit us very well. I feel very lucky to know Diane, and am delighted to find more strengths and abilities the more I get to know her.

Di is enjoying teaching English and maths to our friends. One local woman (whose husband and father-in-law already speak good English) is particularly keen and comes every day with her two-year-old daughter. One day Di was going through the alphabet and when she got to "v", the only word she could think of was "vet". Our friend had never heard of the concept and thought it was the funniest thing she'd ever come across. Imagine animals having their own doctors! She literally fell about the place laughing, and joked with her friends about the crazy foreigners.

A week ago we celebrated "Phangi" (pronounced Pungi), which has no religious significance but is just a week-long party, probably to relieve the boredom of the monsoon. The main belief about Phangi is that everything you eat there will go straight to fat. Of course, this is a highly desirable and popular concept here. Can't see it going down too well at home.

Everyone in the village who wants to attend pays $NZ24, and the provisions are bought at the market the Saturday before. One of these provisions was a live goat, which sat outside the house bellowing mournfully for two days. The first day of Phangi was a full moon, so the animal couldn't be slaughtered until the next day. Both Di and I became quite attached to him over that time and agonised over plans to set him free. However, hypocrites that we are, we tucked into his Sherpa stew a couple of days later with few qualms.

The parties would start in the mornings, but we had the hospital clinic open until midday. When we'd arrive, the room would be full of villagers, all gambling over cards or an incomprehensible game involving shells, coins and bits of maize, where the player enthusiastically plonks his dice, in a wooden container, on to a base with a great "whoop". The more enthusiastic the shout and the harder the container is thrown down, the better the dice are meant to be. It took me quite a few days to stop jumping involuntarily every 30 seconds or so when this happened. Usually the younger people in the village (i.e., our age) attended these parties and things felt much more relaxed. At first the men gambled together for about $NZ4 a game, while the women stuck to 1 Rs ($NZ0.04) a game. However, as the week went on, men and women all played together. In the background, a ghetto blaster would be blaring out the latest Nepali hits or, after our arrival, Madonna, Michael Jackson and country music from our collection. People drank chang, but mostly chiyaa. Mingma, Di and I would settle down to some serious (non-gambling) canasta. At about 3.30 we'd be served lunch, but the gambling would go on until about 6 pm.

Then there'd be cries of "Game last!", and soon all the mats and tables would be cleared away for the Sherpa dancing, which went on until about 11 pm. Chang drinking would start in earnest. The Sherpa dancing was very relaxed, with the young children allowed to have a go, and the normal hierarchy of dancing order ignored. Women would dance with a babe actively suckling. Various jokes would be played on people. The most popular was a plaited hair piece, which would be secretly stuck on one of the men's collars, and he would wonder why everyone was giggling at the "new girl". People would break ranks and lapse into groups of two or three, who would go around in circles and wave their arms about in a prescribed fashion. Full of chang, I happily joined in. Obviously, my arm waving wasn't quite right, judging by the hoots of laughter that came from everyone, but it just added to the fun.

Some nights the ghetto blaster would be put on and we'd Nepali or disco dance. We, of course, being the local disco-dancing experts, were dragged up to show them how it was done. After we'd got a bit sick of wiggling our hips around to Michael Jackson, while everyone stared in awe and tried to emulate, we decided the time had come for a bit of line dancing. Sadly, on that particular night, we hadn't brought any country music, so we treated them to the "Tush Push" to Madonna's "Material Girl". I was full of chang by this stage, but I'm very impressed with Diane, who managed this exhibition sober. It was a real hit, with one of the women leaping up and thrusting her hips provocatively around the room, while a few of the young men bounced around us trying to follow the steps. Everyone thought it was hilarious and laughed delightedly with us. At the end, everyone "whoooed" (a great compliment) and clapped enthusiastically. We did another line dance to yet another Madonna classic, and then disco danced to some techno music we'd brought. The next morning our health worker was still grinning from ear to ear, enthusing about how much everyone had loved our dancing. "We've never seen proper disco dancing before, mostly we just wiggle our hips around not knowing what we're doing." Stand aside John Travolta, the "experts" are here.

On the third day of Phangi, they had a mock wedding. One of the older characters of the village was dressed up in his traditional gear, while the "bride" (a young man from the neighbouring Khumjung village dressed in an ingi) made a procession up to the village. Women were dressed as Nepali or Sherpa men, or wore jeans and dinner jackets. Some of the men wore dresses, or flashy earrings, or false noses, moustaches and silly glasses. Instead of the wedding cake, they had decorated a raw turnip. Later we all had a slice to celebrate the "couple's" happy future. (It was actually quite nice. My taste-buds must be getting hardened.) People made speeches, in Sherpa unfortunately, which from watching the crowd were obviously hilarious. A gay old time was had by all. It's certainly the best time we've had since we arrived.

Longin has brightened up and is working enthusiastically on regaining her weight loss. She has even forgiven us for the suppositories, and I must admit that it's a job I'm glad to be finished with. Di and I would spend quite a time each morning chasing Longin around the hospital, while she waddled with her tail fixed firmly down between her legs. I would have a lubricated glove on one hand, and the antibiotic suppository in the other, while Di would finally catch and hold Longin's tail up for me to do the deed. She would then scowl at us and storm off indignantly up the back of the hospital.

We are delighted that she is back to her normal self. She was looking quite svelte for a while, but after attending the Phangi parties she managed to regain all of her previous weight and more. There are always leftovers (since it's rude to finish your plate — implying that you could still eat more and that the hosts have not provided enough for you). Longin is the only village dog allowed at the parties and she guzzled ecstatically all night. She seems to have no stop button and at the end of one party had eaten so much she couldn't walk, so we had to carry her home. Once home she just lay on her side groaning with her overfilled stomach. I tried to give her some antacid, but after the suppositories she wasn't having a piece of it.

62 A few days later, Kami and I went to the annual army party in Namche.

I was sat at the head of the room between the major and his wife, on the only padded seating available. Everyone was very kind and considerate. Fortunately, most of the people around me spoke English, which was a pleasant change, and made for much more lively conversation. The captain (who had just returned from training in the Middle East) chatted to me for quite a while. He asked how many doctors were working with me up at Khunde Hospital. When I said I was the only one, he put his hand on my shoulder, gazed intently into my eyes, and said earnestly, "You are a very brave man!" Oh no, I thought, with my short hair and trousers, he thinks I'm a bloke! In response to my embarrassed laugh, he explained, "I know you are a woman, but in Nepal all women are vulnerable and weak. This is why I call you a brave man." I was at a loss as to how to respond to that, so decided to just accept it as the compliment intended.

The food was very good, highly spiced and a change from Sherpa fare. They kept handing out little titbits and, being very hungry, I accepted fourth and fifth helpings, thinking to myself that this was a bit of a stingy do. Unfortunately, this was only the entrée, and an enormous buffet meal was soon presented. The major stood up and announced "ladies first", which produced giggles from the men, and considerable discomfort for the women, who all stood back, not quite knowing what to do. I insisted that the major's wife start off, and then followed her. She interpreted my hesitation as unfamiliarity with the buffet system, and took me under her wing, filling my plate to almost overflowing. It was hard work to do the meal justice. Then came dessert! Custard, with hard dried lumps of coconut in it. The major looked so hurt when I turned down seconds that I had to give in.

Soon our plates, and even our half-filled glasses were removed. I remembered the previous doctor's letter describing the disco dancing performances of the last army party and had been looking forward to this. YEEHAA! I'd even practised up a line dance routine. To my great disappointment, however, everybody started putting on their jackets and, among many "Namastes" and "Namaskars" we all toddled off home.

We have escaped most of the disastrous flooding in West Nepal, where over 300 people are dead and 200 missing. Eight major road suspension bridges have been washed away, and communications (other than air) were cut off between most of the main centres. Three porters were killed crossing the bridge over the Dudh Kosi, just below Nuntala, as it was washed away. On our trek up we noticed that the right-hand terminal suspension wire was broken and tied on to the end of the bridge by a thin

ONE OF THE BETTER
BRIDGES ON THE TRAIL
TO JORSALE.

DOKAS BELOW
NAMCHE MARKET.

coil of wire. Our guide said it had been that way for a very long time. Another porter slipped on the Phakding bridge and drowned. However, the rain does not seem to have been particularly heavy in our area.

We have been seeing quite a few people, despite the monsoon, ranging from 56 people one Sunday (which Kami says is a record) to a low of about 12. An American school group has been planting trees for the National Park and working on a water project in Ghat. All seemed to get diarrhoea and/or upper respiratory tract infections, so we saw them frequently. They were also suffering from sore necks, having carried the seedlings from Phurte in dokas (packs carried with a band around the forehead)! They kindly donated $NZ500 to the hospital when they left.

We have also had our share of idiots here, first-time visitors on their own without guides or trekking books, who know so much more than any of us about the place. They tell us that they are "travellers" rather than "trekkers", and find out about things by talking to the locals. One guy had been told that it was only one day's walk from Namche (3441 m), to Gokyo (4750 m). I came across him in a teahouse before he left and spent considerable time and effort explaining why his trekking plan wasn't such a good idea, and drawing up a reasonable plan for him, which he ignored. His pulmonary oedema stopped him halfway up, and he had to cut his "travels" short with a rapid helicopter descent to Kathmandu. Often these "travellers" don't carry medical insurance, and this causes enormous hassles radioing their embassy in Kathmandu to see if they will guarantee the cost of evacuation. The helicopter will not leave Kathmandu until the $NZ5000 is paid.

We have had a really distressing time with the woman we admitted with the breech baby. I examined her again last week, as she looks very close to delivery, and was horrified to discover that the baby has turned around and is now in a transverse lie. This means that it is lying sideways, and there is no way it can come out normally. I explained this to the woman and her husband and offered to have the Trust pay for them to fly to Kathmandu immediately to have a Caesarean section.

The husband refused. After many long discussions he stated that he didn't want his wife to have an operation because it would leave her weak and unable to work hard in the fields. We kept saying that she would die if she didn't have the operation, but still he wouldn't let her go, feeling that it would be better to find a strong new wife than keep a weakened one. Of course we tried to get the woman to go by herself, but she would not disobey her husband. When we told her she would die she just shrugged and said it was up to the gods.

The husband became angry with us because we were so insistent and he made his wife pack up and move home. I pleaded with them to stay in the hospital so that at least I could help with the delivery, thinking that at the last minute we could kick the husband out and I would have a go at a Caesarean section. The woman might well survive and, even if she didn't, it would be better to die under an anaesthetic than painfully in obstructed labour.

But off they went to their tiny village two hours' walk from the hospital. We found out a few days later that the husband had gone to the lamas to ask their advice. They had thrown the dice and read the books and told him that yes, she would die soon. It is considered very bad luck to have someone die in your house, so he sent his wife up into the yak fields another three hours' walk away.

Di and I were distraught thinking of this woman struggling and dying a painful death alone in a field, five hours' walk from the hospital. The locals would "tutt tutt" and say the husband was a bad man, but nobody stepped in to do anything about it. It was apparently his right. Sometimes I hate this place.

Our mail runner still hasn't returned from his "ten-day" holiday and we haven't had any mail for over a month. We get so desperate to hear from home. I would like to kick him when we next see him.

Di and I celebrated our birthdays this week. They are three days apart. We had a party with potato pancake and a chocolate cake. I had brought a candle that sings "Happy Birthday" from New Zealand, which impressed the health workers. We miss our family and friends. I wish we were home.

*D*ear Friends of ours who have never even written us ONE letter, even though we've been away for six months now.

We really want to hear from you. So, to make things easy, just tick the appropriate responses below and return this sheet to the above address.

❏ I am alive.

❏ I am not. (Please remove me from your mailing list.)

❏ Alzheimers has set in. WHO ARE YOU? Who am I?

❏ I am missing you terribly.

❏ I was only pretending to be your friend. Really, I'm glad you've gone.

❏ Have you gone already?

❏ What were your names again?

I WROTE YOU A LETTER BUT:

❏ The dog/kid chewed it up.

❏ I thought you were in Naples, Italy.

❏ The gift that I enclosed was so expensive that customs wouldn't let it out of the country.

THE REASON I HAVEN'T WRITTEN IS THAT:

❏ I am so miserable with you away that I can't bear to read your letters, and just burst into tears every time I try to write.

❏ I've been waiting for something exciting to write to you about, but my life's so dull, nothing's happened yet.

❏ I've met someone new. You know how it is.

❏ I've become a Fundamentalist Christian and now abhor your depraved (I only wish) lifestyle.

AS AN APOLOGY:

❏ I have enclosed a money order for $US1000.

❏ I will be coming to see you in Nepal!

❏ I will send k.d. lang instead.

Looking forward to hearing from you,
Love from Liz and Di

*I*t's been a busy time around the village. All the grass fields have to be cut and made into hay. No lawnmowers here, not even scythes (since the ground is so uneven). The villagers kneel down with their little sickles, grab a bunch of grass, hack it down and move on. (A bit like scrubbing the kitchen floor with a toothbrush — but this is the easy bit!) Then it has to be dried before it rots. Now the problem with the monsoon is that it rains a lot. So all the grass is spread out thinly over the field and any other spare flat area, then it starts raining, so it's all rapidly raked up into piles until it stops, then it's spread out again until it rains, and so on, for days. People just sit patiently in their fields waiting for the rain to stop, so they can spread it out again. If they don't take advantage of all the sunshine the grass will rot, so they can't go off and do any other jobs until it's finished. I'm sure drying the grass would leave me a screaming hysterical wreck after a day or so, but the locals just get on with it. Once it has finally dried, it is piled up very high in a doka and carried home to be stored downstairs in the house. The "walking grass" looks quite delightful as it moves around the village.

Once that's finished, the riggi crop has to be harvested. Because of the large amount of rain this year, people have to dig a lot for a small number of sad-looking riggis. Speaking now as an expert on riggi eating, the new potatoes are delicious.

Mingma has taken two weeks' holiday to dry his grass and dig his riggis. Some holiday!

The Gen Lama at Khunde died 12 days ago, aged 84. He was placed sitting in meditation position shortly after he died, and remains like this.

The local people are very impressed and are travelling from far and wide to view his body. It is very auspicious that he has "meditated" for so long, and it is extremely likely that he will be reincarnated.

When a lama is reincarnated he may take on the body of a young boy, born around the time of his death. (They don't seem to have lamesses.) This child at two or three years of age will not act like his siblings and will talk about prayers, monasteries and Buddhist principles well beyond his expected knowledge. At the age of five or six, if the parents think that their son is a reincarnate lama, they will take him to the Rimpoche to be tested. The boy will be asked about personal details of the Gen Lama's life and asked to pick out his belongings amongst many replicas. Kami says that the testing is very rigorous, and there is no way that the boy could study up or fluke it.

NUN PRAYING OUTSIDE THE DECEASED GEN LAMA'S WINDOW.

If it is decided that the boy is the reincarnate Gen Lama, he will be taken from his family and educated in Buddhist practice, probably by the Dalai Lama in Dharamsala (in India). It is a great honour for the family, so the parents don't seem to mind "losing" a son. It is felt that he wasn't really theirs to start with.

The Tengboche Rimpoche has chosen the 25th of September for the Gen Lama to be cremated. This is almost a month after he died! They have been waiting for him to "fall" from "meditation" so they can preserve him in a large vat of salt, but I suspect they may need to give him a wee nudge, since he looks well settled in to me. We pop up every second day or so, and it's interesting to see the subtle changes in his appearance. When he's cremated, samples of the salt will be handed out to the villagers to take when they're sick. Maybe the hospital should get in a load.

He has an ornamental silver cup tied under his chin, and after about four days of meditation, some mucous is supposed to come from the Lama's nose. This is his life force. It can be either red or white, denoting the masculine or feminine part of him. It is very important that this is collected and used for religious purposes. However, nothing has come yet.

At the back of the gompa the men have been breaking rocks with sledgehammers and picks to make a flat area for the Gen Lama's cremation oven. They have done an enormous amount of work, breaking up other rocks and carrying them to the area to make a large retaining wall. There will be an enormous number of people at his cremation, and they have turned a steep rocky slope into a flat platform in a matter of days, all with very simple tools. The oven is about 3 m x 3 m, made of rocks and covered with clay. Once the Gen Lama has been cremated this will be demolished and a proper chorten will be built as his memorial.

A lot of firewood has been collected. Each piece is chipped straight with a knife then smoothed off with a plane. Each faggot that goes around the Gen Lama will have prayers written in marker pen on its sides.

Meanwhile, the monks have been busily printing and sewing the brightly coloured prayer flags that will adorn the oven. Pieces of wood have prayers carved into them and are then covered with black nugget. The cloth is placed on top, then the pattern is pressed on with a rolling pin. The cloth is then sewn together, using small hand-turned treadle machines, into quite elaborate patterns, such as a wind sock of blue, red, yellow, white and green. Then the seams are ironed flat with a metal iron repeatedly heated on the fire. Nothing comes easily in Nepal.

We are totally spoilt every time we go up there, and are fed buckets of chiyaa and food. I feel very privileged, since they asked me to photograph the Gen Lama "meditating". Only men are allowed in the room with him, but I was able to do this through his bedroom window. They were also keen for me to photograph the nuns and monks praying and doing their pujas. The prayers are quite hypnotising, the deep mumbling of the old monks combining with the high-pitched voices of the nuns, some as young as 10.

On the 22nd of September the Tengboche monastery will be reopened. It was accidentally burned down about five years ago, and an obscene amount of money has gone into rebuilding it. Many "big wigs" will be flown in by helicopter for the ceremony, including Ed and June Hillary. Unlike the Gen Lama, who was highly respected and a very good, kind man, especially to the poor, the Tengboche Rimpoche seems to have fallen prey to the material gains available from trekkers and Westerners. Only one monk is training at the Tengboche monastery and most of the religious people here have lost faith in it. But it is a great tourist attraction and a mighty earner for the area.

We will combine the opening with a clinic visit to the nearby villages of Phortse and Deboche. I am fascinated to be visiting Phortse at last. It's only two hours' walk, so we see quite a number of their people at the hospital. Phortse has a rather unfortunate reputation. The pocket of land where it is based is particularly lacking in any sources of iodine. As a result, a large number of children were born to hypothyroid mothers and became cretins. Cretins tend to be of short-stature, deaf-mute with low

DEBOUCHE
NUNNERY.

71

intelligence. This was a problem throughout the Khumbu, but a generation ago almost one in five Phortse inhabitants were cretins! With iodine treatments this situation is righting itself, and the percentage of cretins in the village is now far lower. But the stigma remains. Phortse is referred to as the "toilet-bowl of the Khumbu", and people from the village find it very hard to marry outside the village. Hence there is inbreeding, which increases the problems of mental retardation. Phortse people do tend to have a certain look about them.

Because cretinism is so common in the Khumbu, anyone with any disability is called a cretin. One in five Nepalis have significant hearing loss, and an awful lot of them seem to live up here. In some ways being deaf is not too much of a handicap, since almost everyone knows a form of sign language, and people can communicate simple messages quite well. Unfortunately, anyone who is deaf is considered to be a cretin, however bright. They will get married only if they come from a very rich family, and are treated very much as second-class citizens.

One of our friends, Temba, is deaf but of almost normal intelligence, and is a very gifted painter. From selling his paintings he brings more money into the family than anyone, yet is still regarded as a cretin, will never marry, and is treated like a servant boy and made to do the most menial of tasks for his brothers and parents.

THE AUTHOR WITH TEMBA.

Another of our good friends has had a much luckier life. He was very bright at school and was awarded a scholarship to attend the university in Kathmandu. On the way down he contracted meningitis and became deaf. His father was a climber and one of his Swiss friends paid for the boy to have a cochlea implant in America (which didn't work), then trained him in photography and financed a very impressive lodge in Namche for him. He is an extremely intelligent, well-read guy, yet most of the villagers consider him to be a cretin. We find it very frustrating and cruel.

You really do have to be very bright to do well in school up here. The schools used to be good and strict when Kami and Mingma went there, but have deteriorated since the Nepali government took them over from the Trust. There are very few Sherpa teachers, and down-valley people do not want to work away from their families in a cold, remote area. Consequently, the only people who accept jobs here are those who through incompetence, alcoholism or other problems cannot find work anywhere else. None of them are happy to be here, and they care very little about their work. Most have opened shops or lodges and spend more time working at these than at school. It is common for Mingma's three girls to go to school, have the role taken, and be sent home. Other days the teacher may be there, but is too drunk to do anything, and often the teachers just don't turn up. They get paid for the whole year anyway, so why should they bother?

Because the teachers are Hindu, they celebrate all their holidays, and school is shut then. It is also closed for all the Buddhist festivals. Dumje only lasts five days, but the teachers didn't come back for two weeks. Being Hindu, they don't even participate in Dumje! School closes for two months over winter, so there are only 130 official days of schooling in a year anyway! This does not include the official days when no teaching occurs.

Most of the teachers are down-valley Nepalis, and very few speak Sherpa. All of the classes are taught in Nepali. This is also the language of their textbooks and examinations. Now most of the children around here only speak Sherpa, with a few words of Nepali. It would be as if I were taught geography, history and maths in Maori. Yes, it's relevant to the country I come from and arguably a language I should know, but I don't, and I'm sure I couldn't learn in it. The kids come home from school and have no idea what they studied that day! Recently one of the Khunde Buddhist monks was employed to teach religious studies. Great, we thought, a bit of their own culture at last. The monk is a really nice guy, but he's Tibetan, and, you guessed it, doesn't speak any Sherpa either. So now the kids not only have to struggle uncomprehendingly through classes in Nepali, but are faced with Tibetan as well! No wonder few people from around here get School Leaving Certificate.

Not only is the standard of teaching appalling, but there isn't a lot to motivate children to study hard. Most of the money made here is through tourism and trekking. To run a tea shop or be a trekking guide you only need a little English and to be able to add up the bill correctly. Anything else is seen as quite irrelevant, and I guess really it is. Unless you can become a "rich, greedy doctor in Kathmandu", which costs a lot anyway, most of the professions are very lowly paid government jobs, with surprisingly low status. Little boys dream of being expedition Sherpas, and little girls dream of marrying them. That's just how it is here.

Kami's nine-year-old daughter started boarding school in Kathmandu this year. She was to be in Class Five at Thami School with two other girls, but one was sent to Kathmandu to train as a nun, and the other girl's parents decided that she didn't need any more education. The school wouldn't provide a teacher just for Kami's daughter and offered that she could repeat Class Four. Since she took most of the top prizes last year, that seemed a bit of a waste of time. We suggested to Kami that his daughter come and live at the hospital and go to Khumjung School, but he was concerned that people would talk about him, saying that he was taking advantage of his position. She'll end up in Class Two in Kathmandu, but will still get a much higher standard of education. Those in the Khumbu who can afford to send their kids to school in Kathmandu. The rich Kathmandu parents send their children to school in India. Families are separated all over Nepal.

Last week Kami and I ran a basic first aid course for the local technicians working for the hydroelectric project. The previous doctors had negotiated an electric stove and wiring and lighting for the hospital in return for this service. The foreign company have come across a major problem. None of their engineers have ever stayed here through the monsoon, and they based their designs on the clear water that they'd seen. They hadn't calculated on the amount of silt in the river in the monsoon, did not put in any filters, and this silt has eroded away the turbines, which are apparently ruined. So it could be quite a while before it's sorted out. Maybe the next Khunde couple will be the first to experience electric power at the hospital.

The first aid course was really enjoyable. The men were very keen and participated enthusiastically. We covered burns, cuts, strains, sprains, fractures, choking, and cardiopulmonary resuscitation, with the (now distant?) threat of electrocution and of children drowning in the lake at the hydroelectric scheme.

I discovered some interesting (and sometimes frightening) traditional Sherpa ways of treating injuries. A burn is often treated with heat, so oil or butter is put on it immediately, then later a piece of metal is heated and placed on the burnt area to encourage healing! OUCH! Whenever people are seriously ill, they are sat up and given chang or water. This seems to hold even if the person is unconscious. While teaching cardiopulmonary resuscitation, one lad kept saying enthusiastically, "So we give them water now then." I suspect he was missing the point.

After six hours of instruction, over two days, we decided to give everyone a teaching exam. That is, we go through the whole syllabus with each person and reteach them what they are weak on until we are comfortable that they understand. This took a very long time but gave satisfying results. The first three men (who fortunately turned out to be the three worst) took an hour each! We managed to examine the 12 men over six long hours, fortunately just before Kami and I became too silly with tiredness. We both got very sick of asking the same or similar questions over and over, and they started to sound ridiculous after a while. Towards the end, we would have to stare fixedly away from each other, stifling giggles, as we'd watch the last few men earnestly demonstrating CPR on Diane's teddy bear (our substitute for a baby-sized mannequin). We also expected our mannequin (made of a sack filled with packing chips with a pillow tied on for a head), to explode at any time, with the enormously enthusiastic compressions made. If it had, I think we both would have collapsed on to the floor in hysterical laughter and would have had to finish up for the day.

The men are very proud of their certificates, and the foreign company were so impressed they are now talking about offering us a 200-litre electric water heater as well.

I have been lucky enough to be able to see a little of the other forms of medicine practised in the Khumbu.

There are four main types of health practitioner available to the people here. Most will attend more than one of these practitioners when they or their family become unwell.

Western medicine is available at Khunde Hospital and the Trust health clinics, attended by an estimated 85 per cent of the local Sherpas. Most of these people would also attend one of the other more traditional healers. Who they choose to attend first depends on their own belief of the cause of the illness, the availability and skills of the particular practitioner, and the nature of the illness.

Almost everyone attends the local lamas for advice and help concerning important life events. Some reincarnated lamas, or very knowledgeable senior monks, have also been trained in the healing arts

NGAWANG TENZING
DOING A TEEP PUJA IN
OUR SHORT-STAY WARD.

over many years. Eighty per cent of villagers would, at some time, approach a lama for health advice.

A number of lhawas (spirit mediums) live in the area. They are also very popular and probably 80 per cent of Sherpas attend them for their health care.

Lhawas are people with special clairvoyant gifts, who find that they are able to see or feel the presence of ghosts. Usually they will have a dramatic awakening to this talent in their teens, and will disappear from the village for a number of days, experiencing unusual phenomena and behaving in an odd way, such as speaking in tongues. When they return from this spiritual experience, they will announce to the local people that they are now a lhawa and will start treating patients, without requiring further training.

There are also mendungs, or "junior lhawas", who have some special powers such as being able to identify which bad spirit is causing the illness, but do not have the ability to go into a full trance and commune with the spirits. These mendungs are often consulted for advice when a proper lhawa is not available.

The fourth group of practitioners is the Tibetan doctors or amjiks. They tend to be consulted for long-term problems such as swelling, chronic obstructive airways disease or neurological problems. Amjiks are considered to be particularly effective in treating depression ("loong"). Most of their patients tend to be elderly, and they see very few children.

Only about five per cent of the local people would consult the amjik who lives in Namche. He has not had any formal training, "inheriting" the job from his brother, and is not as skilled as the amjiks in Kathmandu and Tibet. Many of these amjiks have trained in Dharamsala, studying anatomy, physiology and herbal therapy for six to eight years.

As well as understanding the Western medical/scientific theories of disease, many Sherpas also believe in four other major causes of illness.

People can become ill by angering a lu or water spirit, or by the activity of a nerpa (ghost) or pem (bad spirit) belonging to someone still living.

Being involved in certain polluting acts (teep) can produce some sicknesses. Some people believe that they are unwell because they have been poisoned.

There are two types of lu. Many people have their own lu, which lives on their own property. This is a good spirit which, when kept happy, will bring wealth to the family.

There are also general lu, which do not belong to anyone in particular. These lu can be very powerful, and live in well-known areas, usually around juniper trees near spring water. There is a very powerful lu living in the third Gokyo lake. Local people make pilgrimages to pay homage to this lu in the hope that this will bring them wealth or enable them to conceive if they have fertility problems.

If a lu is made angry by some disrespectful act, such as spitting, defecating or urinating near its home, the offending person may become unwell. The Sherpas believe that there are bad ages, when a person is more likely to have bad luck or become unwell, called Thok years. People aged 9, 12, 24, 36 and 60 years of age are considered to have bad luck, and are more vulnerable to illness due to an angered lu.

Typical sicknesses caused by an angry lu would be skin sores/impetigo, abscesses, or neurological problems, such as sciatica.

People may visit a lama or lhawa to identify which lu they have angered. Reparation must be made, and this is done by tying a nenga (a cross made of juniper wood, connected by a bright cotton web) to a juniper tree near to where the lu lives. A sur (a hot coal with nak butter melted on to it) is also placed either at the lu's home or, if the lu lives a long way away, then pointing in the direction of where it resides.

It is believed that most people after they die spend a certain period in limbo while they wait to be reincarnated. It is expected that five to ten per cent of very good people will go straight to Nirvana or Heaven. An unfortunate two per cent with very bad karma will never be reborn and are sent straight to hell. Most of the remaining people eventually become reincarnated as another person or animal, depending on what kind of karma they have earned in their previous lives.

Some of these people may become stuck in this limbo phase, and become nerpas, who roam around the place often causing trouble for the living. It is believed that bad people, those who have experienced a violent death such as suicide or murder, or those who have not had the proper funeral rites read, are at more risk of becoming nerpas. The nerpa often follows its living family members about when they go visiting. Nerpas are more likely to cause problems to the living if they are hungry or thirsty, and the family is expected to organise extra funeral pujas and provide food and drink for any troublesome nerpa who is identified.

Nerpas tend to cause sudden illnesses, such as bad stomach cramps. The patient also tends to suffer a similar illness to that which the nerpa died of. For example, a nerpa who died by hanging may be considered responsible for causing a suffocating type of illness such as exacerbation of chronic obstructive airways disease.

It is also believed that people who are sick are very vulnerable to "superinfection" from a nerpa, which may convert a moderate illness into a life-threatening one.

Since, from time to time, people do die at the hospital, some patients are frightened to stay there when they are unwell, because of the nerpas that apparently live around the place and may kill them.

Similarly, a pem can make someone unwell. The offending person tends to be widowed or old and unmarried, and is considered to be very jealous of his or her victim. Pems do not cause such serious illness, and are typically held responsible for a bad diarrhoea illness.

This is very much the domain of the lhawa, who will attend a sick patient and identify which nerpa or pem is responsible for the illness. The bad spirit will then need to be exorcised. The lama may occasionally identify a bad spirit that is making the person unwell.

A number of activities are considered to be unclean, and may contribute to illnesses such as conjunctivitis, or anything that confuses the mind, for example, meningitis or intellectual disability. One of the most significantly polluting activities is to help with a delivery. Exposure to the blood from childbirth is considered to be very harmful, and this prevents many women from helping others in labour, since they believe that this can give them difficult labours in the future and/or shorten their lives.

Close proximity to a dead body, or even a relative of the dead, can be troublesome, as can spending time with people born into an untouchable caste. There are three main Nepali untouchable castes, the Kamis (blacksmiths), the Damai (tailors) and the Serki (shoemakers). The Tibetan butchers are also considered untouchable. People believe that they can become sick by wearing these people's old clothes, sharing cutlery, or even being in the same room as them, and they tend to be shunned.

It is also considered that a lot of teep exists in areas where many people congregate, such as the market place, the junction of a trail, or the flour mill. A small percentage of pregnant women will not visit these places, for

fear that their boy foetus will be turned into a girl, or they will have a difficult labour.

The lama (or occasionally the lhawa) will treat teep by a ritual of drinking and throwing holy water.

Some people believe that bad-hearted, money-hungry women will poison others in order to make themselves rich.

A poison is mixed in the following way: A number of live creatures such as lizards, snakes and frogs are put together in a large pot and allowed to fight to the death, until just one animal remains. This animal is starved to death, dehydrated, then made into a powder.

A special puja is performed by these women while the poisonous powder is prepared. During this ceremony, the onset of action will be allocated. For example, the person may become unwell one month after ingesting the poison.

The witch then hides a small amount of this poisonous powder under her fingernail, and will surreptitiously introduce it into the victim's cup of tea or glass of chang, by dipping her finger into the brew as she serves it.

Tuesdays and Sundays are considered to be the poison-giving days. Most people are not willing to visit the home of any woman who might be a witch on these days of the week.

The poison produces a sharp stomach ache, like gastritis, attributed to the animal coming back to life in the person's stomach and biting away at it. Another possible outcome of the poison is jaundice.

Some people with these symptoms will attend the amjik, or occasionally a lama, who will give them a herbal medicine made from a common root called Phogmar. This root induces vomiting and diarrhoea, which allows the offending poison to be expelled. Probably 10 per cent of Sherpas would carry this root with them when they travel, to take in case someone poisons them along the way.

When a patient attends a lama, the lama will particularly want to know exactly when that person became unwell. The lama will throw some dice and look up a specific chart that correlates the outcome of the throw with the onset of illness and the patient's year of birth. This will direct the lama to the appropriate part of his religious/fortune-telling book. He will then interpret these findings to determine diagnosis, management and prognosis of the patient's condition. This process is called soongtaak.

The books may say that the patient has made their particular god unhappy, or that they have a bad Thok (unlucky age). They may have eaten polluted food, or made a lu angry.

The lama will then suggest some form of reparation, such as appeasing an angry lu with nenga and sur. He may instruct the person to do maintenance work on the trails, local chorten, or mani walls. The patient may be directed to make a good luck tree and place it high up on a mountainside or ridge.

The lama often also suggests a good luck puja. There are some 40 types of such pujas, all varying in length from 15 minutes to several days.

The patient may be given a blessed necklace for good luck.

There are some specific treatments that can be administered by the lamas. Holy water is used to clear any teep. Very old, brightly dyed butter from the altar can be rubbed on a painful area. A rilu (herbal pill) made by a very renowned lama can be given to promote general good health.

Often the patient will also be instructed to attend the hospital, and to take our medicine. We have a close and mutually respectful relationship with the local lamas, and often refer to each other.

The cost of a consultation varies considerably, and it is really up to the patient to decide what a reasonable payment is. Most local people would bring about $NZ1.67 and a khaarta for the consultation. The price of a religious puja varies depending on how long the lama thinks the person needs. Generally accepted rates are $NZ6 each day for a monk, and $NZ12-$16 each day for a lama, plus food and accommodation.

Most lhawas are very good showmen, often dressing elaborately, and only performing at night. Consultation can be a very exciting process. The lhawa always visits the patient's own home, and will ask a lot of questions about when the person became unwell. He will particularly want to find out if anyone came into the patient's house the day they became unwell, especially if the visitor had been recently widowed, or was from an untouchable caste.

The lhawa will start chanting in his own special language until he goes into a trance. He may just sit there, or run screaming around the room, throwing objects about. Eventually he will change his own persona and act as if he is the nerpa or pem causing the illness. He will adopt the mannerisms and speech of this person, changing his language back to that person's normal language.

While the lhawa has been taken over by the bad spirit, the patient or family member will start talking to the spirit. He will ask the possessed lhawa what the bad spirit wants. The lhawa will usually answer that the nerpa or pem is hungry or thirsty and will demand the spirit's favourite food or drink. After this is given and consumed by the lhawa, the patient will tell the spirit that it now has what it wants and that it should go away and stop bothering them. The family will abuse the spirit, telling it that they do not want it around anymore, that it will never be reincarnated if it keeps making trouble for the living, and that its living family is being shamed by its behaviour.

After a while the lhawa will take on the persona of the bad spirit's personal god (for example, Khumbila), and speak in yet another special language, telling the bad spirit to go away and allow the patient to get well.

The lhawa will then become himself again, and will ask the bad spirit to follow him out of the house. He will take a hot fire outside, and place some of the nerpa's or pem's favourite food, such as butter or meat, on to it. He will also produce a nenga to appease the bad spirit's own god. These ceremonies are performed just outside the patient's property, and pointing towards the bad spirit's family home. It is again told to go away and leave the patient alone.

The identification of a specific nerpa or pem is always meant to be kept confidential. This avoids embarrassing or upsetting the family of the bad spirit, who are not considered to be responsible for the behaviour of their pem or family nerpa.

If the exorcism does not make the patient better, the lhawa will suggest another attempt, or may need to look for another nerpa or pem who is continuing to make the person unwell. The lhawas generally have a low opinion of the other three types of practitioners, and will not refer on to any of them.

A lhawa with a good reputation for success will charge $NZ40 plus food for a night's work.

A mendung, or "junior lhawa", might charge $NZ2-4, for a consultation.

The amjik (Tibetan doctor) will ask about the person's symptoms. He will always examine the patient's urine, looking mostly at its concentration, determining whether it is thick or cloudy. He will also feel the pulse, decreeing it as either strong or shallow.

Amjiks have a vast array of herbal tablets, which are used for specific illnesses in the same way that we prescribe medication.

Acupuncture is often performed, and the older, more traditional amjiks use a form of moxibustion. A short (one centimetre) hollow metal pipe is placed over a specific acupuncture point. Then dried herbs, specific to the person's complaint, are pushed inside the pipe and set alight. This creates a distinctive burn/scar over the area.

A formally trained amjik in Kathmandu will charge $NZ3 plus the medication cost. This is the same fee that a Western-trained Nepali doctor would charge. Our local amjik does not charge for consultation, but his medicines are quite expensive.

Some very traditional people believe that the hospital is only good for treating cuts and broken bones. Fifteen per cent of the local people would never consider attending a Western medical practitioner. Twenty per cent of the population would only come to us, and do not visit the lamas, lhawas or amjiks for their health care. This leaves an estimated 65 per cent who routinely combine the efforts of Western and more traditional practitioners when they become unwell. For these people we need to be aware that our treatments may not be the only ones they are taking. We also cannot take for granted that they perceive illness in the same way that we do.

Quite a number of our patients are reluctant to have injections. Some people who believe that they are unwell because a bad spirit has invaded their body are frightened that sticking a needle into them will make the bad spirit even more angry, and may kill them. Sometimes we will suggest that the patient attend a lhawa or lama to exorcise the bad spirit, and then return for an injection.

Most people are resistant to having a blood test or operation such as vasectomy, in the belief that it will make them weak and unable to do heavy physical work for the rest of their lives.

If someone has been born with an unusual lump or bump, such as an extra finger or pre-auricular skin tag, they will usually go to the lama for an opinion about it before consenting to its removal. Sometimes these extra parts are considered to be valued gifts from the gods.

Some of our Tibetan patients, especially refugees escaping to Dharamsala, will wear a tsengi in their right axilla. This is bag of herbs, prepared and blessed by a well-renowned lama. Others will wear a pouch blessed by the Dalai Lama. People believe that wearing this will make them invulnerable to penetrating injury such as attack by a knife. They also believe that our needle will break against their skin, and will take their tsengi off before receiving an injection. If we are having difficulty getting an intravenous line in, they will often remove their blessed protection to allow us easier access.

Many women cannot understand why we perform an antenatal examination. It is believed that the foetus sits upright (just like people), and what causes the pain at delivery is the baby turning around so that it comes out head first. Some women are not at all impressed when we inform them that we are concerned because their baby is a breech.

The local people generally feel very comfortable with the idea of taking pills to treat illnesses, and most of our management is well accepted.

The cheapness of our medical service can occasionally work against us, since people sometimes perceive our treatment as not being worth much, and thus not very effective.

It is very frustrating to hear of a patient who is sick with something I think I can treat, but not being able to help them until asked. Dehydrated babies with gastroenteritis can be blessed by lamas, exorcised by lhawas, and burnt by amjiks before they are carried to the hospital, days later, at death's door. Of course some are so far gone by then that Western medicine's reputation of being pretty ineffective is merely confirmed.

I am not saying that Western medicine has all the answers — far from it. Fortunately, many conditions get better on their own, whatever you do, thanks to the miraculous ability of the body to heal itself. And some illnesses are, as yet, beyond any help from treatment. But there are many problems that we can cure, and others that can be managed very well. The really exciting thing about medicine for me is that it is based on scientific method. New theories are tried out in an unbiased manner. Ideas are updated and treatments are improved. Concepts and "facts" that were "true" when I was in medical school have been shown to be wanting, and better ways of tackling problems are found. It is a demanding and exciting job, and I feel very fortunate to be involved in it.

I am sure that many aspects of alternative medicines are very valuable. Western medicine has the luxury of enormous financial backing from pharmaceutical companies and the professional classes to fund research based on scientific method. It is unfortunate that similar backing does not exist for many other forms of healing, so that the theories can also be tested in an unbiased way. It is difficult to support wholly a regime based on anecdotal evidence alone, yet statistically significant surveys can be difficult to perform or financially unviable. Without the "proof", the powers that be will understandably not accept the theories, but without this backing it can be hard to find the truth. Catch 22.

The Minister of Tourism has announced that 40 per cent of the Everest expedition fees will be put into projects in the Khumbu. This is quite exciting, since there will be five expeditions twice a year, each paying $NZ100,000, thus providing the Khumbu with a $NZ400,000 a year. We met Kami's cousin (who is doing his PhD in forestry and is married to a New Zealand woman), who is holding meetings in each of the villages to find out how the local people would like the money to be spent. People's main interests are reforestation, fixing the suspension bridges, and water supplies. Some voiced concerns about who would be in control of these large funds, considering past experiences with a few powerful corrupt individuals. Kami keeps reminding us that the Minister of Tourism has put nothing in writing yet, and that with the recent flooding disaster in the Terai, the money may be used for that instead. He makes a good point and we shouldn't get too excited about it yet.

On Black Friday, a 55-year-old woman trekking with a group back from Gokyo slipped and fell about 20 metres to her death, just above Sanassa. Her companions attempted CPR for two hours without success. By the time I saw her she was well dead. Her husband and two friends stayed with her in the classroom while one of the Khunde lamas perfomed an all-night puja for her. Her body, completely wrapped in beautiful white silk khaarta, was to be taken back to her country, and we all waited the next morning for the helicopter. The Namche police had ordered the chopper and sadly it went to Namche instead of Khunde. By the time this had been worked out and her body carried down to Namche, the cloud was too low to take off, so they had to wait until the following morning.

I had started the morning by explaining to our health workers that

Black Friday is a very bad luck day for Westerners. I am sorry that my prediction was so accurate, but the local people are very impressed.

Each time he goes home Kami passes the village where the woman with the transverse lie baby lived. He'd been asking about her each time, but no one knew anything. We felt she must have been dead by now, and probably picked down to bones by the crows up in the yak field.

Kami and I conducted a clinic in Thami and were shocked to see the woman walk in with one baby under each arm, beaming from ear to ear. Her husband made us drink chang and gave us khaarta, and was full of gratitude to us. I have no idea why; I would have thought he'd consider me to be a complete idiot. What I was feeling when I examined her abdomen was obviously the second twin lying sideways. She was big for her dates because of twins, and that's why it took her so long to deliver. She said she delivered on her own up in the yak field, pushing out the boy headfirst, and then the girl breech. No problem, she said. Then she picked her babies up and wandered the three hours back home to show them off to her husband.

The twins were 12 days old and tiny. The girl looked particularly sickly, but they insisted on me examining the boy first. He was well, but the girl was thinner and had diarrhoea. I gave them medicine for the girl and they went happily on their way. I was so delighted with such a good outcome.

Pus got into a bad fight with another cat and sustained an impressive injury to his left elbow. (Do cats have elbows?) His left forelimb was swollen to twice its normal size. We considered doing an X-ray but decided that we would probably end up more injured than him from attempting the procedure. Two days later he went off his food and sulked about with a hot swollen limb, so I added amoxycillin to his regime of nonsteroidal anti-inflammatories. This was an adventure in itself. Pus is not the kind of animal to let you stuff balls of butter infiltrated with powdered medicine down his throat without a good fight, sick or not, and I rapidly found a once-a-day regime to replace the three-times-a-day one.

He must have become more fed up with this than I had, and disappeared. Di (who actually likes Pus) moped about with increasingly morbid imaginings of how he was faring. Generally Sherpas don't like cats, considering them to be bad luck, and our health workers were pleased that Pus was gone. Di and Longin were, however, absolutely delighted when he returned three days later, all better. The rest of us pretended to be pleased so as not to hurt their feelings. While not wishing any creature the fate of dying alone in pain, one of Pus's near-constant, ear-shattering meows reminded us of how nice it was when he was gone. Longin, who thinks she's the cat's mother, is back to dry-suckling him.

Kami told us that when a few years ago the hospital cat went missing for two weeks, everyone assumed that he'd died. He returned with a Swiss trekking group having gone up with them to Base Camp and back!

Apparently there are quite a number of dogs at Base Camp. Stray dogs meet trekking and expedition groups at Lukla and spend their lives walking up and down with them, since there is always someone happy to feed and pet them.

We have found some more cute little white caterpillars, just like the ones we saw on our trek up from Jiri. Kami thought it was hilarious, and he explained that these were in fact leeches!

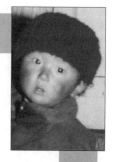

Socially and culturally, life has been very exciting lately. Fortunately, the hospital has not kept us too busy. The monsoon is over and we now bask in the sun, looking for hours at our beautiful mountain views. The riggis are almost all dug up and the animals have returned from the up-valley pastures, so we are serenaded by the gentle tinklings of the yak bells all around.

With the good weather come the trekkers. Some of them are very likeable, interesting people, but mostly it's hard work mustering enthusiasm, answering the same questions over and over, and making small talk with people we're unlikely to see ever again. The tourists descend on the hospital in small or large groups, all feeling that we should be delighted to drop everything and entertain them. Some people seem to forget their own customs and will just walk into a consultation to say "hi", or will try to wander into our private flat just to have a look around. Since we come across an average of 20 trekkers a day, the novelty wore off pretty quickly. Di is wonderful and has taken over the job of showing them around, while I will at times mutter, "Not another bloody trekker," and hide in the surgery or the darkroom. So many doctors come to the area, and while it is interesting showing them around and discussing practice with them, they all seem to feel that they are pretty special and we should be more excited to see them. We must see 10 doctors or medical students a week!

The Gen Lama actually stayed sitting up in "meditation" for 22 days. I got our health workers to take photos of him on days seven and 21. What impressed me was that he did not appear to have decomposed much at all, despite the warmth of his room, filled with permanently lit butter candles.

GEN LAMA'S BODY
BEFORE CREMATION.

Because women are "dirty", neither Di nor I were able to go into the room where he sat, but we could stand outside the open window and watch him quite closely. Neither I nor the reluctant health workers (who were instructed to take a good sniff next to him) could smell any odour from the dead body. In fact he looked better towards the end, sitting up straighter, and had even grown more hair. I remember in medical school being taught that hair and nails continue to grow after death. They really do! Certainly the local people are very impressed. No lama in known history has ever "meditated" for so long.

He "fell" at exactly the time of the Tengboche Monastery reopening. Kami rather cynically thinks he was probably pushed. The Gen Lama was then placed sitting in a decorative box full of salt. His head was covered with a cloth and a special hat, and he sat in the gompa for a few days. People continued to come from far and wide to be blessed by him.

The next day, I printed one of my black and white photos of the Gen Lama sitting in his box. I came out of the darkroom, with the print dripping wet, to check the exposure, and a group of nuns who had just arrived saw the photo, grabbed it, thrust it to their foreheads, and stood around praying to it. And I'd been worried that the local people might be offended by my photography. Our mail arrived with a colour photo of the Gen Lama sitting in meditation seven days after he'd died, and I raced up to show the married/defaulted nun who runs the gompa. She was delighted with it and asked me for a few copies. Four or five hundred! They have since all been handed out and almost every house we visit in the Khumbu has the photo in amongst the shrine.

We attended the Gen Lama's cremation a few days later. Women are never allowed to view an ordinary cremation, but everyone could come to this one. Unfortunately it was a miserable rainy day, but quite a crowd still turned up. We all huddled on top of each other under the shelter of a large blue tarpaulin. To get better photos I had the clever idea of climbing halfway up a large rock, and managed to get a couple of footholds. Three old women from the village decided to join me and clung on tight. I now had one foothold and my arms full, grabbing on to various parts of people to stop us all crashing down into the crowd. Then my leg started shaking uncontrollably, and since it was the only limb attached to anything solid, I decided to give in and crawl down. This did not make me popular, as I brought a few others down with me, at least at a slower, safer pace than the avalanche I envisaged. Finally I found a safe place, in the rain, with a long-distance view of what was going on.

GEN LAMA'S CREMATION OVEN.

They carried the Gen Lama, still in his box, up the steps to the cremation oven. Many people brought khaarta and prayed before him for their final blessing. Rather than sad, it seemed more a festive atmosphere. He was then placed sitting on a chair in the oven. I think he had been taken out of his box, but I was at the wrong angle to see him. The fire was lit around him, and people came to the doorway, bowed down and prayed and threw in various offerings. Most of the crowd must have been able to see him burning, but it seemed quite unemotional from where I was. At the same time, the monks were blowing their clarinets and horns and doing various pujas. Others surrounded the outside of the oven with khaarta and decorations.

When the fire was really raging, they filled up the doorway with stones. I had wondered if there would be a smell of flesh burning, but smelt nothing except the sweetness of juniper branches smoking. We all wandered down the hill, where large tents had been set up, and everyone settled down to chiyaa or chang and a large meal of Sherpa stew. It was rather like a picnic. I felt a little freaked out at the thought of someone I knew being incinerated while we all sat around having a nice time.

Five days later the oven was opened. We were again invited to attend. It was said that often when a reincarnate lama is cremated they will find a baby's footprint in the ashes, pointing towards where the next reincarnate lama will be found. However, most of the Sherpas would tell us this with a bit of a smirk on their face.

We arrived there just as they'd opened the doorway. What I thought was the chair he'd been sitting on turned out to be the intact remains of his lumbar spine and pelvis, resting on the metal stand that was all that was left of the chair. It was very emotional, and almost every member of the small group gathered was in tears. We stood around the opening while one of the monks sieved through the ashes, piling the bones on to a tray. I stood with my arm around the married nun (who had cared particularly for the Gen Lama) as she shook with her sobbing. She and many others had not shown much emotion up until now, and we found it very hard to watch.

The Gen Lama's skull was intact, and was blessed by one of the monks, then wrapped in white and red khaarta and placed in a special copper urn. Then the rest of his bones were brought out on a plate, and again wrapped up. Finally the ashes were collected in a large urn and brought out.

We were taken into the oven individually to view the "mandela", which is a religious drawing in the ground, apparently there since before the Gen Lama was cremated. The monks sat around interpreting it, and it was obviously good news, since everyone started smiling again.

Then the clarinets, horns and drums began, and the monks ceremoniously carried the Gen Lama's remains around the monastery and into the gompa. Occasionally, people would race in front of the various urns, bow their heads, and be blessed by them. We were all fed in the gompa kitchen, with people dropping in for many days.

While this was going on, we also attended the Tengboche Monastery reopening. We were asked to come early because a very important lama was flying up by helicopter and would be at risk of altitude sickness. The Tushi Rimpoche has been reincarnated seven or eight times and is highly respected in the Solu-Khumbu. Kami and I visited him and his companions quite a few times for their various medical problems. He is a delightful 70-year-old man with a bald head and bright cheerful eyes. He had lived most of his life on the side of Mt Everest, in Tibet, but had to flee to Nepal when the Chinese invaded. He spoke only Tibetan, so consultations at times involved a series of translations from English to Nepali/Sherpa to Tibetan and back again. I brought Di to meet him one

TUSHI RIMPOCHE *(LEFT)* AND COMPANIONS AT THE REOPENING OF TENGBOCHE.

day, and he must have misinterpreted who she was. I'd been blessed a few times and had given him khaarta and money, as is the custom (the only house calls I've ever had to pay for!), and had had my hand shaken. When he was introduced to Di, his eyes lit up and he instantly returned the khaarta she gave him, placing it around her neck. This is a great honour and I was quite impressed, until our interpreter showed considerable surprise when he sorted out what Di was doing there. Under false pretences or not, Di will certainly treasure that khaarta. Of course the Tushi Rimpoche could have just taken a real liking to Di, and who could blame him!

One of our Sherpa friends managed to get us into the private gompas on our own, to photograph the inside. Certainly a lot of work has gone into the monastery, and it looked very impressive. I think it will look even better when the brightness of the colours fades a little. The large golden Buddha was certainly interesting to see, as were the displayed relics that had been saved from the fire. It felt more like visiting a museum than a spiritual place, but maybe that was just the busy, expectant atmosphere of preparations for the reopening.

On the day of the reopening, the weather was appalling. We had expected the Trust helicopter at 9 o'clock in the morning. The cloud was low, but a small helicopter (containing an international news crew from India) was buzzing around in a Kamikaze fashion, televising everything in sight. The Indian crew had arrived the day before, but would not get off the helicopter when they discovered they could not have heated rooms

and showers, and went away to spend the night in Lukla. Apparently they had come unprepared for the rigours of staying at Tengboche.

At 8.15 a Super Puma helicopter arrived and, to our surprise and delight, out popped the Trust group. We hadn't realised how much we'd missed seeing people we knew from home, and there were great hugs and greetings all round. We were initially ushered to an upstairs covered balcony, but soon were ordered to come down to the monastery steps to wait for and greet the Prime Minister. So we all waited, and waited, and waited. In fact, Di and I were quite pleased. The atmosphere was really friendly and it was a great opportunity for us to talk to everyone and take photos of various combinations of us grouped together.

The Prime Minister had been invited to stop off at the local foreign hotel for breakfast, in an attempt to encourage him to lift the recent ban of the Pilatus Porter flying into Shyangboche. We decided that he must've had quite a few refills of his cappuccino while we were all made to stand and wait for him.

The Tushi Rimpoche had a seat, and about half an hour later they produced one for Ed Hillary. His wife, June, was busy explaining to us how she and Ed had been at a ceremony with the Tushi Rimpoche that had involved them having to drink his urine! I was rather pleased that this privilege was not extended to his physician. Then another chair arrived beside Ed, and I assumed it would be for June, but she muttered "some luck" and in fact Ed's brother Rex was escorted to the seat! I guess my upbringing of "ladies first" is fairly well ingrained, even after six months of living here.

The Prime Minister finally arrived at 10.30, and we all squeezed back to our seats. There followed many long speeches in Nepali, relieved by a brief speech in English by Ed. The Tourism Minister waved his arms about and was obviously getting very excited about something, but the crowd seemed pretty unaffected. We all went a little pale when they announced that they would now translate into English, but fortunately this only involved a precis of the Prime Minister's speech. He certainly wasn't into vote-catching, and his basic message was "Don't expect the government to help you, you'll have to help yourselves." No wonder a lot of the crowd had talked amongst themselves during his speech.

Towards the end of the speeches it started to rain. We were all fine, up in our balcony, and people raced up with umbrellas for the Tushi Rimpoche, Tengboche Rimpoche, and the Prime Minister. However, poor Ed, June, and Zeke sat more and more miserably in the drizzle. After a while the Prime Minister called Ed over to share the shelter, but it really was a bit grim for them. Then the rain became very heavy, the crowd dispersed, and everything finished. It was a pity, since I think they'd planned some monk dancing.

While the Prime Minister had lunch with the Rimpoches, we sheltered in the gompa and later went to one of the teahouses for rice stew. The weather had really closed in, and members of our party were starting to look decidedly seedy. I handed around acetazolamide (to counteract the effects of altitude sickness), and we all jollied each other along, trying to pretend we weren't feeling very anxious about the possibility of the new arrivals having to stay at this altitude overnight.

I was beginning to get very concerned about the Trust members. They had flown straight from Kathmandu, (about 1230 m) to an altitude of almost 4300 m. The problem with a rapid ascent to high altitude is that after a few hours the body fails to acclimatise to the lowered oxygen content and barometric pressure, producing nausea, headache and, finally, life-threatening cerebral and/or pulmonary oedema.

The visitors were supposed to stay only three hours, but already they'd been there for six. The cloud was thick and some were looking decidedly unwell. I had already been called to see one ambassador, who was not faring at all well. We had only one Gamow bag with us. (A Gamow bag is a portable recompression chamber, like a big sleeping bag, which is sealed and then pressuried with a foot pump. It simulates a 2000 feet descent, and is an excellent, temporary, life-saving measure while awaiting evacuation. The effects wear off after a few hours.) Kami began organising some Sherpas to run back to the hospital (probably two to two-and-a-half hours' run each way) to get our other Gamow bag and some oxygen cylinders.

I imagined horrific dilemmas of who to treat first. We had the Prime Minister, a number of overseas ambassadors, Ed Hillary, as well as about 10 other less-famous but just as worthy people at significant risk. Would I be able to treat the sickest people first? Or should I concentrate on the youngest, strongest, and most likely to survive? Or would I be bullied into concentrating on the famous people first. It is only human nature that I would have resented being forced to try to save the Prime Minister and ambassadors, and having to neglect the people that I know. Was it feasible to fit more than one person into a Gamow bag at the same time?

Just as we'd organised some Sherpas to go, we saw the Prime Minister coming out of his tent. His helicopter was parked at Tengboche. The Trust helicopter was at Phortse, unable to land until he left. There was an almost imperceptible gap in the cloud, and he and his party left rapidly. I didn't see him take off. We were all too excited running to the others to get them ready to leave.

It all happened so quickly. The Trust helicopter arrived. Great hugs and rapid goodbyes as we all raced to the take-off area. Some had to be helped to walk. Di was ahead, and had a physical scuffle with one of the policemen who was trying to stop our group (including Ed Hillary) from getting through to the helicopter. I vaguely remember Di throwing him sideways into the crowd. We later found Ang Dooli in tears. Another policeman had blocked her path and, despite Temba's valiant efforts to beat him away, she had missed her chance to say goodbye to Ed and June. A few seconds later the helicopter rose up (blowing Ang Dooli right over, even though she was standing against the crowd) and disappeared over the side of the cliff into the thick cloud. Everyone ran to the side and with relief saw the aircraft making its way down the valley below the cloud.

It was all very emotional, and I burst into tears at the relief of the Trust people getting away safely. I never, never want to be placed in such a difficult position again. After they'd gone, Di and I went for a long walk, both feeling sorry for ourselves and sad at seeing a little piece of home disappearing after such a short contact.

Our walk was interrupted by a local boy running after us, shouting, "Doctor sahib, come now." We ran after him to find a horse with an enormously swollen abdomen swaying on its feet. The poor animal had been gored by a zupchok (yak crossbred with a cow) several days before, which had obviously perforated it's bowel. The animal was shocked and in pain, and as I started to examine him he fell slowly to the ground. There was nothing much I could do, but I ran back to our teahouse to get some morphine out of my bag. I didn't have much with me, but hoped I had enough to put the poor animal out of his misery. By the time I got back, the horse was dead. Kami explained later that it would have been wrong for me to put the animal down. People are suspicious enough of injections without letting them see one that would kill almost immediately. I just hate to think how that horse must have suffered over the previous few days.

STARTING THE GENERATOR FOR THE SATELLITE PHONE.

A few weeks ago, Mingma and I wandered down to Jorsale (two hours away) to see a trekker who was suffering from altitude sickness. He turned out to be a newspaper photojournalist who was on his way to Base Camp to cover Brian Blessed's second attempt at Everest.

He wasn't too bad and we sorted him out. We got on well and decided that he could stay at the hospital with us, since he didn't feel confident enough to ascend further. His accompanying journalist had gone ahead to Base Camp, and they had set up three mail runners. One arrived each day with photos and the story to go into the next day's paper. A computer and satellite phone were set up in the classroom, both run by two generators. Colour films were processed in our dark room, then the negatives sent through the phone, sort of like a fax! The computer separates the negative into its colours of magenta, cyan and yellow, then sends each segment separately to the computer in the office halfway across the world. Their computer then puts the three colours together, and can adjust this if it doesn't seem quite right, then prints the photo to go in the next day's paper. All in a matter of minutes! After such a long time of isolation, waiting an average of six weeks to get a reply to even an urgent letter, it is completely mind-blowing.

Best of all, we both got to ring home, courtesy of the photojournalist's newspaper — at $NZ40 a minute! It was marvellous for us both to talk to our families. My parents even put my dog on the phone. When he heard my voice, he immediately raced down to my old bedroom and then started searching the house for me. Diane and I were both on such a high talking on the phone, then very soon after were in tears and went into a real homesickness slump for a day or two. Still, it was worth it.

I am getting called out to the occasional rescue for altitude sickness. With no telephone or radio at the hospital, messages can be very confused at times. Last month, Base Camp radioed the National Park Office and a messenger ran two to three hours to let us know that a "sahib" had severe pulmonary oedema and was somewhere between Lobuche and Pangboche. It was the middle of the night. Pangboche is six hours' walk away, and then it is another seven hours up to Lobuche. The trekker could have been staying in any one of hundreds of possible lodges in the area. Kami refused to let me go, saying that it was too dangerous and not feasible to attempt a rescue. I didn't sleep much at all, worrying about this guy. He turned up two days later, not really very sick, having spent the last couple of nights one hour's walk from the hospital on a completely different trail! We are learning to take messages with a grain of salt.

I find the psychology of altitude sickness fascinating. People who are fixed on climbing to a certain point, and have paid a large amount of money to do so, are prepared to ascribe their symptoms to anything but altitude. I find that the large groups are the worst, and the most dangerous. We're all used to a bit of discomfort when we trek at home. If someone has a bit of a headache and/or nausea, it seems a bit "wet" of them to even mention it, let alone make the whole group stop for a day and wait for the symptoms to settle. So people stay quiet and continue to climb with symptoms. Also, some group members can be very unsympathetic to the "weaker" ones, and will bully them on or just leave them behind. The previous doctors rescued a woman who had been left alone in a teahouse, with cerebral oedema, by her husband, who was determined to see Base Camp! She was carried unconscious down to the hospital (only one day's walk), where fortunately she recovered!

I see people with nausea, headache, shortness of breath, white frothy sputum and insomnia who get very irritated by my advice to descend. They insist they just have a cold, demand antibiotics, and continue on against my advice, only to be evacuated by helicopter later. There seems to be a "macho" attitude that only "weak" people suffer from altitude sickness and really tough (may I substitute stupid) people can push themselves past the symptoms. It is very sad when these "heroes" die.

Another interesting aspect of living up here is the aircraft. There are only two modes of transport. The most common is by foot (or if you're rich, lazy or sick, there's yak, horse or porter). The other is air travel. There is an airfield about 20 minutes' walk from the hospital. This caters mainly for patrons of the luxury foreign hotel. Tourists fly straight up to 3840 m, pay $NZ320 a night to stay at the hotel, feel miserable with altitude symptoms for a couple of days, and then fly back to Kathmandu, usually having never left the hotel. The hotel has a recompression chamber —

which leaks. Each year they do more and more work on it, in the hope that it will be right for the next season. Some helicopters land outside the hotel doors, so the tourists don't have to walk more than 20 m.

The hotel very kindly allows us to fly out emergency cases from their airfield, which is of great use to us, though it is expensive and not done lightly. I love going down in the mornings to watch the Pilatus Porter land and take off. Up here amongst the clouds, some of the conditions in which the pilots fly are very frightening, especially considering that there is no tower, and all take-offs and landings are done visually.

Recently, the government banned the Pilatus Porter from flying into Shyangboche, saying that a single-engine plane is no longer safe in the area. This is the official reason, although the general view is that one of the high-up politicians, who owns a helicopter company which just happens to want to open up in this area, is responsible for the ban. This is a great pity for the area. The foreign hotel patrons will still come up, paying more for the helicopter, but this puts it way out of the locals and our budget.

The nearest airfield is now at Lukla, a day's walk away, and emergency cases are now carried down there. Ed Hillary helped build this, and people tell us that when he found it too bumpy for landings he organised a big party, with plenty of chang, and got the Sherpas to dance up and down the airstrip for two nights to flatten it out. This is a larger airfield and has a Twin Otter plane flying back and forth most days. In the trekking season there can be five or six flights a day, depending on weather conditions. There is too much cloud during the monsoon, and there is ice on the runway in the winter, so there are very few flights at these times.

It's been a very exciting time for us, though also rather sad. Ang Doolie's husband, Ed Hillary's sirdar and long-time friend has gone into liver failure. I have told him that there is nothing that can be done and that he will die soon. Understandably, he has chosen to have a second opinion, and the Trust has flown him down to Kathmandu. The family are organising the monks to do pujas for him, while we wait for him to return.

Our very good friend, Gaga Doma, is also very unwell with chronic obstructive airways disease. She is on maximal oral therapy, and not really responding. I have wanted to give her injectable medication, but her family have warned her that she is too weak for such strong medicine, which would be sure to kill her. We have become very fond of Gaga Doma, who is widowed and lives with her son. She is 89 and has a wicked sense of humour. As we walk past her house she often calls us in to have a cup | 97

DIANE AND GAGA DOMA.

of tea with her. She speaks no English, but we manage to have a great time as she uses sign language and acting-out to have a laugh with us. Some days we just sit together, holding hands and watching the fire. She is particularly fond of Diane, and teases her mercilessly, grabbing hold of her large breasts and making signs of "Where is your baby? With these so big, it is such a waste!" Gaga Doma was born in Tibet. She married a travelling Tibetan and, after having some children with him, came with him to Khunde. She was shocked to discover that he also had a wife here and expected all of the family to live together. Gaga Doma had a fiery temper and couldn't get on with his other wife, so he had to build another house in the same village, and lived between the two families. We can hear her "death rattle" from the other end of the room, and I'm pretty sure she's going to die soon. We will miss her a lot.

We are also worried about Soni Aamaa, another old woman of whom we have become very fond. She is 72 and was married with three children. One child died, and a few months later her husband and other two children did not return from a trek downvalley. She does not know if they left her by choice or came to some harm. She has not seen any of her family for over 40 years. As time went on her cataracts became very bad and she was unable to see anything much. Unable to work she eventually had to sell her land and house to survive, and moved into a cave just below the Khunde gompa. Several years ago she came to the hospital and explained that she was going to throw herself in the river, since she could not work and had no further money to live. The doctors convinced her to hang on for John McKinnon's visit. He was the first Khunde doctor, and visits every few years to do eye surgery. He repaired her cataracts, and thick-lensed glasses gave some vision back to her. This literally saved her life, and she survives by slaving away digging people's gardens, cutting grasses and carrying light loads around the village. Her cave gets very cold in the winter and the Gen Lama used to let her stay at the gompa over winter. With him gone we aren't sure that she'll be able to stay up there any longer.

When people go missing, some local people blame the yeti. We initially thought that they were joking, but many take the yeti very seriously. There are apparently two kinds of yeti: one that kills humans, and another that attacks animals. A few years ago a woman was brought to the hospital with severe tearing injuries to her arm. She says she was outside her house when a yeti ran past her, throwing her aside and picking up her yak, tearing its head off and running off with it. She would have no reason to lie, and the doctors involved certainly felt that her injuries were consistent with a large animal attack. We have met and talked with her and she certainly seems to be a very sensible and sane woman.

We have just heard that the twin girl of the woman who delivered in the yak field died a few days ago. The parents decided that they were too poor to care for two children. They fed the boy, but left the girl to starve. It took her a month to die. I feel so angry. If they didn't want her, we would have taken her and given her a good loving home. When we asked Kami about it, he explained that it would be very shameful for the family to give their child to someone else to bring up, since it would be admitting to everyone that they couldn't afford to do so themselves. But if a child dies, it just dies. Bad luck. No shame.

SONI AAMAA AND A SERVANT BOY RIGGI DIGGING.

Yesterday Kami returned from a meeting of the Sagamartha Pollution Control Committee. The Minister of Tourism has now promised that the Khumbu will receive $NZ160,000 each year from the expedition fees. This will be administered by the Sagamartha Pollution Control Committee. Considerable concern was voiced about who would have access to the money, and how thoroughly they could be made accountable for its distribution.

Kami also heard that a foreign trekking group who had come over to "clean up the Himalayas" sent some of their Sherpas to sneak into Pangboche in the middle of the night to fill six large sacks from the local rubbish pit! They carried this back up to their camp and took lots of photos, saying that they had collected this from Everest Base Camp and Ama Dablam. This was to raise donations for future Everest expeditions! Maybe we should send a Sherpa group to clean up Europe!

CHAPTER

11

I have just got back from a few days' trekking up the Gokyo Valley. We met two women who are trekking and climbing their way across the entire Himalayas, going through Sikkim, Nepal, Tibet, India, Pakistan and China. They are being sponsored and are raising money for the Himalayan Trust. We hit it off instantly, and when they said they were going up to Gokyo the next day, I asked if I could tag along. The walk is really pleasant. Because you climb up rapidly in a short time, (although don't seem to climb too many hills), you can walk only for two to three hours each day, which makes it quite a leisurely pace.

The first day, we walked from Khunde to Dole, and spent a very cold night in a tiny lodge. I was wearing three Polartek longjohn tops, a weather-proof thick Polartek jacket, and a down jacket, longjohn bottoms covered by Polartek/fleece trousers, Polartek socks under thick Polartek trekking socks and woolly sheepskin slippers, Polartek gloves covered by woollen mittens, and a Polartek hat. I was still cold and couldn't feel my feet until well after I'd crawled into my minus-20 sleeping bag, (fully dressed), at 6 pm.

In the morning, I was disappointed to look out the window into thick fog, only to realise when I got up that it was a beautiful sunny day — the window had just been iced over.

We moved on to to Macchermo, which was only two hours' easy walk away, and sat dressed to the eyeballs in our Polartek and sunscreen, eating vegetable soup and drinking herbal tea out in a field. Macchermo is 2000 feet higher up than Khunde, and yes, it was even colder than Dole. We huddled around the lodge owner's wood and yak-dung stove, forcing ourselves to keep up beyond six o'clock. Some of the porters from other trekking groups came in, drank some chang and sang into the night, which took our minds off the cold for a while.

The next morning was again beautifully clear, and I wandered around on the icy ground watching the yaks covered in a cold blanket of ice gradually rouse themselves and shake off their white colouring. It certainly made me appreciate being able to sleep inside.

We then wandered up to Gokyo. Now the trip became really exciting. Until then, it had all been a bit grim. Not only was it very cold, but travelling with vegetarians made the diet a bit limited. We wandered up a river that had small waterfalls crashing through blocks of ice — very spectacular. The trail was now marked with "cairns", picturesque piles of

View across Gokyo's third lake.

stones that are offerings to the gods. We arrived at the first glacial lake — an amazingly deep emerald green — continued past another similar lake, then on to the third, which is where Gokyo stands. It looks like a small fishing village, and was so beautiful it made me very homesick for the sea. I'd forgotten how much I miss being near water.

We stayed at one of my patient's lodges, where we were spoilt to an embarrassing extent. The lodge was full, yet we could wander in, order our meal and be served in about 10 minutes, only to discover from the grumbles and mutterings around us that other guests were still waiting for meals they'd ordered an hour and a half ago.

I made vague attempts at looking guilty, but soon just lapped up the pampering. The lodge owner had a kind of pot-belly stove that she filled with firewood and yak dung patties, which heated the dormitory for most of the night, and, luxury of luxuries, a kerosene lamp which was so bright it seemed to burn your retina, but with dark glasses or a sun visor on enabled you to read! So, thankfully, I didn't have to experience the natural night-time temperature at 4750 m.

The next morning, we had planned to climb Gokyo Ri, at 5318 m, for

A VIEW FROM
GOKYO RI.

beautiful views of the surrounding mountains. Usually the mornings are very clear, but tend to cloud in later. I was so excited about the trip that I woke my friends at 5 am, despite the obvious surrounding thick fog. They were surprisingly pleasant about it, but pointed out that there wasn't a lot of sense in climbing the peak in this weather. I was too excited and cold to sit around, so decided to climb it anyway. Off I went through the mist, crossing the icy stepping stones on the lakeside. It was eerily beautiful, with small plants iced into amazing patterns. After about 45 minutes' climbing, I discovered to my delight that it was just valley cloud and the day was clear and sunny above it. I raced up to the top, another 45 minutes of gasping, and sat watching the sun rise just to the right of Mt Everest. The view was unbelievable, including Cho Oyu, only about three kilometres away, bordering Tibet, and the Khumbu valley, also covering Khunde Hospital in cloud. I sat there for two very quick hours, and could have stayed all day, but I was excited about getting down and exploring the areas I had seen.

The following day we all set off for the fifth lake, a two-to-three hour gentle climb of about 300 m. Again we were blessed with a beautiful clear day, and had incredible mountain views, even better than from Gokyo Ri, including the whole of Mt Everest's North Face. I began to fall in love with Cho Oyu. The pass where the Tibetan refugees sneak over looked so close and enticing, but you'd need proper climbing gear to get over it safely. The Chinese border guards would be a bit off-putting too. Most of the Tibetans manage the pilgrimage in sandshoes and normal street clothes, though I'm sure they're made of tougher stuff than me, and not a few perish in the attempt.

We'd just returned from our five-hour trek when I was handed a message from one of the young men from Khunde. He had run from the hospital to Gokyo in five hours. Diane had written saying that one of the women in the village had been in labour for 37 hours. A passing doctor had examined her and thought the baby was dead, but she couldn't stay, and could I come down as soon as possible to maybe do a Caesarean section to save the mother? It was 3 pm and it would get dark around

5.30 pm. I didn't relish the thought of walking all the way back to Khunde in the dark, but couldn't bear to think of the woman dying an agonising death of obstructed labour. I also thought that Kami and Diane wouldn't be having much fun, dealing with the situation. Neither had even done a normal delivery, and I couldn't see them sharpening up their pocket knives to have a go at a Caesar.

The Khunde boy was perfectly happy to head back down with me, as was one of our porters. It was pretty dramatic, as we dropped everything and raced off. Our lodge owner came racing after us, upset that I hadn't said good-bye, embracing me, and stuffing a chocolate bar into my hands to give me strength for the trip.

We moved very quickly. I wanted to make the most of the daylight, and we motored to Macchermo, halving the time it took us to come up. About half an hour before Dole it became so dark we had to use our torches, which certainly slowed us up. I'd started to stagger a bit with tiredness, so our porter made us stop at a lodge and forced milk tea and boiled noodles into me.

We pushed on through the blackness, down a very steep gully to the river. I kept slipping on the dusty trail, and finally the Khunde boy went in front, holding my hand, while our porter would grab my elbow from behind if I looked like falling. I was quite scared, as a lot of the track was on a cliff edge, so a slip off the trail could certainly have been the last one. Fear for my own safety was soon replaced with concern for the Khunde boy, who insisted on walking on the cliff edge of the trail to give me room to walk comfortably! It took a very long hour and a half to get down to the river, with me getting more and more exhausted, and a little hysterically frightened towards the end. I was also very touched by the great concern and caring that these two men had for my well-being, and felt it to be a very special experience. As we wandered through the forest I started thinking about bears, yetis and snow leopards, and it felt really comforting to have a hand to hold on to, and someone at the back of me. Oddly enough, to calm myself, I went step by step over how I would do the Caesarean section. I felt quite calm about this prospect, even though I had never done one on my own.

We stopped for another cup of tea, and though it was only a little after 7.30 pm, I longed to join the sleeping trekkers in their dormitory. We then climbed a hill, in half the usual time (so maybe my adrenaline was buzzing a little), then the men guided me down the slope and around the cliff-faced trail where the foreign woman had fallen to her death last Black

Friday. I couldn't get her out of my mind and was shaking with fear and exhaustion as my friends practically carried me around. The Khunde lad continued his kamikaze attempts to give me a comfortable, safe walk. Once past the cliffs, I suddenly got a burst of energy, realising that there were no more high places to fall from between there and the hospital. We made it home at 10.30 pm.

Meanwhile, Di had been doing her own heroic stuff. One of our neighbours had gone into labour, and Di and Kami had been called to the house after dark. Everything seemed to be going normally. The family is very traditional and wouldn't consider bringing the woman to the hospital. Diane said reassuring things to the family and headed back to bed at the hospital. She was woken at 3 am by the family and again things looked all right to her. She muttered soothing words and wandered back to bed. The next morning, Kami told her that the family had come four more times for her to check that the baby was all right, but he had sent them home.

Things did seem to be taking a while and Diane sent Kami off to the local camping areas to see if there was a doctor about who could help. Di also wrote a note to me and sent the runner off to Gokyo. Kami turned up with a European doctor who hadn't done obstetrics for 25 years but was willing to give any advice she could. She examined the mother and told Diane that she couldn't hear a heartbeat. She couldn't be sure but thought the baby was probably dead. She was very apologetic, but could not stay to help because her group was heading down to Lukla to fly out to Kathmandu the next morning.

Diane and Kami tried to continue the hospital clinic, but soon the family arrived again, saying that the baby had moved down and the mother wanted to push it out, but it wouldn't come. Could Diane cut the mother and pull the baby out?

Diane explained that she is not a doctor and had never delivered a baby before, and really didn't know what she was doing, but the family pleaded with her to try. It was still daylight, so they insisted that nobody see her going to the house. Kami and Diane hid the necessary equipment in a backpack and wandered nonchalantly around the village until they happened to meet up with a family member, who loudly asked them to come and have a cup of tea.

Once inside, Diane fought her way through the pile of blankets on the floor covering the mother and, by lying on the floor, was able to see a tiny bit of the baby's head. She bravely cut an episiotomy, which didn't seem to make a lot of difference. After five minutes or so of watching, Kami suggested they try the Ventouse extractor. Di had seen me use it once before when I'd done the symphysiotomy. She fitted the suction cup on to the baby's head and Kami pumped up the pressure. When the mother had her next contraction Diane pulled. The suction held for a bit, baby stayed put, and then with a loud "pop" the suction gave way. The cup came out and stuck to the mother's thigh. This was all too much for Diane, who suddenly realised that she didn't have a clue about what she was doing. Kami was keen for her to try the suction cup again, but she wouldn't have it, and instead sent him off to try the local villages to see if he could find another doctor who could help.

After an hour, Diane went outside to relieve herself. She had just got her pants down when she heard, "memsahib, hurry." She raced back upstairs to find the mother on her hands and knees, with baby's head hanging out. She grabbed the baby and pulled the body out, only to have it snatched from her by the anxious grandmother, who wouldn't let her touch baby or mother again. It was only with great insistence that she was allowed to clamp and cut the cord. She had to leave the placenta still inside the womb, as tradition said that the family would take care of that after they had all (baby included) eaten chang porridge.

Kami had missed the birth and had been unable to find a doctor. It would have been too late anyway. In the end nature took over. When I staggered into the hospital at 10.30 pm, Di just threw her arms around me and howled out that she'd had a boy and he was alive.

DI WITH TASHI TENZING, FIVE MONTHS AFTER SHE DELIVERED HIM.

The next morning Diane and I checked on mother and baby. The boy looked healthy and was feeding well, but I wasn't allowed to examine him properly. We could hardly see the mother, who lay miserably wrapped up in the same pile of blankets. The family would not let me examine her, but assured me that the placenta had come out. I offered to sew up the episiotomy that Diane had cut, but that was completely out of the question. Despite all of this they were delighted with the outcome and thanked us endlessly for our help. Diane had made a valiant effort, but I really don't think we contributed much at all. In fact, with no offence to Diane, probably more harm than good was done, but the family still showered us with khaarta and chiyaa.

The grandfather had until then been very dismissive of us, and would at times hurt Diane's feelings by calling her "too fat", "no good worker" and "too slow walking". Since the birth of his grandson, we cannot get past his house without a hearty greeting where he will race out to shake both our hands.

The next morning, a trekker turned up at the surgery.

"I wonder if you would mind looking at my fundi. I'm worried that I may have a retinal haemmorhage".

While we sat in the dark room waiting for his pupils to dilate, I asked, "What kind of medicine do you practice?"

"I'm an obstetrician."

I could have screamed. He had spent the past two days camping with his trekking group in Khunde. He had not told the group leader that he was a doctor because he hadn't wanted to be hassled with fellow trekkers' trivial complaints of diarrhoea and stomach aches. So when Kami had asked if they had a doctor in the group, the leader had very reasonably said no. The obstetrician would have been delighted to have helped Diane out!

Gaga Doma continued to get worse and worse. Kami advised us that even if she wanted injectable medication we shouldn't give it to her. She was sure to die, and the "strong medicine" would only be blamed. She wouldn't come to the hospital, and in desperation we carried an oxygen cylinder around to her house. With a little experimentation we fashioned a type of nebuliser and helped her to breath in asthma medication. I had her on oxygen, asthma medication, antibiotics, steroids — everything I could think of. The lamas spent many days doing blessings for her. One morning we came in and couldn't hear her chest rattling away. My eyes welled with tears as I made my way through the dark room to say my goodbyes. I was delighted to be greeted by a wide toothless grin from under the blankets. Gaga Doma had dramatically improved.

Her son was ecstatic with her improvement, and attributed it all to the breathing medicine. He had given it to her most of the night, and we shuddered with horror as he demonstrated with his perpetual cigarette hanging from his mouth. He was very reluctant to let us take the oxygen cylinder home, but we didn't feel that we wanted to risk an explosion.

Within days, Gaga Doma was up and about walking around the mani wall with her friends. Back to her good old self.

Ed's sirdar returned by helicopter looking yellow and bloated. I had sent a letter with him to show to the foreign doctor, explaining that I had told him there was no chance, and asking the doctor, if he agreed, to confirm this opinion to the family. I was outraged to receive a letter from the Kathmandu doctor giving no diagnosis or prognosis, having put the sirdar on multiple vitamins and asking me to send him a blood sample in three months. I couldn't see him lasting that long. The family had the impression that this was a curable illness, and were disgusted with my opinions and lack of action.

Fortunately for him, the sirdar died within a few days, peacefully and pain free. It was a terrible time for me. The case seemed obvious to me, but the "experts" in Kathmandu disagreed with my diagnosis. There was no one to ask, and doing nothing felt almost criminal, but there really was nothing to do. The last few days, the house was filled with lamas doing their pujas. The local shaman came and went into a series of hysterical trances in an attempt to exorcise the bad spirits. Tibetan herbs were tried. Holy water from the Tushi Rimpoche was given to him. Whether this was urine or water — I do not know. When he was too weak to eat, Ang Doolie would chew the food herself and feed him mouth to mouth, as she would have for her children. It seemed such an act of love.

Early one morning there was a knock on the door and I was woken by a tearful family member saying that the sirdar had gone. They wanted me to check him, and when I confirmed that he was dead, various relatives started keening and wailing. I thought the family would be angry with me, but there was no blame. This was the way of the gods, and I was welcomed as much as anyone else to funeral gatherings.

The sirdar's body was sat up in a funeral box. Early one morning, a long procession wandered through the village, with monks blowing mournful horns and banging drums. Five large tree trunks decorated with flags, piles of kindling, plastic cans of kerosene, bottles of chang and thermos flasks of chiyaa were all carried up. His body sat in the box, magnificently decorated with brightly coloured flags and white silk khaarta, and was carried along in the procession, which made its way slowly up the steep ridge at the back of the hospital. Every so often the procession would stop, and the monks would perform various blessings, burning juniper branches. The village was filled with smoke, as almost every house burnt a sprig of juniper branch on one of their boundary walls.

After about an hour, the procession disappeared behind the ridge to one of the four cremation sites for the village. The five large logs were stood up on top of the ridge, each with a different-coloured flag, representing the elements (blue for sky, white for snow, green for grass, red for rock, and yellow for earth). The next day, the remaining bones and ashes were brought down to the house. These were mixed with clay and made into religious statues to go inside the chorten that would be built. The lamas stayed for many days doing blessings, and finally we all attended the sirdar's funeral, where we drank and ate for most of the day. When we left, everyone was given money, rice, butter and salt from the family.

The sirdar's chorten is set up about one hundred yards left of the chortens for Louise and Belinda Hillary. Ed's first wife and 14-year-old daughter were tragically killed in a plane crash in 1974. The aircraft was headed for Phaplu for the family to meet up with Ed while he was building the hospital for the local people. Someone had taken off the cords attached to the ailerons. The New Zealand pilot was running late and did not do his normal pre-flight checks. It was not until he had taken off that he realised that the ailerons (which control movement in the rolling plane about the longitudinal axis) were not working. He was unable to control the aircraft and it crashed soon after takeoff. It seems appropriate that Ed's wife, daughter and sirdar all have their memorials on the same ridge looking towards Mount Everest.

We were also saddened and shocked to hear of the death of Gary Ball, of "Hall and Ball". He apparently died of altitude sickness while climbing in West Nepal. We met Gary only once, when he, Jan Arnold and Rob Hall dropped in for a cup of tea just after they had successfully summitted Mt Everest earlier this year. He seemed a charming, likeable guy. It seems incredible that such an experienced climber should suffer such a fate.

We have certainly been seeing a lot of trekkers with mild altitude sickness at Khunde. A number seem to have been given very odd advice by their doctors at home, or by trekking doctors they have met on their way. Some have described acetazolamide (which is our main prevention and treatment for altitude sickness) as a poison to be avoided. We admitted someone a few days ago who had skipped Dole and gone straight up to Macchermo, despite his persistent headache. When he started vomiting and coughing up frothy white sputum, a foreign doctor he met there advised him to stay a day at Macchermo rather than descend, to see if the symptoms settled, and not to take any of his acetazolamide. Fortunately he decided to descend, which probably saved his life. However, because of the advice given he required some persuasion to take our treatment.

An idiot guide for one of the support treks to a recent Everest expedition kept contradicting my advice when they dropped in before going up. He maintained that only "weak" people needed acetazolamide, and that if you got really sick they could just put you in the Gamow bag! He kept stating that "really tough people can do two days in one", and similar dangerous rubbish. His entire group became unwell with altitude sickness, and we heard later that two had to be urgently evacuated. I tried to talk to him about it when he dropped by on the way down, but his mind was impenetrable. He kept going on about "what a pack of wimps" he'd brought up. He is a dangerous man, and I casually spoke to two of his company's organisers about my concerns. Their attitude was that "yes, he is a prat, but he's been with the company for many years so what can they do!"

The Everest expeditions this season were mostly successful. I was disappointed that, yet again, only the Western summitters were named by the press, and pointed out to our journalist friends that the Sherpa climbers do most of the work nowadays. The "sahibs" just have to climb up, while their Sherpas carry the heavy loads, find the trails, fix the ropes, set up camp, cook and clean up. Surely the Sherpa summitters at least deserve a mention. Our deaf photographer friend from Namche now has a very fine collection of photographic portraits of many of the Sherpa and Indo-Nepali summitters. He is also setting up a museum of Sherpa artefacts before the old ways are forgotten.

One team really did things on a shoe-string, charging only $NZ65,000 for each individual. To save money, the organisers bought seven permits for Everest (at $NZ20,000 each), and seven for Lhotse (at only $NZ8,000 each). Nine of the fourteen who attempted Everest successfully summitted. They are now in embarrassing and, I suspect, rather serious trouble with the Nepali officials, who may take the official title of "summitteer" from at least two of the climbers, and could in fact ban them from climbing for the next five years. Since this was a commercial venture, and the paying climbers were, I gather, not involved in the cost-cutting deal, I imagine sparks will fly.

Only one of the Spanish team summitted. Their expedition had been more expensive and luxurious. They had contracted a canning factory at home, and each of the climber's wives had prepared their favourite meals to go to Nepal with them! Sadly, their team leader, a doctor, turned back at the south summit when he realised that he was too exhausted to go on. He met a member of another team who had just summitted and was on his own with bad frostbite, and helped him down until they needed to go their separate ways. As the doctor was abseiling down a ridge just above Camp Four something went wrong and he fell to his death. His body was found the next day at Camp Two.

The Duchess of York, "Fergie", is at this time trekking up to Base Camp with a group of intellectually and physically disabled people. Sadly, she by-passed the hospital, so we didn't get to meet her, but we did show her group around. She camped at our friend's lodge in Namche, and celebrated her birthday with a party in his lounge. He found her delightful company. Her accompanying press were, however, thoroughly obnoxious, arrogantly ordering everyone around, acting more as if they were royalty rather than her. Apparently, she got fed up with them and sent them home, preferring to go on alone with the group.

Although we missed out on meeting "Fergie", one of our British friends did come across her on the trail. They got talking and, since he's a volunteer worker, she asked if there was anything she could do for him. Being a quick-witted and obviously devoted son, he immediately said that it was his mum's birthday in a few weeks, and would she ring her up and wish her a "Happy Birthday". "Fergie" thought she could probably manage that.

Apparently, on his mum's birthday, the phone rang, and when she answered she heard a very poncy voice saying, "Would you hold on for the Duchess of York?", followed by, "Hello, Mrs Rogers, it's the Duchess of York here. I'm just ringing you up to wish you a Happy Birthday," to which our friend's mum gave a rather dubious, "Oh yes?"

"No really, I am the Duchess of York. I met your son trekking in Nepal, and he asked me to phone you up." The penny dropped, and then Mrs Rogers didn't really know what to say, but somehow they chatted for a few minutes. When she hung up, she just sat there staring at the phone, thinking, "What do I do now?" So she ran to the bottom of the garden and started telling her neighbours, in excited tones, about the phone call. She lives in a small Welsh village, and it's certainly been the talk of the town. She's obviously a very polite woman. We were imagining a few of our friends' responses to the call: "So you're the Duchess of York are you? Well, I'm the f-ing King of England, so whadda ya want?"

Still, from what I've heard about "Fergie", she'd probably see the humour of it and cope admirably.

A young man from Khumjung was one of the guides who accompanied the Duchess of York and her group on their trek last year. He must have made quite an impression on Fergie, since he is at present in England spending four months staying at her house. His father has mixed up the story a little and is proudly telling people that his son is now living with the Queen of England! Well, it's close enough for around here.

The Crown Prince was also in Namche a few days ago, but he too chose not to come up and see us. All those photos of us with famous people that we could have had to impress our friends with. Ah well, I guess it wasn't to be. At least we've got photos with Ed. We'll just have to bask in his reflected glory.

We've also had a Czechoslovakian group here flying their microlight about each morning. They moved into a lodge at the Shyangboche airfield about two weeks ago, and had hoped to fly around and over Mt Everest. Unfortunately, their high-altitude machine has had mechanical problems and is stuck at Lukla. The one they have here can fly to only 6500 metres.

They have a film crew with them, and zoom off each morning dressed in sub-zero clothing, crash helmet with a nasal attachment to an oxygen cylinder, and various video and still cameras attached to the wings of their microlight. They certainly don't look like your typical trekkers up here. All have big beer bellies and rough exteriors, but seem pleasant enough guys who couldn't really give a hoot whether they get to Everest or not and are just here for a good time. They fly in the morning, then go back to the lodge and drink beer. Only two have even ventured as far afield as the hospital, just 20 minutes' walk away. Most of the locals show a sophisticated disinterest at the "queerie" (crazy foreigner) antics, but it's fun to see the excitement of the local kids, and the oldies "tut-tutting" and shaking their heads as they stare up into the sky.

On the 31st of October we had Sherpa Hallowe'en. This is not a reproduction of the American celebration, but an ancient tradition carried out for many centuries. The young children of the village come in groups to each house after dark, stand around candles and sing heartily outside your door until you come out and give them a few rupees. Then often they'll do a wee dance as a thank you. They don't dress up. There used to be special prayers, but these have been forgotten over time. It is not a religious celebration, and no one is really sure how it originated.

Last week, Kami, Diane and I went down to Namche to the bank to open a third account for the hospital. We had an early lunch and wandered down, arriving at 2 pm. Kami had all the appropriate papers ready, including the bank draft from the Trust administrator with which to open the new account. The manager asked us to have a seat, and we waited and waited while various employees searched for the hospital account. Ancient filing cabinets were fought with in an effort to prize them open. Cloths were found to squeeze through the small holes in the drawers where the handles had once been, and were then dragged open, with many graunches and squeaks. Large volumes were pulled out of cupboards, bashed against the wall to remove the dust, and very methodically gone through. After about three quarters of an hour, the appropriate file was found.

But then we had to take some papers to an important official at the bottom of Namche, for him to certify (in triplicate) that we really were from the hospital, and honourable people worthy of opening an account. Since we recognised all the bank staff as patients whom we had treated very recently, this seemed a little unnecessary, but the appropriate forms had to be filled in — that is, when they found them! So we waited again while these were hunted down. Just before 3 pm, we were sent off to find the official and were told that the bank would close at three, so we'd have to come back tomorrow! Muttering away to each other we found the office of the important man, only to discover that he had gone home to Kathmandu for the Darsain festival, and would not be back for a month. So the new account is on hold until then. I should have known better than to expect anything like that to be easy in Nepal.

We won't be holding our breath for the hydroelectric power either. They are now having staff problems. The two foreigners who are in charge at Thamo sacked one of the Sherpa technicians for "laziness". They then decided that the scheme needed to save money, and announced that they were going to sack six out of the remaining 12 technicians. One of these men had been a very promising student in Class 9, and had been talked into leaving school and joining the scheme with the promise of five years' guaranteed employment! At the same time, the foreign company are planning to employ an accountant and "research officer", who will both be paid very well. The technicians called a meeting and have gone on strike. Good on them!

We have made good friends with Temba, who comes around at least every day. Although he is deaf-mute, he does great imitations and is quite an actor, portraying his stories and made-up adventures. Kami is a good interpreter and we have a lot of fun together. With Diane's skills with people with disabilities, they have struck up a particular friendship, and I suspect that Temba has a bit of a crush on her. Recently he has been buying her small pieces of cheap jewellery at the market, and giving her pencil drawings to keep. He obviously has great taste, but we hope he does not end up with hurt feelings.

We weren't sure that he understood our relationship until one evening he was "talking" to Mingma, who suddenly went beetroot red. At first Mingma wouldn't tell us what Temba had said, but we insisted, and he turned his back, hung his head, and muttered what Temba had told him. Temba had said that he'd come around earlier that afternoon and couldn't find anyone around. He was about to walk into our flat, but heard us having sex, so went home! Temba thought this was a great joke, and has added it to his repertoire of unlikely stories that he spreads through the village. We were embarrassed, but realised there was no malice in the tale, and it certainly let us know that he and the other villagers understood that Diane and I are more than just friends. It galled me a little to think of people imagining us screaming at the top of our lungs in frantic uninhibited bouts of lovemaking, when, in truth, we are both rather shy and discreet in that area of our lives.

Temba's paintings sell very well to the tourists, and he keeps promising that he will do one for us as a going-away present. We would certainly be delighted to have one. He says he is working away in secret on our one, since if his mother finds it she will insist that it be sold to a trekker. Kami says we shouldn't hold our breath waiting for the gift.

Di and I have been enthusiastically collecting yak dung and making it into patties to augment our dwindling charcoal supplies — much to the delight of the villagers.

We felt that they might not look too good splattered along the front of the hospital, so we found a less exposed area to work in around the back. When we'd finished, we proudly showed Kami the 30 patties we had made. He, in as kind a way as he could, explained that this lot would probably last us a day, and we would need to make thousands to get us through winter. Sadly, our private little area very rarely sees the sun, and, as long as it doesn't rain, the patties should dry in about 15 days! Kami wandered back to the kitchen chuckling away to himself, obviously thinking "crazy bideshi" (foreigners). Di has been deterred, deciding that it is an altogether smelly business. I find it rather creative and soothing, and am determined to find a sunnier spot next time. Maybe we could set up a deal with the foreign hotel. They could fly up rich, stressed out business people for touchy-feelie personal-growth weekends. As part of the curriculum, the hospital could teach them the art of yak-dung patty making. It would certainly boost our production rates, and could be a novel way for them to find themselves.

About four months ago, I decided I would have a shot at the Everest Marathon, and started training, going for the odd run down to Namche and back. The race starts at Gorak Shep (5184 m), just down from the Everest Base Camp, goes down to Namche (3446 m), for the 20-mile (32 km) mark, then loops off to Thamo and back to Namche to complete the 26 miles (42 km).

As the race drew closer my doubts of finishing increased, but by that stage I had entered and too many people knew about it for me to back out without losing face. Most of the locals thought I was mad, particularly when they found out that not only was I not being paid for doing this, but the foreigners were paying big money to run the distance.

Ten days before the race I had a house call in Namche and met the marathon group, who had just arrived from two weeks' trekking up from Jiri. The room was full of lean, mean men, earnestly discussing race strategy and times. The Ghurka officers casually remarked that they had all run down from Gorak Shep that morning, and the three fastest had made it to Namche within three hours. They were sure that one of their men was going to win. My confidence was not improved when one of the race organisers rather obviously looked me up and down and said, "Er . . . um . . . and have you done any training at all?" I explained that I'd been jogging for one to two hours every second day for about three months. To fill the awkward silence, I laughed and said that I wasn't really a runner, but just wanted to see if I could finish, and have fun. Suddenly the room was filled with contemptuous and pitying eyes. I left feeling very much out of my league, but still wanted to give it a go.

Two days later, Mingma and I headed off for the clinic at Phortse, while Diane went ahead to Pangboche with his sister, who was working as our porter. Mingma and I saw a few people and as usual were fed the unforgettable Phortse riggi couer (buckwheat pancakes). Our health worker insists on giving us this delicacy every trip. His pancakes are two or three times the thickness of the ones we have at home and are sadly raw in the middle. They are eaten with yuck (yak) butter and well-seasoned somma (rancid cottage cheese). Mingma was very brave and ate two.

We then headed to Pangboche, climbing around cliff edges and negotiating yak trains in the mist. We met one old man whose load had fallen off his zupchok. We stopped to help him reload, since his bags were too heavy for him to lift and he could not manage on his own. A group of trekkers had walked past him just before us and, when we passed them, they mentioned that he was their porter and it was their bags that had fallen down. It never crossed their minds to help the old guy! After about two and a half hours, we were delighted to find Diane waiting for us at Pangboche. We did another clinic there and then settled in for the night.

Mingma showed us the gompa, which is the oldest in the Khumbu, and is reputed to store the Yeti scalp and claw. Unfortunately, the scalp was stolen a few years ago. The monks seemed far too eager to grab our money, and then told us that the Yeti claw had also gone missing. It was a nice old gompa, but I've been in too many to be very impressed by them now.

We spent the night in the dormitory, then Mingma went home, while Di, Mingma's sister and I went on up to Pheriche. I had asked Diane to come some of the way, for moral support. It's pretty lonely trekking and staying in lodges on your own. It was an easy two-hour walk to Pheriche, and we settled into the Himalayan Rescue Association Clinic for the two days of acclimatisation. One of the doctors had gone down to Khunde to cover me for the week and the other doctor had gone up the Gokyo Valley, so we had the place to ourselves. Although the clinic was closed, word got around that a doctor was staying there, and within an hour we had patients lining up. Not quite the holiday we'd planned.

Two days later, Di headed back down to Khunde (carrying her own 20-kg pack!), and I wandered over to Dingboche where the marathon group had arrived. There were a hundred people in the group, all camping, so they weren't hard to miss. I met some of their 10 accompanying doctors and fortunately, some more laid back runners who seemed to have come more for the experience and fun of it than to try to break time records.

I was horrified to come across mad Gertrude again! This woman is becoming a legend. She has been around Nepal off and on for about five years, and has caused untold trouble and embarrassment to people.

When we met her earlier in the year at Thami we had thought she was just a nuisance whom people avoided, but then more stories started coming in, such as her chasing men around Namche with her ice-axe a few years ago. She had also had an affair with the husband of a local woman three years ago. Now Sherpa women will put up with a lot, but become very violent towards the other woman in this circumstance (though never seem to have a go at their husbands). They will group together with friends, and stone and beat the other woman, rub chillies in her eyes, shave her head, and have even been known to cut off the end of her nose. Gertrude was attacked by a group of Sherpa women in this way and, luckily for her, was rescued by some passing trekkers.

She had turned up at Namche a few weeks ago, waiting for the marathon group so she could let the runners know what terrible people they were travelling with. She believes that one of the Sherpa organisers is a serial rapist. She followed the group up, but at Tengboche, where she is well known, the lodge-owner refused to let her stay. She went to the local policeman and complained about this. When he did nothing about it, she tried to attack him with her ice-axe, and beat holes in his door when he managed to lock himself away from her.

FITNESS TESTING FOR THE EVEREST MARATHON.

She continued up to Dingboche, and decided that the lodge-owner there had been rude to her. She grabbed his visitors' book and defaced every page with rude comments about the lodge, writing over and ruining his collection of signatures, including those of Jimmy Carter and Sir Edmund Hillary. He had been very proud of these, and the poor man was in tears. He pushed her on the arm, to which she screeched, "Take your hand off my breast!", grabbed her ice-axe, and tried to attack him. Fortunately one of the Ghurka officers was passing and managed to wrestle the weapon off her.

I decided to wander up to Dugla (two hours' walk) to stay the night. There really isn't a lot to do in Dugla on your own. Mingma's sister was with me, but speaks no English, so we smiled and signed to each other, but mostly I read until it was dark and crawled into my sleeping bag for a very long, cold night.

The next day, I wandered another two hours to Lobuche and fortunately timed my arrival with that of the marathon group. Things looked up from then. It was getting too cold for tents for many of the people, so we all crowded into the lodges. I was invited to join the group for meals, which made me feel far more part of it all.

We would all crowd into the two very long mess tents, shoulder to shoulder with no elbow room, all in our down jackets, hats and gloves. There would be a cry of "soup ready", and hot bowls of water with lumps of ginger and garlic would be passed down the row. We suspected that for added flavour they may have spoilt us by occasionally squeezing the tablecloth into the soup pot, but could detect no other seasoning. Some nights we got a handful of popcorn thrown on the top of the soup! At least I had had this for only the last few days, but the rest of the group had had the same soup every night for the entire trek from Jiri! Then came the shout of "plates, plates" as we bundled up the soup bowls, and wet, iced-over dinner plates were thrown down the table. Then came rice with potato stew, another regular on the trek.

This was followed by announcements and nominations for the "silly hat". One poor guy who won the award had discovered a very large rock that someone had sneaked into his pack that morning. He'd carried it all the way from Dingboche to Lobuche. I felt that the idiot who'd put it in there deserved more of a mention, but no one ever owned up. The award winner had to wear the "silly hat" (a bright red velvet monstrosity, pointed at both poles, with tinkling bells along the top) for the whole of the next day. Although it sounds a little childish, it was in fact fun, and tended to bring the group out of itself.

Then came dessert, which was invariably either raspberry or chocolate glob with canned peaches. Real luxury. After that came the highlight of the meal — hot chocolate. You live in Nepal for nine months and simple things like this will excite you too!

We spent two days acclimatising at Lobuche. Some of the fitter, more acclimatised, or just plain stupid ones raced up to Kalla Pattar and back — a six-hour "rest" day. One runner exhausted herself so much that she collapsed when she got back and had to be carried down to Pheriche on a stretcher.

Few people slept at that altitude. We had a rat in our dormitory, which skittled across the sleeping bags and dropped bits of its nest on some of the runners. Also, for some reason, the lodge owner and her son came in at 2 am with bright torches, and chatted loudly for an hour while they sorted the potatoes. Don't ask me why. There was a film crew with us, making a documentary of the race. They had to recharge their video batteries each night, which involved running the generator outside our window until 3.30 am. The organisers tried to con us into thinking that the sound was soothing and sleep-inducing, but it didn't ever work for me!

The film crew seemed to take miles of footage, but explained that they would only use a twentieth in the documentary. We were told sternly that anyone who waved "Hi Mum" or "Hi Dad" would definitely not appear on the video. Feeling rather as if we'd been treated like school kids, we lived up to their poor expectations and managed to get plenty of "Hello parental figure" and "How do you do, guardians" into their shots, and people competed to get little signs or waves into the background. Infantile but fun — well, for the runners at least.

The next day, we wandered for two hours up to Gorak Shep. Now this is not a place anyone would want to spend a lot of time in. The only thing going for it is that it is one hour's walk to the top of Kalla Pattar (which has great mountain views), and two to three hours from Everest Base Camp. Even in blazing sunlight it is a cold old hole. There are three dreadful lodges, which all compete to see who can provide the most unappetising food at the highest price.

The lodge-owners certainly rubbed their hands with glee as they saw the hundred marathon runners approaching. We were crammed into dormitories like sardines, six of us pushed together on to four half-inch-thick mattresses. The price for these sleeping pits went up and up as the dormitories filled, until one of our camp leaders was charged $10 (instead of the usual $NZ1) for his little space. It was too cold for most people to sleep in tents. Last marathon it had been minus 23 degrees at the start of the race. I was furious when I went back into the lodge I'd booked into two hours previously to find the lodge-owner moving my porter's and my sleeping bags on to the floor. The group of Japanese runners had just arrived and, I gather, offered more for their beds, and we were being turfed out. I made quite a fuss, and finally was squeezed in between the row of Ghurka soldiers. The owner just said that it was bad luck about my porter! The most frustrating thing was that there weren't any options at that stage, so I put up with it. Mingma's sister, fortunately, was able to sleep in the kitchen of one of the other lodges.

Dinner was a sombre affair. It was even colder than the night before, and several of the runners were becoming seriously introverted as they contemplated their race strategies. The rest of us just felt lethargic with the altitude, the cold, and the prospect of another long, sleepless, cramped night. The cooks tried their hardest and, after the tablecloth soup, presented us with real meat (bought six days before in Namche) to go with our rice and potato stew. And then, YEEHAA, they presented us with a large chocolate cake with "Good Luck" iced on top. That felt like a real treat.

THE NIGHT BEFORE THE MARATHON.

We were told that a whistle would blow at 6 am to wake us up. (That got a bit of a laugh, since no one really expected to sleep.) We were to change into our running gear immediately, and crawl back into our sleeping bags to stay warm. Our kits should all have been packed that afternoon. At 6.30 am the Sherpas would bring around rice pudding and hot chocolate for us to consume in our sleeping bags. We were not to leave them until the next whistle at 6.45, when we would all leap out of our bags, pack them up quickly, and make our way smartly to the start line, about five minutes from the lodges. We would call out our numbers in order, then line up waiting for the race start. We had all practised the start earlier that afternoon.

Well, that was the plan anyway. The Japanese contingent got up at 4.30 am, wrapped up their sleeping bags, and noisily unpacked and repacked their kit bags, shining their torches in our eyes. At 5.30 am the Ghurkas got up in unison and, with military precision, got ready. I obediently but rather irritably lay in my sleeping bag awaiting the whistle. At 6 am, I changed into my running gear and spent a very difficult fifteen minutes covering vast areas of my feet in second skin and other protective plasters. Not that easy, half inside in a sleeping bag, in the dark, by torch light, with various other bodies climbing over and around you. Then I climbed confidently back into my sleeping bag, awaiting my breakfast.

I saw the Sherpas walk past, but they refused to believe that I was part of the marathon group, despite me showing them my running number pinned on to my shirt! I still hadn't put my boots on, and had to chase them across the icy ground in bare feet, in an effort to get at least some fluid before the race. One of the Ghurka officers came to the rescue and convinced the Sherpa that I really was allowed to have breakfast, which turned out to be porridge and tea. He said he thought he'd better step in, since I sounded as if I was about to hit the guy any minute. I hadn't realised that I'd sounded as angry as I felt.

I stumbled back to my sleeping back with wet, dirty, frozen feet, gobbled my breakfast, and hastily forced my numb feet into my boots, just before the whistle went. My sleeping bag was stuffed away rapidly and left optimistically on the mattress for my porter to collect when she got there. Then we all blundered down to the start, which went off remarkably well. The fast runners stood in front, the average ones in the middle, and the "just-having-a-go" ones, like me, went to the back. It was only minus 15 degrees and didn't feel all that cold, but we were pleased that they started us five minutes earlier, since we were all ready.

About 75 started off, including 13 women. The first 200 m is soft sand, then there's a sand hill, followed by a steep uphill climb of rocky moraine. Most of us walked the first bit, and those who tried to run soon stopped after about 50 m. At the top of the hill, the fast ones rapidly disappeared, while I plodded steadily on over the first one-and-a-half miles of up-and-down rocky moraine. Finally we came down a steep hill of loose rocks and dust to a flat area, and I jogged beside the river down to Lobuche. At last my feet had thawed out and I could feel them. It was flat for a while, then rose up to a long row of chortens (memorials for Sherpas who have died on Everest). I muttered "Om Mani Padme Hom" (Hail to the Jewel of the Lotus) as I passed them, in the hope that the good karma would get me safely down the steep, slippery, rocky slope to Dugla. At Dugla, I took my boots off, since my knees were killing me, and pulled my runners out of my pack. I ran down the hill almost to the river, feeling great, until I discovered that I'd left my gloves back up at Dugla, so had to go back up that hill to get them. I didn't feel so great after that, but turned back down and up and down again to the three-mile straight to Pheriche.

This was a deceptive part of the course, since it was made up of sand with hidden rocks, and involved crossing the river numerous times, leaping cautiously from one rock to the next, never being quite sure if it was just wet or covered by a thin coat of slippery ice. At Pheriche, I was told I was the sixth woman, so that spurred me on, and I continued to jog down to Pangboche. The track was covered with little iced-over streams, so it involved a bit of leaping and cautious hopping about. I got lost at Pangboche, and went up an unnecessary hill, then swore my way down a scree slope to get back on to the trail. I lost several minutes wrestling with our Deboche health worker, who insisted that I looked tired and kept trying to drag me into her lodge for a sit down and a cup of tea! Up a steep hill to Tengboche (3867 m), and I gasped my way to the drink station at 11.15 am, a little over halfway.

I was worried about "hitting the wall", as I had with my only other marathon in Auckland last year, where I'd had to walk the last 12 kilometres. This time I had been advised to eat during the race. The marshals were delighted when I forced down a large plate of rice pudding and canned fruit. Despite being in about 60th place by this stage, I suspect I was one of the first takers.

I then headed down the steep hill to the river (3225 m). Now, downhills are not my forte. I am pathetically concerned with not twisting my ankle or falling, and I took three-quarters of an hour to get to the bottom. Six people passed me going down! But then uphills I like, and I managed to pass four of those six people climbing up to Sanassa (3597 m). Just before Sanassa, the track goes around some cliff edges, and I came across some locals and their yaks going to market. At one stage, in my impatience, I made the really stupid mistake of trying to pass a yak on the cliff side of the trail. When he veered over to the cliff edge, I only kept my footing by hanging on to his horns, and very rapidly leaped on to the bank side of him. Not something I'll ever try again!

After Sanassa, I was on very familiar territory, and would break out of my walk into a confident striding jog as I passed locals I knew standing by their teahouses crying "Ee-aye, Doctor memsahib," and chortling away. One woman raced after me with a pair of gloves that Diane had left there on her way back. I'm sure she'd expected more than a stunned stare at the articles, and was probably hurt that I wasn't effusive in my thanks. Such a light thing to throw in my pack, but at the time it seemed a bit unfair.

I jogged and walked along the trail I had trained on a number of times before, around to Namche, though I feel sure that they had added a few more corners for the race, and it felt as if I'd never get there. Again I put on a particularly strong, confident stride as I bounded up to the drink station at the top of Namche, where Diane had been waiting devotedly for an hour and a half to cheer me on. This was the 20-mile mark, and it was 1.30 pm.

I continued to Thamo, which also seemed to have moved a lot further away, but coming back was the real challenge. Halfway back my legs suddenly felt like lead, and I thought, "It's not going to happen, I'm not going to get there." I thought I might throw up, and could do little more than a very slow, rather wobbly walk. Somehow I made it back up the gentle incline, which felt like the biggest hill yet, to the top of Namche.

The film crew were there, and, although I was filmed four times during the race, I bet that if I do get on to the documentary that will be the one they choose. My eyes were sunken and rolled back, my mouth open in a gasp and my legs staggering all over the place. I couldn't even muster enough energy to try and look good for the camera.

But once at the top of the hill I had an irrational urge to sprint down to the finish line, and it took all of my self-control to amble down gently without breaking a leg. I think I may have been a little confused, because I got to the Namche monastery and tried to go up the hill to the left of it, as is the custom. The back-up team were just coming down the hill to start the Thamo loop, and kept THE AUTHOR AT THE shouting for me to go down to the right. I felt that if I walked the FINISH LINE. disrespectful right-hand side down, then I might not make it down, but I went anyway, turning all the prayer wheels, and chanting "Om

Mani Padme Hom" all the way down. Then on to the main street of Namche, confidently striding by various locals cheering me on, and down past the finish line. Di was taking photos and had said before the race that she wanted me to run through with my arms thrown up for the photo. But straggling in at about 60th it seemed a bit too pretentious, and while I rather wish I had done it, I couldn't bring myself to at the time.

And guess who was at the finishing line handing out medals? Mad-as-an-ice-axe-Gertrude! I almost felt like running back. Thank God, one of the organisers leapt up and presented me with my medal. So I finished the race in 8 hours 45 minutes. YEEHAA, YEEHAA, YEEHAA! The first man had taken 4 hours 3 minutes. I was the sixth woman in.

There were no injuries, although one guy managed to slip under a yak, which fortunately chose to step over him instead of on to him! Only one man had to pull out, a British minister working in the Bahamas. That was particularly sad, since he had recently turned 60 and this was to be his 50th marathon.

The race, I felt, had been well organised, with safety in mind. Every person had to carry a requirement of warm clothes, a bivvy bag to climb into if injured, a whistle, notepad and pen, and even a torch. A doctor was present at each of the nine drink stations, and she or he would run down after the last runner to the next station. As well as that, a back-up team, including one doctor and three of the organisers, ran the entire race, behind the slowest runner. At each drink station they would check that everyone had been marked off. In the event of someone being missing, two of them would have gone back along the course to search for them. So I felt our welfare was well looked after.

Di arranged a shower for me in a friend's lodge. When I got out I realised that he'd pushed me ahead of about five of the other runners. I was a bit embarrassed, but also chuffed at one of the perks of working up here. After copious cups of tea, Di and I wandered up to our lodge, 20 minutes up a very steep climb from the finishing line. As soon as the lodge-owner discovered what I'd been doing, he presented me with an effervescent multivitamin drink to take immediately, to help me regain my strength.

Next morning we went back down to sort out the donations from the marathon group for the hospital. Three large rubbish sacks full of medicines, a stretcher, a generator, and two gerry cans full of petrol! They had already been very generous. The other runners had paid almost $NZ6,000, (including airfares) to do the marathon, and the organisers had let me do it all for free, so I am very grateful to them.

Di and I walked up the ridge to Khunde. I was so amazed. No blisters and I felt fine. I even carried the heavy pack up the hill. This lifestyle must be good for me. I must be fitter than I thought.

As we arrived at Khunde, the Sherpa grapevine had of course beaten us there, and a number of the villagers came out to congratulate me. That felt really good. Most said, "Oh, Doctor memsahib strong woman." One of our friends topped it off with what she obviously felt was the height of compliments, shouting out, "Eee, Doctor Liz, you big, strong, fat woman!"

One of the frustrating and upsetting aspects of this job is dealing with trekkers who have got sick and have been abandoned by their group, who leave them in teahouses and continue on. Another even more common, and excusable, problem is that of the trekker who becomes unwell and is taken down to medical help by one of the guides.

Two days ago, we saw a 63-year-old Japanese man who had developed altitude sickness at Gokyo. He speaks no English. However, the rest of his group decided to go on over the Chola Pass and up to Kalla Pattar, leaving him to be brought down by a Sherpa guide who speaks a few words of Japanese.

The man had cerebral oedema. This is one of the effects of not acclimatising well to high altitude. His brain had become swollen with fluid, making him confused, drowsy and unable to walk straight. Without treatment and descent to a lower altitude, this proceeds to coma and death. His well-meaning guide had no understanding of altitude sickness, and had him carried slowly down to our hospital, taking four days, when he should and could easily have been brought here in a day.

By the time I saw him he was ataxic and unable to even walk a couple of steps. He looked totally bewildered and was very confused, and had difficulty telling us even his first name. We had a very frustrating three-way attempt at translation, where I would ask a question in English, my health worker would ask the guide in Sherpa, then he was to ask the man in Japanese. Most of the time the Sherpa would just answer for the man without asking him. I would say, "Is Mr such-and-such feeling nauseated at the moment?" And the guide would just say no, without asking him! We would then say for the hundredth time, "ASK HIM!", and the patient would nod his head. I would try to see if the patient could walk, and the Sherpa guide would refuse to tell him, or help, maintaining that of course he could walk, but he was tired now.

When I explained that this man's brain was swollen due to high altitude, and that he was seriously ill and could die, the guide looked at me pityingly and said that he was much better now. "Look he was just tired and now he's having a sleep." In fact the man was lapsing in and out of consciousness and was Cheyne-Stokes breathing! When I insisted that he be carried to a lower altitude, the guide refused, saying that the man was too tired to be moved, and he'd sent the porters away anyway. "Maybe tomorrow."

A GAMOW BAG.

We stuffed the confused, semi-conscious man into the Gamow bag, and left him there for two hours while we read the riot act to the guide. We again explained how important it was that this man was evacuated, and agreed on the compromise of helicoptering him out first thing in the morning, since it was now dark. The nearest radio is one hour's walk away, and we sent the guide off with a letter explaining the need for emergency evacuation.

We watched the man overnight, but it's very hard to determine level of consciousness in the wee small hours of the morning when the patient has a right to be drowsy anyway. We had no language, and the guide was not helpful, since he thought we should just let the poor man sleep anyway.

The next morning we waited anxiously for the helicopter, and then finally asked the guide what time it was expected. "Oh," he lied, "I tried to get through, but there was no one at the helicopter office, so I thought I'd see how he was in the morning." He then went on to explain that because the man wears a visor/sun hat instead of a woolly one, his head got very cold up in Gokyo, and he's just recovering from that. All he needs to do is stay for a few days with the heater going and get warm! Also he hadn't eaten much for the last few days, and he just needed a few meals.

At this point I completely lost my cool. I told him that this man would die if he stayed another night at this altitude, and that if he did not go and get a helicopter this minute I would write to his trekking agency and insist that he be fired. I think he got a fright and raced off, we hoped towards a radio.

Two hours later the enormous army Super Puma helicopter circled the hospital and landed in a field about a hundred yards away. Mingma raced down to it and pleaded with the pilot to wait just a few minutes. (Often if the patient is not ready, they will just take off again and disappear. Fortunately there were some army guys from Namche who knew us, and they talked the pilot into stopping the engine and waiting.) The guide had not returned, so with attempts at sign language we dressed and packed up the man, who still looked totally bewildered, gave up trying to get him to pay his bill, and carried him down to the helicopter. He looked very frightened until he saw the aircraft, then his eyes lit up and he even tried to take a few stumbling steps on his own. At least he knew what he wanted.

Within minutes it was over, and the helicopter disappeared in a large cloud of dust. He'll be fine once he gets to the lower altitude of Kathmandu. I wonder if he'll remember anything of being at Khunde. I doubt it. But what really concerns me is that this man's fate was very much at the mercy of the guide, who had no understanding of his medical condition yet had the power to make the life and death decision for him of whether he would take the doctor's advice or not! I would hope that the patient's companions have some idea of the extremely vulnerable position they left their friend in.

We had another very frustrating time when we heard that a Japanese man from the foreign hotel was seriously ill with altitude sickness. He had been carried down to the Shyangboche airfield in the Gamow bag. We heard the plane, and forgot about him. It's not such an unusual thing up here. Six hours later, just before dark, we had a message asking to borrow our stretcher, so they could carry the man down to Namche. Apparently it had been too cloudy for the plane to land.

I was delivering a baby at the time, but sent a message with the stretcher, asking if they wanted me to see the man, asking which medicines they had started him on, and advising them to take him further down to Jorsale, rather than just Namche. The messenger was very clear that they had everything under control and definitely didn't want me to see him.

The next morning, I heard through the grapevine that the man had been on oxygen, and in the Gamow bag, all night, but they had a helicopter coming for him. Again I offered assistance, which was declined.

That afternoon, we received a message asking me to go down to Namche, since they were still unable to evacuate and the man was looking very ill. Mingma and I raced down, and found it very hard to assess him as he spoke only Japanese. Whenever I asked his companions or the staff to interpret, or see if he seemed confused, they very rapidly denied any symptoms. It was only when he struggled to tell me his first name and had no idea of how old he was that I began to get an idea of how unwell he was. The staff and his friends refused to help me try heel-to-toe walking, and kept saying he was tired, rather than couldn't walk. He turned out to have cerebral oedema, with confusion and ataxia, and had been coughing up frothy sputum. Apparently he was high up in the Japanese Embassy, and no one wanted to shame him by admitting he was confused!

Even more of a concern was that the hotel staff had in fact only used oxygen and the Gamow bag once, while waiting for the plane at Shyangboche, and no medicine such as acetazolamide or nifedipine had been started!

None of the staff would believe us when we explained that this man was in fact seriously ill, and could go into a coma and die. They accepted our medicines, but we had to get very stroppy in order to get him carried down to a lower altitude.

I was upset to find that the hotel staff knew very little about the treatment of altitude sickness, apart from giving patients oxygen, putting them in the Gamow bag, and evacuating them. This is particularly worrying considering that virtually all of their guests fly straight up to Shyangboche from Kathmandu, and are all at risk of having altitude problems. We have decided to negotiate a teaching session for the entire staff in the very near future.

The day after this, who should appear on our doorstep but Professor Igor Gamow himself — the man who designed the Gamow bag! He was a delightful, eccentric-looking man, with long, pony-tailed grey hair, cowboy hat and string neck tie. We liked him instantly. He told us a story of the time he visited his "competitors" in Lyons, France. He originally sold the patent to Du Pont, who retail it for about $NZ4500. Then a French company stole the idea, but use a hand pump, and sell it considerably cheaper. Du Pont are not impressed and there's all sorts of legal and political hoo-ha going on about it.

Professor Gamow didn't give a toss about all that, and ended up having dinner with the other team. After a few drinks he offered to let the vice-president have a go in the bag. All went well, though the Frenchman complained that it was a little cramped, and would Professor Gamow like to see what it was like in their more roomy bag. He very happily climbed into their bag, and the vice-president, not being in great physical condition, gasped and panted away as he hand-pumped the bag up. One of the Professor's companions, a world-class woman mountaineer, decided to take over, pushed the vice-president aside, and pumped away enthusiastically. Suddenly there was an almighty boom, and the bag exploded into pieces! As you can imagine, everyone raced about, and the room was filled with *sacre-bleus*. The Professor was unhurt, and understandably amused. The vice-president managed to save the moment by proposing a toast to "the one way in which his bag was superior to the Gamow bag — it deflates more quickly!"

PROFESSOR IGOR GAMOW.

Two hydroelectric power experts came and checked the Thamo Power Station recently. They have said that the entire system is no good, and will have to be started all over again! So I'm sure we can discount any chance of hydroelectric power for the hospital in our time here.

The Pilatus Porter service will be stopping, and instead Asian Trekking will be flying up a large helicopter each day. It will carry 28 passengers and 1400 kg of cargo!

A lot more trekkers will choose to fly straight up to Shyangboche rather than walk from Lukla. I guess we're in for a lot more altitude sickness work.

*T*he weather is just starting to get cold here, with us waking to minus 5°C in the mornings now. When the sun shines it gets up to about 5°C, but on cloudy days the temperature stays below zero the whole day. On a sunny day we have enough solar water for a hot shower. Other days the shower stall stands unused with a layer of ice covering its floor. The shortest day has passed, but Kami says the coldest weather is still to come. Many of the better-off villagers are deserting to the relative warmth of Kathmandu. All of the teachers have gone for their winter holidays.

I spent Christmas Day in Dingboche, lying in a lodge, surrounded by a group of rowdy 16-year-old schoolboys. I had an altitude headache and nausea so bad that I wished someone would wander past with a Magnum 45 and put me out of my misery. Di was alone in Khunde and cleaned the flat! We have both agreed that that Christmas didn't really count and have postponed the real Christmas for a couple of weeks, which is the first Saturday that all the hospital staff and their families will be free to come and party up.

The reason that Di and I were several days' walk from each other at Christmas was a case of misplaced enthusiasm on my part. A group of 10 boys and their teacher arrived the week before Christmas from an English public school. They bore many gifts for the hospital, including a surgical suction, six barrels full of medicines, a microwave, a food processor, and the promise of $NZ75,000 worth of medicines next year! (Interestingly, the wholesale value of these drugs amounts to only $NZ12,000. Those drugs sure must make a lot of profit along the way.)

Initially the boys were all a bit subdued. Two of the group had become unwell in Namche, and their group doctor had evacuated them to Kathmandu. Because it was a school trip, they were not allowed to proceed any further without an accompanying doctor. They'd spent the last three to four years planning and saving to trek to Gokyo, Kalla Pattar and Everest Base Camp, and now had to turn back. I felt really sorry for them, so I said, "I'll go with you if you like."

We decided that we only had time to get to Kalla Pattar, since they wanted to do half days all the way to avoid any possibility of altitude sickness. It was only later that night that I felt like bashing my head against the wall for being stupid enough to volunteer to go camping in tents, up to the base of Mt Everest in the middle of winter, and miss Christmas as well! Di was very kind, and said she didn't mind, but obviously thought I was an idiot too. Anyway, it was nice to see the look of delight on the boys' faces.

It was very cold. I'm talking about lying in my minus 20 down sleeping bag and fleece liner, dressed in Polartek longjohns, two pairs of fleece trousers, Polartek socks, sheepskin boot liners, two winter-weight Polartek jerseys, two wool-

CHRISTMAS DAY.

len jerseys, a Polartek jacket, a down jacket, Polartek gloves under woollen gloves under Gortex mittens, turtleneck tube, and two woollen hats, and lying on a Thermorest blow-up mattress, shivering in my tent at three in the morning, still unable to get to sleep because of the cold. They were very long nights. I just don't think I'm a winter person. One night, as I climbed into my sleeping bag, I noticed several lumps of ice attached to my trousers, where I must have dribbled some tea about quarter of an hour before in the mess tent. Some mornings, it would take two hours of walking before my feet would thaw and stop hurting.

Apart from the cold, I actually had a very enjoyable time. Despite coming from a very expensive English public school, these lads were good company and not in the slightest bit snobby, spoilt or wimpy.

Our tour leader went to great efforts throughout the trip to make it enjoyable for us. On Christmas morning, he donned his red down jacket and trousers, put on a Santa hat, and greeted us all with presents. It was a "rest day" (when you sleep at the same altitude two nights in a row). To aid acclimatisation, we climbed 923 m up a nearby ridge to get delightful views of Makalu (one of the 8000-m peaks). On the top, a number of us developed headaches, which is not unusual, and we all descended, expecting the headaches to abate. But my headache and nausea and that of the teacher got worse and worse, until we could hardly walk by ourselves at the bottom of the hill. I filled us both up with an alarming concoction of pain relief and anti-nausea medication, to little effect, and we both collapsed on to beds in the lodge.

I have vague memories of a Christmas pudding with flames of whisky on the top, crackers being pulled, a party hat being gently fitted on my head, people around me standing up for "God Save The Queen", after we had listened to her speech on someone's radio tuned to BBC World, and various renditions of Monty Python sketches, interspersed with highlights from the sound track from "Top Gun". So I gather a good time was had by the lads.

I just lay there wishing I was dead.

In the morning, I woke to the glorious feeling of not having a headache at all, and felt perfectly well. I went out to my tent to discover that the local dogs had been in, and had stolen the chocolate bars that Santa had brought me! So, it wasn't one of my better Christmases.

When we reached Lobuche, I saw some down booties in the lodge's shop. Thinking this might be an answer to my frozen feet, I asked the lodge owner how much they were. "Oh, expensive memsahib." I told her I really was keen to buy them, but she just said, "Oh no, too expensive." Finally, I got our sirdar to ask her and was able to buy them for $NZ20. I don't think she was much of a salesperson. After that I was warm at night from the ankles down.

The next day, we finally reached Gorak Shep, ready to climb Kalla Pattar. It was the first cloudy winter's day the Khumbu had had all year. We struggled and gasped our way to the 5545-m peak, and sat there and looked at each other, since there wasn't anything else to see. We couldn't even see Mt Everest, and we were actually right beside it! It was a windy minus 20°C and when it started snowing on us I seemed to be the only one to see the humour of the situation. Anyway, we took lots of enthusiastic photos of the group on the summit, and the boys decided to buy one of the posters available down in Kathmandu to see what they'd missed. They actually coped very well with the disappointment and showed admirable maturity.

When we arrived back at the lodge, I saw an elderly Japanese man, who I'd met down in Deboche. I'd been called to see a cretin man, who was deaf, mute and significantly intellectually handicapped. He had been out chopping wood and had somehow dropped his axe on his face. His "owner" was not going to bother to get him medical attention, since he "wasn't worth much", but one of my health workers heard about him and dragged him back to her lodge. Fortunately, he had only severed his left nostril, which I stitched up, to the sound of this Japanese man, who

THE VIEW FROM THE TOP OF KALLA PATTAR ON A GOOD DAY.

snored his way through the whole business, despite the amount of noise and activity going on.

The Japanese man had impressed me because he was white-haired, trekking on his own, and we'd managed to hold some semblance of a conversation, despite his knowing only about ten words of English (more than my Japanese, mind you). His limited vocabulary included "Mount Cook New Zealand very good".

At Gorak Shep, he greeted me as if I were a long-lost cousin, and I discovered from one of the Sherpas that this man had been coming up to Gorak Shep every year for the past 15 years. Every New

Year's Day, he makes his way to the lake, cuts a hole in the ice with his ice-axe, strips off, and submerges himself completely! Some start to the year! Most people thought he was completely "barking", but I was very impressed, and had my photo taken with this brave, strong man.

The next morning, I awoke in Lobuche to snow everywhere. Our orange tents had all turned white, and we walked over three centimetres of snow, right down to Pheriche. Even the frozen rivers were completely covered in snow, and occasionally we'd find ourselves off the trail and walking down the middle of a river.

On the tenth day of our trek, just as we were walking up our last hill before getting back to Khunde, we came across Di and Longin, who'd wandered an hour's trek down the hill and had waited four hours to meet me. It was great to see them. And it was totally orgasmic to have a shower and get into clean clothes for the first time in 10 days.

The Sherpas played a good trick on the group when they stayed at Khunde. The tents were all put up, and the boys put out their sleeping bags and gear ready for the night. When they were all in the lodge having dinner, the Sherpas sneaked out and moved the last tent in the row around to the front. When everyone staggered out to bed, in the dark, there were a number of indignant lads, demanding to know why their mates were rifling through their gear!

New Year's Eve was a very quiet affair for us. Di, Mingma and I had Sherpa stew and rice, followed by one of Diane's delightful chocolate cakes. I opened a bottle of beer in an attempt to get into the mood for New Year's Eve, but, since neither Di nor Mingma drink, I only managed half a glass. We played a few hands of canasta, then went off to bed. Di was asleep by nine o'clock (a late night around here). I managed to hang on reading my book until nine thirty, but neither of us saw the New Year in.

We get to celebrate five New Years this year! The Sherpas in Khunde, Khumjung and Thami celebrate New Year (called Losar) for about a week, starting on the 12th of January. Then the Namche, Tengboche and Kathmandu Sherpas start their Losar on the 18th of February. The Hindu/Nepali New Year starts in March, and the Tibetans have their own New Year. All have separate calendars, which can make appointments very confusing.

The trekkers are starting to thin out, and we see mainly individuals or couples rather than the larger groups. Last week we saw a 28-year-old Norwegian man who had been trekking alone, walking up from Jiri to

Kalla Pattar. His companion had become ill while they were doing the Anapurna circuit together, so he'd been left to do the rest of the trip on his own. On his first day, just before Bhandar, two men leapt out from behind the bushes. One held him, while the other slashed the back of his neck open with his khukuri (machete)! The trekker fortunately managed to struggle free and run away. He was saved by his thick camera strap, which had to be cut through before the knife reached his neck. At Bhandar, he waited four hours and was seen by a Ghurka Army medical officer who stitched up his 15-cm wound. Finding someone around there to do a house call is a pretty impressive story in itself! There is no doubt that these two men intended to kill and rob him. He is extremely lucky to have escaped. We were also impressed that he was happy to continue on with his trip, though this time with a porter to carry his pack.

Neither Kami nor Mingma seemed to be particularly surprised by this story, and both said that between Jiri and Lukla is a very dangerous place, and no one should trek alone over that area. (No one told me that when we trekked up!) Two trekkers were killed at Puiyan a few years ago, and a Peace Corp Worker was murdered on the trail, very near to where this man was attacked, about 10 years ago. I guess it doesn't compare to the risks of New York Central Park, but it still shook us up. Mani Ram informs us that he always carries a khukuri when he brings our mail.

The Sagamartha Pollution Control Committee are very pleased. They received $NZ120,000, from the Minister of Tourism last week. Not quite the 40 per cent, or even the amount promised, but money in the hand is worth a lot more than any governmental promise. They all seem a bit stunned at actually having received the money at all. There was no comment as to whether this was a one-off or a regular annual payment, but time will tell. There was an odd condition attached to the money, that $NZ30,000 of it would be spent on building and maintenence of "the new airfield". No one seems to have any idea of which airfield they mean, or why we need another one up here.

We have heard that the trekking company who organised the expedition where nine people summitted, only seven of them having permits for Mt Everest, has been fined $NZ200,000, but no one has been banned from climbing, and all of the summitteers retained their title. Most people here think they got off lightly, since they will have made a lot of money from the support treks and publicity generated by the successful summitteers.

The saga of the hydroelectric power continues. Maybe the Trust could make some money out of producing a weekly soap opera entitled "Power Soon Coming — Nineteen Years and Counting". The company had another meeting explaining that their experts had told them that the turbines were all ruined and that, in fact, the entire inlet system was no good. They would have to completely redo it all, and could they please move up the Thami valley and use more of the local people's land to set up another inlet system. It should take them a few years, and we should expect power in about five years. The Thami residents hit the roof, saying that they had waited long enough for power and that already too much of their land and forests had been ruined. Enough was enough! The company now say that they will "make do" with the inlet system that they have, and promise to have power available before monsoon next year. We're not holding our breath.

Kami and I went to the foreign hotel to hold a teaching session about altitude sickness for around 20 staff. We arrived at the arranged time of 3 pm, to find them all enthusiastically involved in a volley-ball game. They finally straggled in to the teaching session held in the poncy four-bed suite (Kami irritated them by referring to it as the dormitory), and we were able to start at 3.45 pm. They were coldly polite, but made it clear that they knew all there was to know about altitude sickness and, really, we were wasting their time.

However, as time went on, the staff members warmed to the subject, and it went surprisingly well. It turned out that their main understanding of the illness was a "cookbook regime" that a passing doctor had taught them. If the oxygen saturation was at a certain cut-off point, then they would give oxygen, put the person in the Gamow bag, and evacuate them. Simple. They didn't know much at all about the symptoms and signs to look for, nor the medications such as acetazolamide and nifedipine that could help prevent problems. The manager was sceptical and annoyed to hear that the oxygen saturation is a good, but not entirely accurate tool, and that other symptoms and signs have to be considered when starting treatment. However, after an initial unwillingness to learn a more complicated regime, they seemed keen to listen to what we had to say.

The only other disagreement came when we discussed the compounding effect of alcohol on altitude sickness. They told me of a very good Sherpa climber who had lived at Pangboche. He was an alcoholic who used to drink heavily at Base Camp, was even drunk while he was summitting. A few years ago he had committed suicide by throwing himself into the river at Pangboche, but he had never had any altitude symptoms, so surely it was OK to drink at altitude! It took a surprisingly long time for us to explain that this was a different situation, and that alcohol could in fact increase the risk of altitude sickness in their guests.

We had great fun role-playing different situations, and ended up putting someone in the Gamow bag to revise that. The two and a half hours of teaching went very quickly and I was delighted that the staff still seemed interested at the end. We left some typed notes to be kept at the front desk, and some acetazolamide and nifedipine, to be handed out only by the manager. Hopefully, altitude-affected guests will be managed a little better in the future.

The helicopter to Shyangboche has been put on hold for a while since the Nepali government have insisted that it be flown by a Nepali pilot. Apart from one part-owner/pilot for another helicopter company, nobody seems to know of any Nepali helicopter pilots, so it could be a while.

Last Saturday, Di shouted me breakfast at the foreign hotel to celebrate my finishing the marathon. As we sat on the balcony, sipping our mango juice and real coffee, we saw a large fire at Phortse. Di never seems to go anywhere without her binoculars, and we watched as some poor person's house burst into flames. The one house contained two households, and we watched in horror as people clambered all over the roof, ripping it apart to stop the fire spreading to the other part of the house. At one point the whole of the inside glowed red, then with a "whoosh", a great burst of flame blasted up through the roof.

BREAKFAST WITH A VIEW.

We heard later that no one had been injured. The local people all stood around doing nothing, but the army branch near Dole saw the fire, raced over, and saved the rest of the house. Fortunately, the family own the other side of the house as well, so will still have a home. Their father ran away a few years ago and became a "married monk", leaving his wife, seven sons and one daughter. However, the children are almost all grown up (the youngest son is fourteen), and two are involved in trekking. One of the sons returned to his trekking group at Pangboche in tears, crying that he and his family now had nowhere to live. The trekking group had a "whip-around", and he received a lot of money to help restore the place. So they haven't done too badly.

We wandered back home and were greeted by an excited Mingma. His sister-in-law had gone into labour that morning. Mingma had started off to go to market, got as far as the mani wall, then decided he couldn't be bothered that day. Shortly after he returned home, his brother-in-law ran to get him, since we were not at the hospital. Mingma arrived just in time. The mother had gone into the toilet, and he burst in to find the baby hanging from her, with the umbilical cord wrapped tightly around the baby's neck. He rapidly freed the baby, rescuing her from the inauspicious beginnings of falling into the long-drop, and undoubtedly saved the baby's life. The baby seems fine and is suckling well. So now Mingma's father-in-law has five grand-daughters. He wonders why he has such bad luck. The family seems to be pretty disappointed that it's yet another girl, but we keep stressing how lucky they are to have a live, healthy baby and if everybody had boys then there'd be no girls to marry them.

One of our elderly patients, a spirit-medium/local healer, who we were treating for heart failure, died the other week. He was doing a puja, walking around the chorten at Phurte, when he suddenly had a stroke. I rather liked Kami's description of the event. "He was just walking around the chorten, then suddenly he stumbled and he was speechless, then he was walkless, then he was gone."

An old Tengboche monk was cremated a few days ago. He had sat in meditation for 22 days after his death, and is said to have maintained an even better posture than the Gen Lama. It feels as if a competition is on. Who will be the next to break the record?

W̶e are surviving the winter well, and feel very lucky when we hear the locals saying what a mild season it is. Some believe that the crops will probably not be good, as a consequence, but we're very relieved that it's not colder than it is.

We've had two days of it snowing, still a new and exciting experience for me. Mingma and Kami both think we are mad, as we dress up in our warmest clothes and race out to walk around the village in the heavy knee-deep snow. The local children are all out there, skimming down banks on toboggans made out of plastic jerrycans cut in half. We are both very impressed with their skiing, managed on short bits of plastic tubing or sometimes just a small rectangle of plastic tied to each foot with rope.

The belated hospital Christmas party went very well. The staff and their families arrived in the late afternoon. Temba had just left, having brought us one of his drawings as a present. I don't think he knew it was Christmas, but his timing was perfect.

We all played a game of "Jenga" (removing wooden blocks from a pile and placing them on the top without making the tower fall down). Di was very keen to have this game, and it was very heavy to bring over. I certainly muttered and grumbled about it. However, it has turned out to be a real hit, breaking all language barriers. Kids and adults alike really enjoy it. A couple of games of that certainly broke the ice. We then gave the children a balloon each, and we all leapt around the kitchen tossing the balloons about the room, while Kami and Mingma heated up tea.

Our menu of hamburgers and chips didn't go down as well as we'd

CLEARING SNOW FROM OUTSIDE THE HOSPITAL.

thought. I think everyone else would have preferred shakpa, (Sherpa stew) and rice, but they made valiant efforts to enjoy the meal. Di and I couldn't help giggling as we watched one of Mingma's children very politely trying to eat her buttered bun with a fork. Mingma put everything together to make a hamburger, but all of the children carefully and slowly ate the ingredients individually. We kept telling them that they didn't have to eat anything they didn't like, but they all pressed on earnestly. Di's apple cake and chocolate cookies were more of a hit, and disappeared quickly.

We gave some small Christmas presents. Tsumje's daughter was a delight. Tsumje became pregnant while she was portering for a trekking group. The father is a married man in our village, and had to pay compensation to Tsumje's family. Her daughter has cerebral palsy, and as an unmarried woman with a disabled child Tsumje has little chance of marrying. We have asked Tsumje to bring her five-year-old daughter with her when she comes to work, and we have fun playing with her. Diane has put in a particular effort, and the girl has improved remarkably, now being able to say quite a few words and walk on her own. She is still considered to be a cretin by the locals, but is less "written-off" than before. The little girl instantly fell in love with a little teddy bear we gave her. She spent the rest of the evening clutching her "baby" to her, and beaming proudly at everyone. I've never seen her smile so much.

Unfortunately, Tsumje's younger brother appears to have developed a form of psychotic illness. He did very well at Khumjung School last year, and was awarded one of the Trust scholarships for special tutoring in Kathmandu, to prepare for his School Leaving Certificate exams. We heard reports that he had "gone crazy", breaking many belongings and beating up the woman in whose house he was boarding. He has been hospitalised, and Tsumje's older brother has gone to bring him home. They have been to the lama and are having special pujas for him.

We have found out more about the Norwegian man who was attacked just out of Jiri. Our mail runner says that the only reason the thieves did not chase and kill him was that four porters came around the corner just at the crucial moment, and the thieves ran off. This certainly sounds more plausible than the trekker's version of outrunning his attackers.

Just a couple of days later, the Sherpa lodge owner near Jiri was murdered. He got into a violent argument with his neighbour, a Tamang man who owns the only other lodge in the village. The Tamang man beheaded the Sherpa with his khukuri and covered the body under blankets on the bed. The Sherpa lived on his own and his body was not discovered until four days later, when neighbours came to check on why his goats were not being cared for. The Tamang man had tried to run away, but because he had threatened the Sherpa on many occasions, the Sherpa had told the police that if he was ever killed, the Tamang man would be responsible. So the police have arrested the Tamang, and he has confessed to the murder.

Another trekker was apparently attacked last week while on the trail. He was just coming into Phakding when a man leapt out and plunged his khukuri into the back of the trekker's neck! The trekker's porter came around the corner at that moment, and the assailant ran off, leaving the knife still stuck in the trekker's neck. The trekker high-tailed it back to Lukla and jumped on the first plane out. I don't blame him at all.

One of the old locals died about a month ago. He has an interesting history. When he was in his thirties, he climbed Mt Everest twice within two days. Each time he summitted he left a picture of the Nepali King and Queen on the top. The King heard about this loyal subject, and granted him honorary captain status in the Nepali Army. As time went on he reached the status of major, never having actually done military service. He was a very well liked and respected member of the community.

A number of "good luck" pujas for the village are being performed up at the Khunde gompa. In particular there have been prayers to hurry up the Gen Lama's reincarnate, who they hope will turn up in Khunde/ Khumjung soon.

When we were last in Thami to do a clinic, Kami mentioned that there were two foreign women staying in the village. They had been in Tibet, and had flown to Kathmandu, then Lukla, then walked over to Thami. They had paid some Tibetans to carry their gear over the pass, because they "couldn't be bothered having it go all the way to Kathmandu, and back up to the Khumbu again". They waited for two weeks, spending each day anxiously looking up the valley with their binoculars. Most of the locals felt that the Tibetans had just disappeared with their gear. We were more suspicious and wondered what they were trying to smuggle in.

A week later, we mentioned this to one of our Canadian friends, who was at Lukla, and she decided to watch the foreign women closely. At the airport coffee shop, one of the women checked her pack and let out an anguished cry. She pulled out something wrapped in an old yellow lama cloth and raced out into the corridor to show the broken article to her friend. The lodge owner's daughter was passing, and said that they had the Yeti claw which had been stolen from Pangboche a few years ago! Something had dropped from the parcel as the woman had run out into the corridor, and when our friend checked, it was indeed a piece of bone.

I don't know why no one confronted these women, or at least told the police, but apparently everyone just let them continue on to Kathmandu! I'm not sure I'd have even wanted to get on a plane with them. Stealing religious artefacts can't rate you very highly on the good karma rankings! Our friend sent a note up to us about it, and we asked Kami to get the Thami policeman to search the remaining gear they had left in the village. Unfortunately, by the time we got the message, all of their belongings had been flown down to Kathmandu, so we have no idea what other treasures have gone missing. The dental technician says that she's treated one of the women, and that she's been in and out of the area for at least a year. I'm sure they'll be back. They're obviously doing quite well out of the place. Neither Kami nor Mingma think that the police will be at all interested, and probably wouldn't have done anything if we'd been able to call them in time, anyway. It's all very frustrating!

Six barrels of medicines arrived from the English public school. Unfortunately, a lot of the equipment is for intensive care or major surgery, and won't be much use to us. We'll keep what we can use, send some to Phaphlu, and are thinking of giving the remainder to one of the hospitals in Kathmandu.

The Sagamartha Pollution Control money is already disappearing into the wrong pockets, as so many of the local people feared. The Member of Parliament for the Khumbu area has just taken $NZ30,000 to build an airstrip in his home village. He lives about four hours' walk south of Phaplu, which is certainly not in the Khumbu. Why would anyone need an airstrip there when the airstrip at Phaplu is so close? Everyone is muttering about how unfair it is, but the committee still just handed him the money without a fuss. At least the corruption back home is a little more subtle!

We should have realised that the "Christmas gift" from Temba was too good to be true. The next day, his mother stormed around and insisted that we give her $NZ240 (the going trekker's rate) for his painting. We couldn't do much else, since returning it would have hurt Temba's feelings, but forking out almost three months' allowance for something we hadn't asked for certainly hurt.

Asian Trekking now has its helicopter flying twice a week to Shyangboche from Kathmandu. They started off flying on Tuesdays and Fridays, but had to change to a Monday when they found that few locals would use the Tuesday flights. A helicopter crash on a Tuesday would be an unpopular move, since it is a bad luck day to die on.

The fare is $NZ250 for trekkers and $NZ80 for locals, each way. The company plans to send a local boy from Khumjung to Russia to train as a helicopter pilot, but are making do with a foreigner until then. The other company's Nepali helicopter pilot has been grounded for dangerous flying and picking people up from outside their hotel in Kathmandu instead of going through the airport.

On the 12th of January we had the hospital Losar party. Mingma, Di and I went around the village at about four o'clock, calling everyone to the party. It took quite a long time since almost everyone insisted that we come in for a cup of chiyaa. Even when we declined, it took a lot of "shey, shey, shey" and "touche, touche, touche" (thank you) to escape.

People soon started piling in, all the men sitting along the far wall and by the stove drinking rakshi and chang, while the women bunched around the table near the door with their chiyaa and chang. The chang tasted particularly nice to me. While I was drinking my second glass, Di and Kami asked me anxiously if it tasted all right or any different. I said it was

THE HOSPITAL LOSAR PARTY.

just fine, but whispered, had they watered it down to make it go further? They just laughed and went on serving the brew. I found out later that Kami had decided it was too weak, and they had thrown in all the leftover rakshi, whisky, gin, and liqueur that's been in the pantry for years! Still tasted fine to me.

By the time we served the dinner of takhari, dhaal and rice, I counted 51 people in the kitchen, and about a dozen children and young teenagers hanging around just outside the door, so it was certainly a full house.

People seemed very shy after dinner, but once they got up to dance things really livened up, though it was very squashed in the dancing circle, and most of the non-dancers had to sit or stand in the middle, since there wasn't any room outside it.

One of the old local men, who seems to be permanently drunk, now greets us every day with, "Good party memsahib! When you go now? Good party coming soon?"

Well, we've been to hell and back! Hell is a place called Bung, which is four *long*, *hard* days' walk from the hospital. Unfortunately we are responsible for the supervision of the health clinic down there.

Mingma and I headed off 12 days ago, slipping and sliding down the ice and snow of the Namche hill. Mingma seemed to cope well, but each time I fell I would slide very close to a steep cliff — definitely a fatal fall. It took forever to get to the bottom of the hill. Usually one-and-a-half hours, this time it was three hours' walk. Poor Mingma didn't know what to do as I'd fall yet again, then sit in the snow crying and saying I just wanted to go home. (And I wasn't talking about Khunde!) It took nine hours to do the six-hour walk to Chaurikharka, and it was dark when we arrived.

On the second day, I donned my snow-trekking boots and we headed for Pangkoma, usually an eight-hour day in good conditions. The snow and ice really slowed us up, and we slithered and slipped most of the way. Our porter had only sneakers with no tread, and fell about more than us. He eventually tied a reed several times around each shoe to give him some grip. Mingma would go on ahead of him, holding his hand and guiding him down the more slippery bits. Other porters we saw had socks on the outside of their sneakers for grip, but others had jandals or *bare feet*!

At a particularly treacherous spot, we met a group of people who had walked seven days each way to a monastery to be blessed by the lama there. One old woman with no feet and a stump for one arm had been carried the whole way on her son's back! He also wore treadless sneakers.

MINGMA HELPING OUR PORTER OVER THE SLIPPERY ICE TRAILS.

When we arrived at the bottom of the high pass, there were no footprints, so the trail had not been opened. That meant that no porters had come to market from Bung, so weather conditions must be worse further on. The snow was knee-deep, and Mingma was keen to blaze a trail for us but wasn't too sure if he'd be able to find our way. Dying of exhaustion and cold in knee deep snow is not my idea of a good way to go, and I said that we should go back, and "bugger the trip to Bung". Then Mingma said, "Oh, there's another track around, much safer, but maybe an hour longer." So we took that, and slipped and slid our way around the side of the mountain.

I was becoming exhausted, and each time I asked how far to go Mingma would say, "Oh, just about an hour." After three more hours it was dark, and our destination was still "just about an hour" to go. By this time I was spending more of my time stumbling, falling and whimpering than actually heading anywhere. We reached a small house in the middle of nowhere, and I just sat down and said, "Go and ask them if we can stay. Pay them anything, I don't care. Otherwise I'm sleeping right here on the trail." The family were not thrilled to have visitors, but let us in. They gave Mingma the only mat to sleep on and twice as much rice. (Since I have about 20 kg on Mingma, and was famished, this seemed unfair.) Mingma slept with the family by the fire, while the porter and I had to sleep on the floor on the porch.

We left early the next morning, and even fresh and walking fast it took us one-and-a-half hours uphill to get to the place where we were supposed to stay the night before! We did a house visit to a man whom everyone said was dying. He was about 50, and had had a fever, cough and kidney pain for a month. He had not sought any medical care (though the health post is only about four hours' walk away). The house and gompa were beautifully adorned with painted butter decorations, since they had had a number of "shetos" already done for him. (Some rich people have their funeral service and their wake before they die.) He certainly lay on the bed

146

looking like a man about to take his last breath. When I examined him, he wasn't actually very sick. He had a left lower-lobe pneumonia and a probable kidney infection. I gave him some antibiotics, told him he probably wasn't going to die after all, and asked him to start getting up and about. The change in him was amazing. Soon he was sitting up with a bemused smile on his face, while his family stood around him beaming from ear to ear. By the time we left, he was gently wandering around the room. The mind is a powerful thing.

We staggered on up over another high pass of ice and snow, and I looked with horror at the near-vertical gully and cliff-like climb we had to achieve that day. We still slid and slipped, but Mingma cheerfully told me that sometimes the trail was completely covered in blue ice and they had to skid down the slope on their bottoms. The trail was, as usual, bordered by cliff faces, and I gasped with horror as Mingma remembered these times as being great fun. After one and a half hours of climbing down, we could see the small pencil line of the large river we were to cross at the bottom. It took three hours to get down. The bridge was impressive, and one of the safest ones I've crossed here. Both the porter and I looked gloomily and hopelessly up, up and up, knowing the climb ahead.

Halfway up, we were met by a man who was off to the local lama to get a blessing for his wife, who was sick. We were soon greeted by her family who ushered us off to their three metre by three metre grass hut, where the nine of them lived. The woman had congestive heart failure, and we wrote down the medications the son would have to come up to Khunde to get for her. They lit an open fire in the middle of the room, and made us chiyaa. My eyes streamed and I could hardly breathe from the smoke, trapped in their little grass box. It seemed a horribly poor way to live amongst the snow.

We got to the top of that damned hill just as it was getting dark. Fortunately, Mingma said it was too dangerous to climb over the high pass in the dark, so we stayed in a small village, again of grass huts, still covered in snow. It was cold, but the woman of the house was welcoming, and her children sat around me in amazement as I wrote my diary by torch light. The written word was a complete mystery to them.

The next morning we climbed the high pass, all holding hands and supporting each other as we slipped and fell. The village we were supposed to stay at took us two hours to reach and was all closed up. We walked down, down and down for hours, finding no lodges for a meal. We tried to buy food from houses we passed, but no one would sell us anything except

A HOUSE IN BUNG.

for rakshi (strong alcoholic spirit), which we did not want. At 3 pm, we made it to Bung, tired, hungry, thirsty, and miserable.

The clinic was closed, and the health worker was typically unfriendly and cool (a particular characteristic of the down-valley Nepalis). We had arranged a meeting that day for the three health workers, but he was the only one there. One was away for a "month's" holiday preparing for her School Leaving Certificate. (She had left three weeks ago, and the exam was not for another two months.) The other had gone home for the day.

Although Bung has 7000 inhabitants, there are only two lodges. We went to one close to the clinic, which was closed, but we were assured that the owner would be back soon. We waited for three hours, and no one came. No one offered us tea, shelter or anything. That would *never* happen in a Sherpa village. It was starting to get dark, so we headed down a very steep climb to the other lodge. We walked for 40 minutes in the dark and, thank goodness, it was open. Our porter had left and gone home for a couple of days, so we had to carry two packs each.

I noticed that the long-drop at the lodge was very clean smelling, but got a hell of a fright the next morning, when I was crouching over the hole and heard a loud grunt. In the long-drop lived the largest black pig I've seen in this country! I thought, what a disgusting life, living on human waste, but Mingma said that he thought the pig would have a very happy life — shelter and plenty to eat! Blurrgh! Anyone for pork?

The next morning, we grunted our way up the steep climb with all of our bags and reached the clinic after an hour, both drenched in sweat. We passed many villagers, but no one stopped to help us. Mingma's top pack kept sliding off and we had to stop frequently to centre it, but people just stood and stared.

No one turned up to the second meeting, which we'd called for 10 am. It was Saturday, and the clinic was closed. We waited until 4 pm, then found that the nearby lodge was closed again. There were no shops open and no one would even sell us some rice. We decided we could sleep on the floor in the clinic. Finally the lodge owner arrived and sold us a handful of rice and some eggs. So we boiled them up over an open fire, and settled down for the night.

On Sunday morning, two people turned up at 10 am for our third planned meeting about the future of the clinic. The Bung health worker said that no one ever comes on time for meetings, so we should plan to start the meeting at 12 o'clock, and see patients until then.

We were very busy, as hoards of people had come for treatment. By 12 o'clock, the two men who had arrived for the meeting had gone home! So we kept seeing patients. At 2 pm, about twenty men arrived for the 10 o'clock meeting, so we stopped and talked clinic business for an hour.

In the waiting room, people jostled each other to get in, fighting about who got there first and who was the worst "emergency". Outside, hoards of people elbowed and jostled around the entrance. We had to lock the door because people kept bursting in. There were always about 10 patients in the room at a time. No confidentiality at all. When we had finished with that lot, we would all take a deep breath for strength, open the door a crack, and start shoving the patients out, while others pushed and shoved their way in.

I was horrified to see one of our health workers take a running leap at the back of a patient who was leaving and throw her into the crowd knocking down a few people, while those remaining standing stepped over or on them to clamber in. Mingma just laughed and said, "It's always like this when the doctor comes to Bung." It felt very out of control to me, and I felt disgusted that people could behave in such brutish ways, but also saddened that their need for health care was so great.

We had initially been concerned that no one would turn up for the clinic! We met some "Care Nepal" health workers who'd been travelling around the area, and nobody they met seemed to know who I was, or that there was to be a doctor's clinic for the next two days. So they very reasonably suggested that we try to advertise our next visit (which certainly won't be from me) a bit more widely.

On the other hand, our health worker said that he'd received a lot of abuse from the patients waiting at the clinic to see me. "Why did you have to tell so many people the doctor was coming? If you'd just told us, we wouldn't have had all this hassle to see her!" You can't win.

I managed to escape a few times (not an easy or painless task) to relieve myself, and found that people wouldn't let me through the crowd to get back into the clinic. It was as if the crowd hysteria had taken over their senses, and I would have to elbow and fight my way to the clinic door. Fortunately, I was the only person who knocked, so the health workers knew to unlock the door and let me in, but then there'd be a great battle as arms dragged me in and pushed and shoved others out, who clung on to me in an effort to be pulled in with the tide. It was just horrible. At one time outside, I tripped and fell, grazing my face and arm, wrenching my shoulder, and hanging from a bank with a six-metre drop — cast and unable to get up. This happened right in front of the waiting crowd, but not one person helped me up. They just continued their sullen, uncaring stares.

At 4 pm the health workers started packing up, but there were about 30 more people waiting, some who had walked five or six hours to see me. The clinic staff were very annoyed with me when I insisted that we would stay on and see everyone who had come, even if it meant working all night. So, there we were, inserting Norplant by candle and torchlight.

The next day was exactly the same, and as we closed the doors at 6.30 pm I had the uncomfortable feeling that so many people in this area needed health care that it could be this busy every day if I stayed on.

I saw some interesting cases, and felt excitement and despair at some of the people who presented.

One woman had been beaten up severely two weeks previously by two of her husband's cousins, which left her unconscious for about eight hours. Her husband apparently has three other wives and doesn't often live with this woman. His cousins reasoned that since he didn't use this wife's place much she didn't deserve the household belongings, so they came to take them away. The woman tried to stop them because her husband would be angry when he returned to find his belongings gone. So they attacked her. Since then she's had blurred vision, loss of balance, headaches and a tremor. I thought she had a subdural haematoma (bleeding between the brain and the skull) and offered that the Trust would pay all travel and medical expenses for her to go to Kathmandu to have a CT scan, and surgery if required. Otherwise, if the bleed continues to expand, she will die. But no one cares enough to take her to Kathmandu, so she just had to walk three hours back to her village, with my rather inadequate and unrealistic advice to try not to do heavy work, and to avoid being beaten up again in the near future. It saddened and enraged me to think that probably she'll soon be dead, and her young children will likely follow, since there'll be no one to look after them.

INSIDE THE CLINIC AT BUNG.

I saw a young woman who regularly portered loads from Bung to Namche for the market. A few weeks previously, she'd walked over the snow with gym shoes on and had got frostbite. This had become badly infected, so she now had a combination of frostbite and gangrene. I put a local block in to anaesthetise the area, so I could clean off the dead rotting tissue, but ended up amputating her toe, since there wasn't any living tissue left and the whole thing sort of fell apart. What a mess!

Some of the more traditional patients or ones who live in more remote areas only speak Rai, and the Bung health workers had to translate. Their English is not too hot and it gave rise to difficulties at times.

One woman presented, and the Bung health worker said, "She burned her kids five days ago."

"Oh", I said, "and where are the children?"

"She's dead."

"Oh, so why has she come here?"

"She wants Norplant," he said with exasperation, looking at me as if I were a cretin.

So I was confused. Did this woman have schizophrenia, and believe she was now a ghost? Why would a ghost need contraception? Was she a mass murderer? I could certainly support giving reliable contraception to someone who would kill her children, but she seemed to have remarkable insight by asking for it.

Finally we got to the true story, which was still rather sad. The "kids" was actually one child — the woman's seventh, and a girl. The mother had been unable to produce breastmilk for her new baby and since she was yet another unwanted girl, the family decided not to waste their short supply of food on her and starved her to death. The little girl died at 10 days, and her mother had cremated her (that's the burning bit) five days ago. She very reasonably did not want any more children.

And I could certainly support that. What really upset me was that the health worker could see nothing wrong with choosing not to feed an unwanted baby. "Her baby, her choice — it was only a girl."

I saw a baby with an enormous inguinal (groin) hernia, and people with eye or other problems treatable by surgery. The nearest hospital at Phaplu is only two days' walk away, but most refused to go, wanting only a "magic" pill or injection to cure them. Most were dissatisfied with my explanations.

Over the two days, we saw 133 patients. I inserted 20 Norplant devices, and removed two from women whose young children had died recently. It was very hard work, and hardly the kind of consultations learnt in Family Medicine Training, but hopefully we did some good.

The second night we were there, I was awakened by the loud beating of a drum, then hysterical screaming and shouting from a nearby house. I woke Mingma wondering if we should try and help whoever was being attacked. He rolled over sleepily and told me it was just the local healer at work. The healer paints his face and dresses elaborately with feathers. He then bangs his drum until he goes into a type of trance, then leaps about the room, speaking in tongues and primal screaming to rid the sick person of their evil spirits.

Bung is not a friendly place, and I was well sick of the sullen stares and the lack of acknowledgement to my "Namastes", and not even a smile or any sign of gratitude as I treated people. I was happy to leave.

Our porter had returned, and he said he knew an easier way home — a bit longer, but not those great big hills. So we went around the long way.

His way seemed to have just as steep ups and downs, but took a day longer! It was also completely off the trekking route, so we would walk for hours and hours before even coming across a house that would sell us a cup of tea — let alone food. I slept on the floor in smoke-filled rooms with rats running around us, and even outside one night. Cold, exhausted, hungry and miserable — I hated every damned minute of it.

I would stomp my way up and down the trails, tired and sore, but realising that the only way out of the hell-hole was to keep going. I was so angry and irritable I couldn't trust myself to speak, and silently seethed the whole way. We would pass the sullen, open-mouthed stares of the down-valley women, and I would feel like slapping them across the face. The porters would invariably rest until I caught up to them, then move on, slowing everything up and requiring death-defying manoeuvres to get past them. When they'd make some obviously derogatory remark about me as I passed, the urge to elbow them off the cliff or stick my walking pole through their backs became, at times, unbearable.

Almost everyone we met would say in Sherpa or Nepali, "Where are you going? Where have you been? Where did you stay last night? Where will you stay tonight?" Fortunately, my language is not good enough for "Mind your own damned business", and Mingma would politely stop each time and go through the ritual of 20 questions. As a variation, I would sometimes be greeted with, "Hello Mister, gimme pen," or "Gimme bonbon," which did not warm me to their company, and I would snarl "Longin" (beggar) at them.

BREAKFAST TIME FOR A GROUP OF PORTERS.

No, I was not your average happy trekker. I was sick of the sullen stares, the smiles only when something was wanted — which disappeared without a thank you when the person got whatever it was. I was thoroughly fed up with the Nepalis' disgusting personal habits, of hawking great gobs of sputum at me, of emptying their nostrils on to the floor, of eating and talking with their mouths full, of burping and farting freely, of peeing in public . . . I hated the whole place, spent a lot of time in tears, and just wanted to get back to Khunde, collect Diane, and go home.

We stopped to do a health clinic at Chaurikharka on the second to last day. We arrived at 2 pm to do the 2-4 clinic. We were back with the Sherpas again — who excel in their hospitality — and the health worker insisted on us drinking copious cups of tea and eating a large pot of boiled riggis. It was utter luxury compared to the rest of the trip.

153

At 3 pm we finally got up to open the clinic. Our porter had not arrived, so we sent a message for him to come up and meet us. He had all of the examining equipment and a badly needed warm jacket for me. At 5 pm, we finally finished, having seen 20 patients, and still no sign of our porter. Then we heard that one of our patients had met him coming up the hill and told him we'd almost finished. If he ran around the other way, he could catch us up at Phakding (a village usually about two hours' walk away). She had been trying to be helpful and had genuinely misunderstood our plans. It was getting dark and cold, and we had already decided to stay the night in Chaurikharka, but all our warm gear was now heading up to Phakding.

So Mingma and I ran to Phakding, to beat the dark, and made it just after 6 pm, to find that our porter had not found us there, and had gone on! I was a great lot of help. I just sat down in the middle of the trail, shivering and howling my eyes out. Mingma ran on ahead, and saved the day by catching up with our porter and bringing him back. To top a perfectly horrible day, I managed to break one of my molars in half on a piece of white rock, hidden in the rice I had for my tea!

I stomped up the Namche hill the next morning to the dental clinic, only to find a sign saying it was closed for a month (it has been a very long month) and please see the Khunde doctor for any emergency dental attention. Oh, just great. So I headed up the hill and was delighted to see Diane coming down the trail to meet me. Home at last.

A hot shower, several cups of tea, a warm hug from Di and her sympathetic ear for me to rave at, and the world seemed a far better place. I do not plan to go to Bung ever again.

*T*he weather is warming up, and views remain spectacular. Trekking season is upon us, which at least gives us a bit of company (mostly very pleasant). We are still bored and lonely a lot of the time, but at least we're not cold. Only about 49 weeks and we'll be home.

Mad thrillseekers that we are, we have tossed our nightly games of canasta aside and have moved on to Monopoly. The guys love it, but I invariably lose, and sit through the games with barely concealed misery. It reminds me that we have absolutely no assets or savings to go back to. What on earth are we doing here? We should be setting ourselves up for a financially secure future.

We feel so isolated at times. We have made some good friends here, but smiles, nods and hugs, with the occasional mutually understood word, is very limiting. We really miss like-minded friends, or even people who speak our own language fluently.

As far as "really making a difference" here goes, I just don't know. I feel that the hospital provides a very good treatment-based service, and many of the difficult years of getting people to trust our approach to health have been already battled out by previous Khunde doctors over the past 27 years. Mostly I feel that we are maintaining a system that works well, rather than doing any earth-shattering stuff. The work is certainly not as medically challenging as I had hoped for. Yes, we certainly save lives that would otherwise be lost, but I am finding that the most good comes from simple interventions, such as pushing fluids in a dehydrated baby, rather than the heroics. I don't know that I contribute much.

We are pleased to see winter gone. I don't know that I can bear another one. Snow was initially an exciting novelty, but it is cold and wet stuff, and hard to walk through. Just as the sensation of walking on the snow changed from that of cornflower to crystallised sugar, we would get a fresh snowfall. I ended up hating the irritating sound of my boots on snow, rather like fingernails being dragged down a blackboard.

The last straw that has really dragged me down happened when some friends came to Kathmandu. We sent them a bag of precious things to take back to New Zealand. This caught them unawares and left them well over their luggage limit. Not knowing what to do, they sent the parcel, uninsured, by surface mail. They may as well have opened it up and thrown it into the streets of Kathmandu. I am unreasonably furious and devastated. The parcel contained photographic negatives, my Everest marathon medal and T-shirt, and a special coin blessed and sent to us from the Tushi Rimpoche. I just can't get the loss of it out of my mind. Although I can rationalise that they didn't know what they were doing, I wish I could tell them what bloody inconsiderate idiots they have been!

GAGA PASSANG.

We have been trying to fight the end of winter blues by spring cleaning. We have tried to keep records and letters of interest, but have also managed to throw out decades of accumulated junk. We have sent quite a lot of medical equipment to Phaplu Hospital and other hospitals in Kathmandu (such as portable cardiac monitors, subclavian catheterising sets, and regulators for ventilation machines, which will never be used up here). We also felt that four microscopes were too many, and have passed two on to the science departments of Khumjung and Chaurikharka Schools. The schools have also been given sets of antique encyclopaedias, and some of the several thousand pencils we seem to have accumulated. I'm sure that the kind people who donated these things would feel better knowing that they were actually being used, rather than sitting in the classroom gathering dust.

We have also made a rule that we must go for a walk together every morning and afternoon. This is to fight the depression that is creeping up on both of us. The other day, Di and I were on one of these walks around the village when we came across two of our favourite people, Gaga Phu (who is 86) and Gaga Passang (who is 79, and spends her days carrying 20-litre jerrycans of water to the yak farm, about 15-20 minutes' walk away). Both have cataracts and can't see very well, but when they do pick us out, they grab our hands with delight and beam toothless grins at us. They are both as deaf as posts, and are always easy to find, since they spend a lot of their day sitting, conspiratorially bellowing into each other's ear, then bursting into hearty laughter. You can hear them all over the village.

Gaga Passang was married with two children. About 30 years ago her husband and son went trekking and didn't return. Nobody knows what happened to them. Her 40-year-old daughter is married to a 60-year-old Tibetan. As is their custom, his husbandless mother-in-law also becomes his wife. Sometimes there is jealousy between the mother and daughter since they both seem to love him very much, but generally they get on very well together.

The old women insisted that we have a cup of tea with them, and we felt our way up the steep stairs and into Gaga Phu's very dark house. We sat on one of the benches, but were rapidly shifted off and made to sit on Gaga Phu's bed, which is closer to the fire, and more appropriate for special guests. Then the two of them bickered and bellowed at each other, Gaga Phu wanting to give us tea in a glass, while Gaga Passang argued that she should use her new china cups. The glasses won, and were dragged down from the shelf. While Gaga Passang rustled up a fire, going bluer and bluer in the face as she blew into the smoke, Gaga Phu searched around for a rag to "clean" our glasses with. She finally found a limp, black rag on the floor, and enthusiastically polished the bugs, smearing the lumps of dirt into a uniform opaque smudge. Water was boiled, then tea leaves added. Milk powder and sugar were whisked together with a forked stick, then added to the brew. We could just see the light brown tea through the glass, and cheerfully drank it, while Gaga Passang sat up against me, beaming in my face, patting my knee and stroking my cheek, shouting merrily on and on in incomprehensible Sherpa. Gaga Phu wandered around the room, feeding Longin boiled riggis. Later when Longin found a bowl full of riggis and tipped it over, she just shrugged good-naturedly and fed them all to him. We suspect that this was going to be their lunch, but nothing seems to phase either of them. They offered us what I thought was rice, and we earnestly made gestures such as a flat horizontal hand to our throats, or groaning noises holding our stomachs out to indicate that we were full. Just as well, since as Gaga Passang threw herself into it with abandon, we realised that we'd been offered chang porridge. This is the fermented sludgy rice that's found at the bottom of the chang barrel when it's all been drunk. Very strong, and very awful. However, like rancid yak butter, it is considered quite a delicacy around here.

After several glasses of tea, we made our excuses and were helped down the dark stairs by our elderly friends, who were concerned that we might fall and hurt ourselves. Times like these are very special.

Last Friday we had the first vaccination day at Khunde Hospital for a number of years. We were delighted by the response, and saw 108 patients that day. We vaccinated 53 children and gave tetanus toxoid to 37 women. The large job of filling out all the forms in Nepali was done by Mingma. Di had the unpleasant task of giving all of the injections. I got to be the nice guy, who handed out the balloons. I also kept records in English, and saw patients who had other complaints. We worked well together as a team, though were all a bit shell-shocked at the end of the day. The vaccines should arrive each month from Phaplu Hospital, and after this initial lot have had their three sets of shots, things should calm down a bit.

Most of the people came from Khumjung, but we were really impressed by the number who came from Phortse (17 children and 11 women were vaccinated). We saw a few Namche patients, and even vaccinated people from Lukla. These families had turned up at the Namche Health Clinic that day, only to be told that the health worker was at the bank, playing cards, and would not see them, so they came up the hill to us. This is fairly typical of the Namche Health Clinic where people complain to us that they can never find the health worker or, if they do, he is drunk or playing cards. And he is one of the better ones they've had there!

We were also delighted to see an eight-year-old girl, who had turned up at the hospital just three days after I'd left on the trip to Hell/Bung. She had a Monteggia fracture (a broken and dislocated elbow which requires an operation with internal pinning to repair). Di and Kami said that the Trust would pay all of their expenses and that they must go to Kathmandu. To Di's horror, her father refused.

This little girl had been gored in the face by a yak, one year previously. The family had taken her to the local healer, who had told them not to go to the hospital, that he had "magic spit", and he treated her facial laceration by spitting in the wound and saying prayers for her each day. She consequently has a very nasty scar on her left cheek, which pulls her lip up in a particularly disfiguring way. Kami explained that she's "not worth much" since she's an | Vaccination day.

unwanted middle daughter, and with her disfigurement will be that much harder to marry off, so is even more of a liability. Certainly not worth going to the bother of taking to Kathmandu!

Di was very upset about her and had shed a few tears by the time I got back. Her mother fortunately brought her back the day after I returned from Bung and, noting that the girl had lost the movement of her thumb, I thought I might try to straighten things out a bit. We gave her some ketamine to knock her out, and I wrenched and pulled and yanked, but really couldn't achieve any particular improvement. Yes, the books were right, she needed an operation to fix her. One that I certainly couldn't do. So we plastered her arm up, and Mum looked delighted until we explained that I hadn't fixed her arm, and that the plaster would make it less painful, but she'd never have a good arm unless she went to Kathmandu. Mum looked crestfallen and said that they couldn't afford to go. We realised that her husband had not told her that we would pay, and when she realised this she was very keen to get her daughter treated. So they both flew down to Kathmandu. The little girl had her elbow pinned and repaired.

When she saw us the other day, she was a completely different child. "Dokta Lijj, Dokta Lijj," she cried as she ran up and threw her arms around us. Her thumb still doesn't work and never will, but otherwise she's fine. Mum was smiles from ear to ear, and presented us with beer, Sherpani aprons and ceremonial khaarta in thanks. Di went all weepy, and I must admit to feeling all warm and fuzzy myself. Days like that, we feel it's worth our time here.

There have been many books written about the Khumbu and its Sherpas. The Sherpas have a wicked sense of humour at times, and will often tell the earnest researchers and authors any old thing, just for a bit of fun. Some of the articles we read are accurate, and others have us n stitches, laughing at misunderstandings or outrageous stories that some-one has earnestly recorded. Probably we too have had our leg pulled at times.

Kami tells us of a time when he was out in front of the hospital mending the prayer flag. A trekker and his son were also there looking around, and the child was driving Kami crazy running around and over the prayer flag he was working on. Kami at last called the boy over and whispered that he shouldn't jump over the prayer flag like that because the Sherpas believe that if you do that, your balls will drop off, and you'll become a girl! The boy raced over and worriedly told his father, who was fascinated, and immediately wrote it down "for his diary". Kami cringes at the thought of this piece of "Sherpa culture" being earnestly retold in a magazine one day.

I am still staggered by the corruption in this country. One of our forestry workers has recently disappeared with $NZ1120 of funds we gave him to buy supplies and equipment for this year's planting. (This equates to just over 11 months wages for him, so is nothing to sneeze at.) He tried very hard to trick both us and the office in Kathmandu into paying this amount, turning up at both places saying the other had not paid him. Fortunately, he failed, but it did show him up as even more of a scoundrel. Nobody seems to have done anything to catch up with him. I casually mentioned to Kami that in New Zealand we would report this man to the police, and he would be arrested, fined some money and probably sent to jail. Kami thought deeply about it, and said, "Yes, I suppose we could do that too, but it would cost us too much, I think." He explained that it would cost the Himalayan Trust a lot more than the amount stolen, in bribes to the police to get them to do anything! Our own police system may not be perfect, but it sure beats the one in Nepal!

The local people are having a rough time with the Nepali "Lands and Survey" officials. The government has decided that people's land must for the first time be formally documented. I guess this makes sense, but for generations land has just been handed down to the next member of the family without documentation. There is no written Sherpa language, and people just knew who owned what, by word of mouth. The Nepali officials are having a field day. They just move the boundary to suit the person who will bribe them the most, and villagers are at each other's throats trying to outbid the other. No one will dare stay away from their fields while the officials are there, in case they "take their land away from them" when they're not there! Mingma has already paid $NZ240 (six weeks wages for him) in bribes to the "Lands and Survey" men, and they haven't even got to our village yet!

Lindsay and Genevieve Strang (previous Khunde doctors 1971-73) have brought a group of trekkers from their home town, Christchurch, up to the Khumbu. It is great to see them, and we had a Sherpa party for them. We went around the village calling people to come to the party at about 4.30 pm, and by 5.30 the place was full. The chang was good, and we drank an awful lot. The trekkers all got up and Sherpa danced, and mixed in well with the villagers. Then someone came up with the great idea of us singing a few songs from our culture. Well, pack of conservative white middle-classers that we were, none of us really knew what to perform. None of us knew any Maori songs all the way through, and would they have been indicative of our culture anyway? I cringe to recall that we resorted to a rendition of "Khumbiya", followed by the National Anthem. It went down well, but was hardly "cool-city". Di and I followed this up with the "traditional" New Zealand "Tush Push", danced enthusiastically to the throbbing beat of Madonna. Well, I don't know how to do a haka!

Then we put on Tina Turner, and each of us dragged an unwilling villager on to the floor, while we "disco" danced. Soon the cookboys turned up with their drum, and the Nepali dancing started. Sherpa dancing is fairly staid, but the Nepali men really get into the beat, sensuously waving their arms about and thrusting their pelvises about in time to the very seductive beat. Soon all of the Westerners and quite a few of the local Sherpas had joined them and were boogeying down! We were a bit concerned that we'd gone over the top with this break from tradition, but the party went on for hours longer than usual. It really was great fun, and the locals have been saying "good, good party" to us ever since. I have had my first hangover since I got here. I may never drink chang again, but then never's an awfully long time.

The Asian Airlines helicopter service is proving to be so popular that they will be flying daily during the trekking seasons. The service is certainly changing the quality of life up here. People hardly need to bother going to the Namche market, since the Shyangboche shop has so much available, and special requests from Kathmandu can be ordered and brought up in a matter of days. We can now buy fresh fruit and vegetables (such as, swoon . . . tomatoes), chickens, and bread. It is much cheaper than Namche market. Last Friday, the trekking company had 200 chickens killed in Kathmandu, brought them to Shyangboche, and sold them all on the Saturday. Although this is all very handy, it will have devastating effects on the downvalley porters, who will have to reduce their slim profits even more. It may not be worth their while coming up to Namche for market anymore.

Already there is a new lodge at Shyangboche. I think there will be more, since trekkers will tend to stay there waiting for their flights out. Soon the souvenir stalls will come, and I wouldn't be surprised at a Shyangboche market, maybe on Sunday or Monday to sell what hasn't been sold on the Saturday. Shyangboche may become the new "Namche". The Tamangs from Namche are putting pressure on the airlines to stop them bringing food up here, because it is bad for their businesses. They can be a powerful group so it may not go on for long.

The helicopter service is very popular with the Sherpas travelling to Kathmandu. It is fascinating to hear people saying that they would no longer dream of walking *all the way* to Lukla anymore. It also seems that the process of purchasing a ticket is easier up here, and so far doesn't seem to involve the bribes required by the "Lukla Mafia". However, I was very upset when we saw one of our friends off yesterday. We had weighed her pack before we took it down, and it was just under the 15 kg allowed. The Sherpa who weighed it moved the scale away from her and told her it was over 15 kg and she would have to pay excess baggage. She said, "No way," and demanded that he let her see the scale. He just grinned and said, "Yeah, well, fair enough." They must trick a lot of trekkers who don't have access to scales and will take their word for it. Mingma feels that a lot of local people will also be at risk because they cannot read.

We continue to use "old-fashioned" transport and have our hospital supplies flown to Lukla then carried up by donkey or porter. Recently we employed three porters to meet our supplies in Lukla, carry a load up in one day, then go down the next. They continued up and down like this for a week. They are paid $NZ0.50 per kilogram carried up. After we weighed one porter's load at 110 kg, we decided to weigh the porter. At 52 kg he had carried more than twice his body weight up a trail that we struggle to complete in a long day.

About a month ago, a trekker was free-riding his way up from Jiri. He would order large meals and expensive items such as Coca-cola, then the next morning would order breakfast and disappear without paying his bill. By going off the usual trail from time to time, he managed to get away with this all the way up to Deboche, when he was confronted by a European couple who, like many of us, had heard rumours about him. They certainly put the hard word on him, and took a large amount of his cash to pay all the lodges he'd ripped off. They gave this money to their guide, who said he would go back down the trail to Jiri and repay the lodge owners. This seems to me naïve in the extreme, but Diane says I'm getting too cynical in my old age. Anyway, even if the guide does walk off with the money, at least the trekker got caught — though in my mind he got off very lightly. I'd have felt the urge to slip several hundred laxatives into his dhaal bhaat! What a sod.

PORTERS BRINGING SUPPLIES TO THE HOSPITAL FROM LUKLA.

We received a letter from the Phortse Community Committee about a month ago, asking us to sack their health worker and choose another. We talked this over with the health worker (who we do find to be unsatisfactory), and he seemed to be philosophical about it all. We have paid him up to the end of March. Since then, his family has demanded $NZ1248 as "rental" for storing the health worker's medicines at their home, since we did not provide a clinic for the village. Well I suppose they deserve points for trying, but I assure you that they won't get very far with that one!

We advertised for a new health worker and have chosen a 28-year-old woman. She seems to be a very pleasant and well-presented woman. She has one three-year-old daughter, is educated to Class Six, reads and writes Nepali, and speaks a little English. The Phortse Community Committee specifically asked us to employ her, so we very much hope that she will work out.

We have also chosen the new Monzo health worker, since the last one left to follow her husband's job transfer. He is a 26-year-old man who has passed Class Nine and has a good command of English. He and his wife run a lodge in Monzo. None of us know him but the guys have asked around and have heard nothing bad about him. Kami reports that "he doesn't get drunk, he doesn't go trekking, and he has a strong wife". He and the new Phortse health worker will come to the hospital for two weeks at the beginning of March for training. This will be the beginning of a three-month trial, at the end of which we will assess whether we wish to continue employing them.

Today, Mingma was on holiday, and Kami had to go down the hill to talk to the Namche health worker (whom he couldn't find anywhere), so we closed the clinic for a few hours. Temba's mother, Ang Doolie turned up with some chang for Kami, and wanted to know why I wasn't seeing her friend from Thami, who couldn't wait around for Kami to return. When I explained that I didn't know enough Sherpa to talk to her, Ang Doolie volunteered to translate for me.

Well, it really was a hoot! I wish someone could have videotaped the consultation. Ang Doolie explained that her friend wanted her injection. "Ah," I thought, this will be easy. We found her name in the Depo Provera book, and yes she was due, so I got the injection ready. Just as I was about to give it, Ang Doolie said, "Oh sorry, sorry, she wants the five-year-injection." "Ah-ha, Norplant," I thought, still unfazed.

Now the forms we fill out for Norplant are a bit involved, since we try to collect as much data as possible for future doctors who may wish to do a study on it. I began with, "How old is she Ang Doolie?" This started off a long and involved discussion, while they both stood counting the animal years off on their fingers.

"Twenty-two."

"Um, no, Ang Doolie, she looks quite a lot older than 22. How many children does she have?"

"Six children, and two dead."

"So, how old is she?"

Again, engrossed counting, "Twenty-two," replied Ang Doolie confidently.

"Hmm, how old is her youngest child?"

"Ten."

"I think she looks about 40 to me, Ang Doolie. What animal year was she born in?"

"She not know," says Ang Doolie as they finished another few minutes of counting animal years off on their fingers. So I guessed 40, and gave up on the other questions.

When it was time for me to insert the Norplant, I tried to get Ang Doolie to explain what was going to happen to the woman. Instead, Ang Doolie went pale, and said in a quavering voice, "Cutting operation? Ang Doolie goes outside now."

I convinced her to stay a little longer, but she seemed to be talking about anything apart from the "cutting operation" to her friend, and instead informed me that her friend was very happy that it was only us here because she was too embarrassed for Kami to know she was on contraception. To do Ang Doolie credit, she really hung in there, and it wasn't until I picked up the scapel that she squeaked, "You no need no more talking now. Ang Doolie going outside," and disappeared.

The insertion went well and, after it was finished, I wandered out to ask Ang Doolie if she could explain a few things about follow-up care. There was no one about, but when I checked the kitchen I was vaguely annoyed to find Ang Doolie, with Kami, polishing off a glass of chang. He did, however, leap up and help explain things to the Thami woman. (She was 42 and her youngest child is two.)

Kami later told me that he'd arrived back from Namche just as Ang Doolie burst out of the surgery door. She grabbed him by the arm and dragged him into the kitchen, and immediately started pouring chang down his throat. When he could get his breath, he asked where I was.

"Oh, Doctor memsahib doing operation. You no worry."

When he tried to go to the surgery, Ang Doolie said, "Oh no, woman's operation. Doctor memsahib say you not to come." Kami managed to work out from her gestures that I was inserting a Norplant, and felt I could probably manage on my own, especially when it looked as if he would have to gag and tie Ang Doolie down to get through to see me. So Ang Doolie continued to pour chang into Kami and keep him occupied to save the honour of her friend.

I thought Ang Doolie was very sweet to help me — and her friend — but I don't think we'll be employing her as a health worker quite yet.

Three weeks ago, a Japanese man working as a guide for a trekking group was found dead in his tent at Namche. The group had come up from Lukla. Apparently the man had not been well the day before, and had had to come up the Namche hill on the back of a horse. The local people think it was altitude sickness. Other trekkers we met had heard he'd had a myocardial infarction. I guess we'll never know. We only heard about it when his body was flown out two days later.

Two weeks ago an Italian man died of altitude sickness on Cho-Lhotse. Two days later, another Italian man became ill at Macchermo with altitude sickness. His Sherpa guides tried to get him to descend, but he refused, and also died. Once again, we only heard about these two men when the helicopter came to collect the bodies.

Apparently there are two Australians lost on Cho-Oyu. No one seems to be looking for them, and they are assumed to be dead.

There will be four expeditions to Everest this season and also *thirteen* from the Tibetan side! One group arrived in Namche a few days ago. They decided to do a bit of climbing around the area to help their acclimatisation, and, unfortunately, they chose to attempt to summit Khumbila. (This sacred mountain is considered to be the God of the area, and climbing it is forbidden by the local people.) As the Khumjung villagers realised what the climbers were up to, there was a great uproar, and some of the young men raced up after them, screaming at them to get off their mountain! Eventually the group worked out that something was wrong and came down, but they have certainly not made themselves popular. Even Kami seemed disgusted and unimpressed when I said, "But how were they to know it was a sacred mountain?"

This group was also the first to fix ropes across the icefall, and are now charging $NZ1110 for *each person* who would like to use their ropes instead of setting up their own! I was horrified, but apparently this is now common practice, and works out cheaper for the other expeditions than paying for the extra time and work of their climbing Sherpas. It all seems a bit too commercialised for me.

Most of the expeditions are now having all their gear flown straight to Shyangboche, and Asian Airlines is pushing for permission to land higher up the valley, as close to Gorak Shep as they can. It will cost half the price to helicopter their gear up to Shyangboche as it would to fly it to Lukla. Some of the Sherpas make a great deal of money portering the loads up to Base Camp on their zupchoks, so would not be thrilled if the airline is able to land higher up.

We were visited by a Spanish climber with frostbite of his fingers. Di was a little taken back as he raced up to her and planted a kiss on each cheek, explaining that he wasn't able to shake hands. She very decidedly thrust her hand out to his companion before he felt that a similar greeting was called for. They'd assumed that she was the doctor, and I just chortled in the background. The five climbers had set off together to climb Cho Oyo, but as these two men descended from the summit they were distraught to find the bodies of their two Swiss companions. It was too dangerous for them to reach the bodies, so they had to leave them there. They assume that they must have fallen.

Jan Arnold and Rob Hall dropped in on their way up to Base Camp. We were delighted to see them. We'd been so lonely, we couldn't stop ourselves gabbling on to them. It was sad to hear the details of Gary Ball's death, but so exciting to hear news from home.

They are taking three Americans, one Norwegian and a German on the expedition to Everest this season, for a mere $NZ156,000 each. We have been invited to stay at Everest Base Camp at the end of April. I wonder if I can talk Rob into letting me on to the icefall. It is illegal without a $NZ20,000 permit, but just a few steps into it would be a real thrill for me. I could always pretend I was on a housecall! We have promised to bring up lots of Diane's wonderful ANZAC biscuits, so are assured of a warm welcome when we arrive at Base Camp.

The Thamo Hydroelectric Saga continues. Who needs television here? (Incidentally, there is now a satellite dish in Namche, and for $NZ0.80 a session — local rate — you can watch Indian TV, Star TV, MTV etcetera.) The foreign company are now threatening to pull out completely from Nepal. The Nepali Government has decided that they will take all of the proceeds from the Thamo Hydroelectric Power Station when it begins running. (Seventy per cent to the Water Ministry — I didn't even know they had one — and the remaining 30 per cent to the Nepal Electric Corporation). The company had always maintained that the project was to be run locally, with any profit going directly back into the Khumbu area. They seem to be at loggerheads, and the foreigners have stopped work on the project. Since the likelihood of Thamo producing any power at all this decade seems remote, we can't really see what all the fuss is about. However, now the Sherpas are starting to get a bit militant about the situation. Three people from Thami are to go to Kathmandu and join other Sherpas there. They plan to go to the government and voice a protest demanding that their workers at Thamo leave and the government backs down, so that the foreign company will start work again. If this is not effective, they plan to go to the Thamo Hydroelectric Power Station, threaten the government workers and make them leave! Kami has assured me that they don't plan to get violent about it, but it still sounds pretty stroppy for around here.

Some of the wiring that the Sherpa technicians and their helpers have put up in the local houses seemed a bit dodgy to us. Di and I had muttered to each other about it but, since we're certainly not experts in electricity, had kept our concerns to ourselves. Last week, we met up with an electrician trekker, who went pale when he visited a few houses with us. It appears that the wiring is not uniformly colour-coded, so that a blue wire may be positive in one house, and neutral in the next. In Mingma's house, both of the wires going to his lights are the same colour blue, so there is no way of knowing which of the wires is live!

About a month ago, the main part of the Tengboche roof blew off during a windy storm. Apparently the nails were too short! The local wisdom about this is that the monastery is having bad luck because the Hindu Prime Minister and other members of parliament attended the opening ceremony. There is strong feeling that the Tengboche Rimpoche and Tushi Rimpoche should not have gone through the Buddhist ceremonies with them present, and especially should not have bowed down to the Hindus. Apparently it was OK for the foreigners to be there.

Kami and I were asked to sit on the selection committee for the Assistant Project Officer for the Sagamartha Pollution Control Committee in Namche. This person's job will mainly be as a sort of Tourist Information Officer, with an emphasis on looking after the environment. Kami and I voiced doubts as to whether this was the most effective use of another employee, but, as with most organisations, once the money's been allocated in the budget it has to be spent promptly or lost next year, so we proceeded with the interviews. Five young men applied. Unfortunately, the only applicants who spoke good English have other jobs which they are not prepared to give up. One applicant felt compelled to tell us that he was related to someone important in government and that he had already been promised the job, and that these interviews were only a formality. Not a great interview technique, but I guess he thought that it would improve his chances. We have given the mayor our comments on each applicant and have left the final decision up to him. He could change the job description to fit one of the applicants already employed elsewhere, but Kami rather cynically comments that one of the young men with little English is related to the mayor and will probably get the job!

We have had three groups of school children around the hospital lately, on treks organised by Peter Hillary. We have been impressed by their enthusiasm in working around the hospital. The long-stay kitchen and ward have been thoroughly cleaned and relined, and the plastic has been replaced on the greenhouse. Local carpenters have fixed the chimney in the long-stay kitchen, and the Sagamartha Pollution Control workers have dug three large rubbish pits in Khunde, one just behind the hospital. So things around here are really getting spruced up.

The tooth I broke on the way back from Hell/Bung is unfortunately a little too tricky for the local dental technician. But delight of delight, I will have to fly to Kathmandu to get it fixed. If I'd known I'd get a chance to get away from this place, I'd have been at my teeth with a hammer and chisel weeks ago! Ed Hillary, his wife and some other Trust members are flying up here in a couple of weeks, so Di and I will catch a ride in their helicopter back to Kathmandu. Di also has a broken tooth (no — not self-inflicted). The porters carry rice up from Jiri or Lukla and are paid by the kilogram carried, so just before they get to the market they mix white stone chips in with the rice so they are paid more. We try very hard to sieve the rocks out, but some are always missed. I have in fact broken five teeth so far eating rice. I was going to leave them until I got home, but the one that broke in half is starting to hurt a bit too much.

We receive some interesting letters and requests from time to time. A recent letter from a French climbing group, very kindly offering to bring some medicines over for us when they come in October, delighted us by being addressed to the "Sigmund Hilary Hospital". Could this have been a Freudian slip?

*I*t was just getting dark on a cold February evening when I wandered out from the kitchen to go into the flat. A flash of movement caught my eye at the gate, and I saw someone duck down behind a small juniper bush. Pretending I saw no one I continued as if to go into to the flat, then quickly turned around to see a frightened and wild-looking Tibetan man cowering by the gate. I immediately called Kami to find out what he wanted before he ran away.

He turned out to be part of a group of Tibetan refugees who had become ill after crossing the Nangpa La on their way to see the Dalai Lama in Dharamsala. He was soon followed by another 10 men, two guides and a small boy. The atmosphere was very tense as we tried to get information from our patients, who looked more like a pack of frightened animals ready to make a run for it any minute.

We started with the first five, removing their cheap sandshoes and nylon socks to reveal badly frostbitten toes and feet. Bare hands showed similar injuries to fingers. The freezing had occurred about six days previously, and they had all suffered the very damaging freeze-thaw-freeze cycles over the past few days. It was too late for immediate first aid or medications, so we soaked their feet in lukewarm, antiseptic water, and tried to document some personal details and specific injuries.

They were very anxious about giving their names, and one person kept telling us she was a man. She certainly was dressed in male clothing but looked definitely female to us. But we didn't push it, deciding that it wasn't going to affect our treatment, and maybe she felt safer disguised as a man.

They all looked exhausted, and many had other health problems. Of the ten, seven had pneumonia, two were swollen from congestive heart failure, and another had difficulty breathing with severe chronic obstructive airways disease/emphysema. One had his first ever epileptic fit shortly after arriving. Eight had frostbitten toes or fingers, though three were only mildly affected.

They were so poorly prepared for the trip, and we wondered what kind of people would be foolish or desperate enough to walk through snowy passes in winter wearing only cotton clothing, no gloves, nylon socks and cheap sandshoes.

Both the guides were in fine health, and well-dressed in warm coats and sensible footwear, as was the young boy, who was a relative of theirs and had been carried. They told us that they had been caught in an unexpected snow-storm, but every year Khunde Hospital admits Tibetan refugees with frostbite, and the difference in the group's wellness and preparation concerned me.

We dug through our box of clothing that had been donated to the hospital, and managed to outfit the worst-dressed people with warmer socks, gloves and hats.

The guides charmed us with a gift of a zee. The real ones are worth thousands of dollars, but these were undoubtedly fake. Still, we were pleased by the present. The woman guide explained that she was the mother of one of the little boys we had treated the year before. He and his companions were safely at school in Dharamsala, and she wanted to thank us.

We treated the whole group for a few days, then the guides announced that they and the fit people would continue on towards Kathmandu. This would leave the five weakest people with the worst frostbite injury. We were concerned about how they would manage in hospital. As with other hospitals in Nepal, we provide medication, treatment and somewhere to sleep. Patient's families usually move in too, so they can collect firewood, buy food, prepare it for the patient, and perform most nursing tasks, such as carrying someone to the toilet. These services are not provided by the hospital, and we worried about how the remaining patients would manage. We were not prepared to feed them, nor carry out the 24-hour care that some of them required.

Fortunately, one young man volunteered to stay behind with the other five and care for them. The group was still suspicious and distant from us, but we warmed to them as we saw them in tears at the thought of the group splitting.

The group had enough money for the five patients to fly to Kathmandu from Shyangboche in the helicopter. I wrote a letter, which Kami took down to the booking office, requesting that these patients be given a seat on the next flight. We had to wait a day to find out that the airline could not risk flying Tibetan refugees, since the government could close them down. In fact they had just recently had a visit from journalists asking if they flew Tibetan refugees, after some confusion at Kathmandu airport when Tibetan traders with green cards were mistaken by police for refugees and arrested. If we could get an official letter from the police allowing their transport, they would reconsider.

The group pleaded with us to try our best to get their friends to Kathmandu, and we promised to do so. That night when I wandered through to the flat I saw the group disappearing. I told Kami and Diane that they were leaving, but we decided not to frighten them more, and just let them go.

There is a police checkpoint in Namche, but most Tibetan groups travel past them safely by night. In fact if they are caught, usually the police merely "arrest" them, and although they are supposed to escort them back to the Tibetan border they just take them back out of Namche, and the group waits until nightfall and goes through again. However, about two years ago one Tibetan man tried to go past the checkpoint in the middle of the day. The officer on duty happened to be drunk, and raced out and shot the man. As a warning he left the body lying on the trail for a whole day before it was removed. So our group were probably very nervous, and did not know us well enough to know whether we would report their movements to the police.

However, they must have had a change of heart, because after they went through the gate they turned back and knocked on the door to tell us they were going, to thank us for helping them, and to plead again for us to get their friends to Kathmandu. It was very emotional, with Kami and I holding or shaking their hands and wishing them "Tashi Delek" (good luck) for their travels.

A number were still hobbling from their frostbite and I was able to grab a box of aspirin for them to use on their walk. They would go to Jiri (five days' fast walk for someone fit and well) and try to get on the bus to Kathmandu. Sometimes they are refused passage, which means at least another eight days' walk.

The next morning, we continued with our thrice-weekly dressing changes, but the five remaining Tibetans looked lost and forlorn. They sat

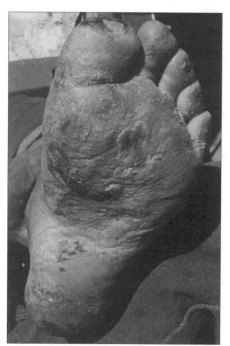

FROSTBITTEN, BURNT
AND INFECTED FOOT.

out in front of the hospital, looking miserable and gazing with horrified disbelief at their frostbitten digits, all hope apparently gone.

They shared the area with our two other frostbitten patients, who had been here for a couple of weeks and were more used to us. One was a 29-year-old Sherpa who had got drunk one night and fallen asleep in the snow on a mountain pass (four days' walk from the hospital). When he awoke the next morning, he realised one of his feet was frostbitten and visited some friends, who advised him to put it in boiling water! By the time we saw him about a week later, his foot was frostbitten, burnt and infected.

Another Tibetan had turned up one night just as it was getting dark, in a similar way to the others. He had left his group to go on while he came here, and he was terrified of us to start with. He had no money, filthy clothes and long hair, which stuck out in all directions, making him appear wild and menacing. His eyes constantly shot to any sound, and he cringed like a beaten dog if we moved too quickly. Twice in the first week he ran off and hid from us, frightened of what we might do to him, or that we might tell the authorities. Kami and Mingma both speak Tibetan, but unfortunately he came from a different area of Tibet, and spoke a dialect unknown to our health workers. By the time the other Tibetans arrived this man had relaxed and showed himself to be a delightful 23-year-old young man, full of smiles. His feet were very badly frostbitten. We had hoped that he would help settle the others in, but sadly they could not communicate with each other either.

It was upsetting, though interesting, to see the Sherpa patient's reaction to all the Tibetans in the hospital. While he had been happy enough to stay with us when just one Tibetan was there (and each had a separate room), he soon arranged to stay with one of the Khunde villagers, and only appeared for his thrice-weekly dressing changes. The trekking season was just beginning and occasionally trekkers who came to look around the hospital would arrive during dressing time (which took about two to three hours). Our Sherpa, who spoke some English, went to great pains to explain to the trekkers that his type of frostbite was quite different from the Tibetans' frostbite, in an attempt to be disassociated from them. After a while he insisted on coming on alternate days to them, so he would not have to be treated at the same time.

At first we could not understand this at all. We were beginning to get to know our Tibetan patients, and found them to be pleasant and admirable people. However, Kami and Mingma explained that many Sherpas consider Tibetans to be lower-class people compared to them, believing them to be dirty, dishonest and unreliable. This stereotype is reinforced in some ways by the kind of Tibetan who is seen in the Khumbu area nowadays. Many Tibetan traders come here officially to sell carpets and "genuine" Tibetan artefacts. They are usually single men who live as nomads and tend to be scoundrels who are reputed to sell fake articles for high prices, and drink and fight a lot. We found the Tibetan traders exotic and wild-looking, with their unkempt clothing and long hair plaited with a red tie and placed around their heads. However, they didn't look altogether trustworthy. The other Tibetans the Sherpas see are the refugees, who because of their long and difficult journey look scruffy, dirty and tired. All they own is what they can carry on their backs, and often they need to beg

TIBETAN TRADERS.

for food and money, and even resort to stealing from the local people to survive. They are in Nepal illegally, and are frightened of the Nepali officials, and as a consequence may be understandably suspicious of strangers that they meet. These groups are, I am sure, not characteristic of Tibetans, who from most reports I've heard have suffered decades of atrocities from the Chinese invaders with the utmost fortitude. I can, however, understand, if not admire, the racism that exists.

Over time, we came to know the six who had been left behind. One man was 55, with nasty frostbite to both hands and feet. His feet were swollen and he was breathless from previously undiagnosed congestive heart failure. He had a strong presence, and seemed rather severe. I was a little shy and frightened of him to start with, especially when we saw the whole group defer to him and take particular pains to care for him. At first he had to be carried on someone's back for dressings, and could not use his hands at all. The others fed him, scratched his head, and even massaged his shoulders. He was a monk, and we decided he was probably a high-up lama, though never really found out. He was very stern and exuded seething anger. It was many weeks before we ever saw him smile.

THE FARMER LOOKING AT HIS FROSTBITE.

Another was a 69-year-old farmer with very bad frostbite affecting all his fingers and some of his toes. His wife had died recently and he had given his farm to his son, and he and his daughter (who had originally tried to convince us that she was a man) had decided to go to Dharamsala. He felt that it would give her a fresh start in life, and all he wanted to do was see the Dalai Lama before he died. His 26-year-old daughter had very badly frostbitten feet.

The farmer spent the entire first week sobbing and praying. He had decided that his and his daughter's injuries were a punishment from the gods for leaving Tibet, and he particularly blamed himself for "ruining her life". His daughter would sit and stare dejectedly at her feet, or scowl sullenly at us and the world in general.

One 26-year-old monk with frostbitten feet would shyly sit with his head down through all the dressings. We didn't see much of him at any other time.

Another 29-year-old monk had minimal frostbite to a few of his toes. Although he had regular dressings along with the others, he had been well enough to leave with the rest of the group and had stayed behind to help his companions. He seemed to grin perpetually, and was a particular delight during the early difficult times for them.

It was not until after a month that we began to understand some of their despair and anger. They had all come from different parts of Tibet, and met their guides in Lhasa. All were from reasonably well-off families, and they had arrived with snow boots and other warm, appropriate clothing for their trip. They were told by their guides that it was seven easy days' walk to Dharamsala (it took them 20 days to get to Khunde Hospital), and that they certainly wouldn't need all that heavy gear, which would only slow them down. They were made to leave their good expensive clothing behind, and set off with only cheap thin gear. Undoubtedly the guides sold the gear left behind!

The Tibetans soon settled into our long-stay ward. The three younger men would hobble out around the village and beg for food. This began to make them quite unpopular, and soon the villagers were asking us how long the Tibetans would be staying. People began to become more concerned about security, believing that when some of the villagers started refusing to give them food the Tibetans would steal their firewood and supplies. Others complained that because some of them were monks it was very hard for them to refuse their requests, but still resented them. At the same time, we were also impressed by the number of people who, on hearing of the Tibetans' plight, brought food, money and chang off their own bat.

The begging also made me feel very uncomfortable. In the West, patients' food is the responsibility of the hospital, and I have never felt good about making patients provide for themselves. This was even worse when they couldn't, and we found ourselves making extra for our meals, so we would have to give the leftovers to the Tibetans to save wastage. Diane suddenly began spring-cleaning the pantry, and a lot of old excess food was handed on to them — though even this seemed rather insulting. Kami and Mingma kept stressing that the hospital was not to feed them, or everyone else would expect us to provide for them too, but Diane and I would feel guilty every time we saw one of the young men hobbling off to beg, especially when we found that they were now having to travel one to two hours' walk from the hospital in search of "fresh territory".

It was about this time that our Sherpa patient stopped coming for dressing changes. He could not leave the village, since he had to work for the villager who had taken him in to repay him for providing a place to stay. We would often see him staggering about carrying water or firewood for his host family, and chase him to come and let us change his soggy, infected dressing. Remarkably, he had almost completely healed. He had lost a little off the top of two of his toes, and raw bone stuck out from their ends. However, he refused to let me trim the bone back and give him a covering skin flap. Unfortunately, he was so frightened by the prospect that he didn't come for treatment again. However, we saw him paying off his debt for quite a few weeks afterwards, and he seemed well and happy.

The secret to managing frostbite is patience. Gangrene can look similar to frostbite, but the tissues underneath are usually worse than they look from the outside, and it tends to get worse over time. Frostbite works in the opposite way. It tends to heal from the inside, out, and thus looks worse than it really is. The adage "freeze in January, amputate in July" refers to the fact that, in general, the longer frostbitten areas are left to heal, the less tissue will eventually be lost.

However, after a few weeks of dressing changes, and antibiotics for infection, it became obvious that some of our Tibetans' toes and fingers were never going to heal.

When they arrived, the affected areas were pale grey, boggy and sometimes covered in blisters. Soon some areas became black. We were delighted when we debrided a thin, black outer layer from a couple of their hands and feet to discover perfectly normal, healthy, healed tissue. Others' blackened toes and fingers were becoming mummified and dry, like pieces of petrified wood, and then started to separate from the healthy tissue.

After a few more weeks, some of the digits looked as if they were in danger of auto-amputating. I had never deliberately amputated anything before, and was very reluctant to give it a try. It was easier to ignore the reality of the situation, and keep being "patient", putting off the inevitable.

All this time, we had been trying to get permission for our patients to fly to Kathmandu. Despite their begging, they had kept the money for their airfares safe and separate, wisely refusing to spend it in case it was their only hope of escape. We wrote to and visited the local branches of both the airlines that fly from this area, with no luck. We wrote to Tibetan organisations in Kathmandu and Dharamsala for help. We were too frightened to ask the local police for help. Last year when we had tried to get our young Tibetan boys to Kathmandu, the airlines had insisted on a letter from the police. The Namche police wanted to contact the main district branch near Phaplu, but this was not long after the Tibetan man had been shot, and we feared that if central authorities found out about them, they could be arrested and sent back to Tibet, or worse. We felt that there would be even less sympathy for a group of adults.

During our efforts to get our patients evacuated and referred to surgeons with more expertise, a European woman turned up at the hospital. We still tended to do the dressings out in front of the hospital

because it was sunny, warmer and more pleasant for our patients, and it left the consultation room free for other patients who turned up. We also found that locals and trekkers were more keen to donate food and money to our patients after they had seen their injuries. We were, however, not unaware that our patients found this attention embarrassing, and we were all becoming sick of the occasional trekker who would flick off a few photos for their scrap album. The woman presented herself saying that she was writing a book about Tibet. "Who isn't?" I thought irritably, feeling annoyed at her barrage of questions, and too busy to pay her a lot of attention. After the dressings were finished, I saw a few other patients and wandered around to the long-stay ward, and was furious to see her interviewing and photographing our Tibetans! She explained that she had ties with the United Nations, and could get them officially registered as refugees, and evacuated. I thought it a very unlikely story to cover her own self-interest in finding something juicy to put in her book, but soon forgot her after she left.

We continued on with dressing changes in the same way. With gentle debriding, they took a long time, but the infrequent need for antibiotic cover is a real testimony to Diane, Kami and Mingma, who did most of this tedious work. After a while the Tibetans seemed to come to terms with their injuries and really enjoyed the caring attention involved. We explained to a few of them that their frostbitten areas had changed too much, and would never heal, but even this was accepted philosophically.

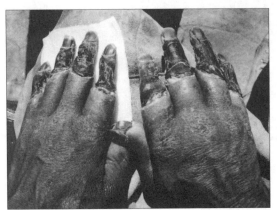

THE FARMER'S
FROSTBITTEN HANDS.

I don't know how long I would have kept on with the same treatments, ignoring the obvious. The day after the party for their trekking group, Lindsay Strang convinced me that I was only delaying the healing process. It was obvious that some of the digits had to be amputated, and if our Tibetans were going to have to walk to Kathmandu after all, my reluctance was only holding up their pilgrimage. He could understand my hesitation, but was happy to show me what to do and help me with the amputations.

This news both delighted and horrified me. I knew that Lindsay was right, but the act of amputation seemed so violent and final. It really quite frightened me. After a sleepless night, I decided that the patients knew it had to happen, Lindsay knew it had to happen, and so, really, did I. I was fooling no one.

The old farmer's hands were the worst, but fingers seemed too personal to me, and I couldn't bring myself to start with them. We decided on the original Tibetan, whose toes of his right foot were black, mummified and separating. Interestingly, the toes on his left foot, which had looked as bad to me when he arrived, had healed completely under a very thin layer of blackened skin.

This man had turned out to be a happy, easy-going type of chap, who just grinned at us while we explained what we would do. He seemed to have accepted it well, and looked forward to healing up quickly so he could leave and join his companions, who were hopefully in Dharamsala already.

We put local anaesthetic into one of his toes and Lindsay showed me how to remove the black digit and cut the remaining bone back until a covering flap of skin could be sutured over the area. After he'd removed two toes, I'd got over my squeamishness, and wanted to have a go myself. The local seemed to work very quickly and, in my nervousness, I realised that I was halfway through amputating a toe that I hadn't yet anaesthetised! I looked up in horror, into the patient's calm, smiling face. Kami checked it out, but he hadn't felt a thing!

The "healthy" skin just at the margin of his frostbitten digits had become depigmented, and when we tested the remaining areas, he had no sensation in that area so I was able to amputate the fourth toe without using local anaesthetic. His big toe didn't look too good, but we left it on in the hope that he may get just a little more growth out of it.

By this time, I was becoming a bit carried away with my new surgical skill, felt rather pleased with myself, and was already losing sight of my initial worries about the "violence" of the act. I must admit I was beginning to enjoy myself. Things were going well, and we decided we'd sort out the farmer next. While Mingma sterilised our equipment, we went to tell him we would amputate his fingers. No problem!

I was suddenly shocked back into the reality of the situation when the farmer burst into tears after we had we told him of our plans. He was truly horrified at the thought, and we realised that despite our many comments to the contrary he still firmly believed that his fingers would heal completely, just like the lama's had done. Denial is a powerful thing. I desperately wanted to believe the same thing myself, but Lindsay sternly reminded me that there was no chance of that ever happening.

The farmer was very brave as he climbed up on the operating table, and although I don't think I could have coped if he'd been crying, somehow his stoicism made it worse. I kept repeating to myself that this was the best thing for him overall. Fingers are a bit different to toes, and I still wasn't entirely confident to amputate them on my own. It was better to do it with Lindsay here to support me, and he'd be gone trekking tomorrow.

AMPUTATING FROSTBITTEN FINGERS.

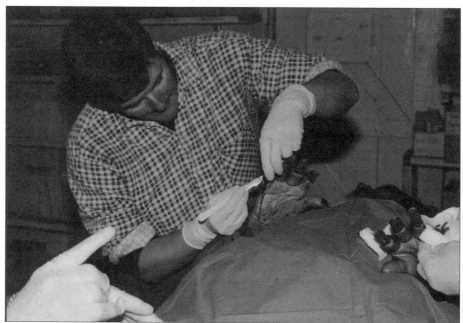

But I still wasn't completely convinced. We then had a long discussion deciding how many of the farmer's fingers were to be amputated. Lindsay was confident that the thumbs could be left, but all eight fingers needed to go. I was losing my nerve and started making hopeful comments about one or two fingers that might achieve a little more healthy tissue. Another doctor on the trek was assisting us, and made the very good point that if we weren't sure about a finger, we should leave it on. This, however, only increased my ambivalence and hesitation.

We finally decided on two fingers on each hand. Lindsay worked on the farmer's left hand while I did his right.

I still remember cutting into the first finger with a sick feeling. Fingers are definitely different from toes. We used local anaesthetic, so the patient was awake, and couldn't really look anywhere, so just lay there with his eyes closed, probably pretending he was somewhere else.

Part of me wanted to be somewhere else too!

After we had removed the first finger, it became obvious that we were doing the right thing. I don't think I'll ever forget the sound of his finger clanking on to the surgical tray like a piece of rock. When I examined the finger, it was mummified and black all the way through, and there really was no possibility of any healing.

With only brief consultation, we decided that all eight fingers were useless now, and should be removed. Lindsay had removed the four left-hand ones, as I was suturing up the skin flap over the third right one.

I suddenly had the nauseating and panicky thought that we had got a bit carried away. Maybe we shouldn't have done so much, but another inspection of the amputated digits calmed me, realising that they all were very dead bits of tissue.

Lindsay suggested that we leave the remaining digit, so the farmer could see what would have happened to his other fingers if they had not been amputated. We all agreed that this might help him come to terms with his loss.

I had expected the farmer to be a bit upset about the amputation, but was not prepared for his or his daughter's reaction. He spent the next two days staring at his dressed finger stumps with tears pouring down his face. One of the hardest things I've ever done in my life was to go and see him regularly, to check that he was all right. Each time I entered the room he would give me a hurt look from his tear-stained face and shake his head slowly at me, as if to say, "How could you do such a cruel thing to me?" His

daughter would glare sullenly at me and turn away whenever I came near.

I just wanted to hide in my room, the horrible monster that they obviously felt I was.

I was also amazed at the amount of guilt I experienced. What if I'd been wrong? Should I have waited? Maybe the fingers would have healed by themselves? I tossed and turned all night, agonising about having just cut someone's fingers off.

But life goes on, and after a couple of days their anger and resentment resolved. The farmer forgave me and made great efforts to be brave and friendly to me. As we watched the remaining finger over the next week or so, it became obvious to all of us that we had done the right thing after all. It continued to deteriorate, while the amputated areas healed rapidly. Only 10 days after the initial amputation, he asked me to amputate his remaining frostbitten finger, and his daughter asked me to do the same with her badly frostbitten toes.

In the end, all five ended up having amputations. The farmer lost eight fingers. His daughter had all five toes of her right foot and both little fingers amputated. The young monk lost all the toes of one foot, and both ring and little fingers. The first Tibetan had his big toe amputated as well, leaving him with no toes on one foot. The lama only lost both of his little toes. Sixteen toes and 14 fingers in all.

Each dressing change, I would silently rage at the injustice that had created this situation. These good people had been misled by their guides into leaving behind appropriate clothing which would have prevented any such problems. Looking at the larger picture, why should they feel they have to leave their country at all, just because of the despicable oppression of the Chinese. These were just good, kind people who wanted to live somewhere where they could practise their religion of Buddhism in peace and with freedom.

Very slowly, over time, they told us a little more about the lives that they had escaped from. They did not tell of the awful atrocities that the Dalai Lama has spoken of, and I believe still occur. The only time I saw the lama in this group show uncontrolled anger was when he explained that the Chinese would not let him practise his religion. If I was him, I would have raged at the guides who tricked me, and been bitter at the outcome of losing parts of my body, or frustrated that the Nepali officials would not help. But all of those things seemed to be accepted with resignation, maybe as his karma. It was the Chinese oppression of his religious beliefs that he felt so badly.

They told us of the time Jimmy Carter visited Lhasa. It turned out to be one of the important Buddhist religious days. The day before, the Chinese announced that this day could be celebrated. Of course they did not say that the President of the United States of America would be visiting. The Tibetans were delighted, and the next day the streets of Lhasa were filled will happy Tibetans, practising the rituals of their religion, kowtowing happily to Buddha, thrilled with their new sense of freedom. Suddenly a diplomatic car with tinted windows was driven down the main street, and Jimmy Carter was able to see for himself how happy and free the Tibetans were. He was even able to take photographs to take home and show other Americans the good news. As soon as Jimmy Carter left, out came the troops to stop the celebrations, and the religious ban was on again. Fortunately, some Western tourists in the city at the time were able to later disabuse Jimmy Carter of his mistaken impression.

We were not sure that three young people, each with no toes on one foot, and two old men with heart and lung problems would be able to walk all the way to Kathmandu, but their hands and feet were starting to heal up, and it seemed time to prepare for the long trip.

Then, in April, we received a letter from one of the airlines saying that our patients had become registered as official refugees with United Nations, and they would be flown out to Kathmandu within the next two or three days. The European writer had actually come through! We were very surprised and delighted!

So their meagre belongings were packed, medications handed out, medical referral letters written, and we all sat on tenterhooks over those days, ready to drop everything at a minute's notice and transport the Tibetans to the airfield, about 20 minutes' walk away.

We waited, and waited, and waited. After a week, we sent a message to the airlines, who just told us to be patient. Two weeks later, they said, "Where is your official letter from the police saying it's OK to fly them out?" So we went to the police in Namche with our letter proving that our patients were official refugees under the protection of United Nations. The police inspector was angry that we hadn't told him that the Tibetans were there when they first arrived, two months before. He said that he would have to contact the central district branch near Phaplu, who would ask the police department in Kathmandu! So there we were back at step one.

Fortunately, a man from the Tibetan community down-valley had been contacted by the Tibetans in Kathmandu, and came up to negotiate with the police on behalf of the Tibetans. The meeting went on for hours, while the police inspector filled out many forms and detailed each of our patient's injuries. We were devastated when he said that he could see no reason why the whole group couldn't just walk back to Tibet, where they belonged. The man seemed to have no compassion or sense of what they had all been through.

In my anger, I undressed the daughter's foot and showed him the granulating area of healing tissue, snarling at him, "How do you expect a person with a foot like that to walk even to Namche, let alone Tibet!" He was obviously shocked and unused to seeing wounds, and it seemed to have the effect of making him realise how ridiculous his suggestion was.

He agreed that the Tibetans should fly somewhere, and going to Kathmandu was cheaper than Tibet. I couldn't understand his concern about price. United Nations was paying the airfare, or, at a pinch, these Tibetans could pay for themselves, but I was happy with his conclusion.

Later, I foolishly told him that the youngest monk had recovered completely, but had selflessly chosen to stay behind to help his companions. His reward for this kindness was to have the police inspector say that he could walk to Kathmandu then, and didn't need to fly! I felt furious with the inspector and myself for putting my patient in this position.

Anyway, the Tibetan negotiator left saying that he would have it all sorted out within the next two days, so we should be ready to have them leave at any time. I voiced concerns about whether anything would actually happen, but the Tibetan negotiator said he would not leave Khunde until he was sure our patients would also leave.

Well, two days later he left, and we heard nothing from the police inspector. Another two weeks passed with no news, and we turned our thoughts to how our group could walk to Jiri or Kathmandu.

Most of the areas were now well-healed. The farmer's only complaint was cold "fingers", and I found a pair of woollen fingerless gloves for him to wear. He spent the rest of the morning chortling to himself, and remarking to the others that they were perfect, made specially for him. I was very impressed by his acceptance and bravery.

We gave up on the chance of the Tibetans flying out, but one evening we got the news for them to be at the airfield at 7 am the next morning to fly to Kathmandu! We raced around to the long-stay ward, excited and delighted about their news. The farmer burst into tears, and the lama repeatedly squeezed our hands. We were all in tears by the end of it.

Everyone was going to be able to fly out. While we were away, Kami had met the police inspector and explained to him that I'd made a mistake about the youngest monk. I'd confused him with another patient who had already left, and he really did have significant injuries too.

At daybreak, the group moved slowly up the hill to the airfield. The youngest monk carried the lama almost to the airfield, but just out of sight. He then ran back to the hospital, where Diane was waiting to bandage his feet. He grinned from ear to ear as she gave him lessons in limping, and found him a stick to lean on.

Meanwhile, Kami and I were at the airfield dealing with the officials. The tickets and baggage were all sorted out, but then a police officer appeared and insisted on searching our patients and their belongings. We had expected a customs check, and had warned them all to leave any knives behind. (Tibetans characteristically carry a small knife attached to their belt.) I was still angered at the humiliation of the search, where personal items were dragged out for all to see, and each of our patients had to strip down to underclothes.

The officer became angry that the youngest monk had not yet arrived, until I explained that his feet were pretty bad and he was slow, but he'd definitely be there. He finally arrived, and half hobbled and half ran across the runway in his excitement. He attempted a pained expression, but would frequently burst into a wide grin, with his simple excitement at the "trick", and finally being able to get on his way.

We heard over the radio that the plane had left Kathmandu half an hour ago, and would be due soon. I went to each of my patients, realising that they had now become good friends, and gave each a khaarta and wished them "Tashi Delek". We clasped each other's hands or hugged, and all shed tears of relief and delight that they were finally getting closer to their goal, but also sadness at the fact that I am unlikely to ever see any of them again.

As I watched them hobble to the plane and fly off, I felt an overwhelming gratitude for the experience and privilege of knowing these courageous people. Ordinary people who had been forced into bravery and suffering because of the country and culture they were born in and their belief and desire to live a life free from religious bans and the oppression of many basic human rights. There is no going back, they can't undo the injuries they suffered, but it seemed that they had come to such sad, unnecessary harm. I wondered how the rest of their lives would be and if, after all that had happened to them, it had all been worth it.

We had a great time when Ed Hillary, his wife June, Zeke O'Connor and Larry Witherbee came up to the Khumbu for a few days. I had been worried about them coming straight up to altitude (and still wouldn't advise it), but they were lucky and all stayed well for the three days they were up here.

Their visit started on April 6th, when we'd been invited by the headmaster to attend the official reception at Khumjung School. I wandered down with my camera, while Di stayed at the hospital to make sure things were all ready for our guests. At 10 o'clock, all the local school children were lined up in two rows, with great excitement. They'd certainly gone to a lot of trouble. The beginning of the line had a large red "WELCOME" sign from the Khumjung Village Development Committee. At the end of the lines was another red "WELCOME" sign, this time from the Khumjung School.

A table was set out, with many chang bottles and thermos flasks of chiyaa at the ready. About six chairs were placed behind the table. A carpet was placed over one chair in the middle, for BaDaasahib. Then another carpet was placed on top of that one. One of the local men then brought two more carpets, and these were placed on either side. I commented that there were four important people coming, and who were the carpeted chairs for? "Oh, BaDaasahib, Zeke Sahib and Larry Sahib." "And what about June memsahib?" I said. "There are four carpets. Each of them should have one." This started a very worried and heated discussion amongst the organisers about what was appropriate. It seems that some people felt that it was very important for BaDaasahib to have more carpets than the other three. Most felt that only the men should have carpets. I assured them that the VIPs would not feel this way and that they would insist that June have a carpet to sit on and go without themselves. This thought horrified them, particularly when I suggested that Ed, as her husband, would probably be the one to forego the privilege of the carpeted seat. Finally, they decided to take two of the carpets away, and left two for Ed. The rest of the chairs were left bare.

The battery-operated microphone was being well used as the children practised their routine. One of the teachers would bark out, "Doublevoo. . . iiieeee. . . lel. . . chii. . . ouu . . . eymm . . . WIELCUUM, WIELCUUM," and the children would repeat each letter and word. The rest of the teachers marched up and down the row, waving their sticks vaguely to make sure that the children kept in a perfect straight line. A number of times they would decide that the line was not quite right, then they would redraw it in the dust, and reorganise the rows yet again. I guess it kept the kids occupied. They practised their welcome for over half an hour until we heard the helicopter coming from Tengboche.

I was very impressed to see the children stay in their lines as the helicopter circled over us. There was great excitement in the air. The teachers' sticks were rapidly thrown aside, and everyone stared up at the Super Puma. The shout of "WIELCUUM" became even louder and more enthusiastic. Temba grabbed me and dragged me to the front of the line. We were both arranging our khaarta when the headmaster raced over anxiously and explained that *he* had to be the first one to greet BaDaasahib, and we were to stand right back out of the way.

THE INFANT CLASS AT KHUMJUNG SCHOOL.

It was all organised and the whole school had practised it over and over again. He would greet the party, then they would sedately march through the rows of children as they called out their welcome. The party would then join the headmaster for a cup of tea in his office. Then, when they came out, the important people (that included us) could give them our khaarta, then the locals (he said with a dismissing wave) could give khaarta. This would be followed by speeches and chiyaa and chang. So it was all organised and we must stand back and wait our turn. I grinned at this and wandered back into the crowd to watch the show.

Well, the headmaster just managed to get to Ed first. The four VIPs got to the beginning of the line-up of children, and began to be covered in khaarta and garlands of flowers. It really was quite emotional with the children clapping, shouting their welcome routine, and all leaping up to present their gifts. By the time the four made it out the other end, I felt quite tearful and excited at the obvious aura of love and respect that emanated from the crowd.

The important people (which turned out not to include Temba or me) were ushered into the headmaster's office for chiyaa, so after getting in a rapid hug and hello to June, Zeke and Larry (I couldn't get to Ed), I zapped up the hill to meet them in Khunde.

When I arrived at the hospital I was greeted by a European film crew, who'd just been interviewing Dr Kami Sherpa, and were interested to know how long I'd been a nurse here! Kami was embarrassed, and though I wasn't pleased about the sexism of assuming that being female I was the assistant, I was rather pleased to see that they hadn't assumed that Kami wasn't just a peon because he's a local.

Peter Hillary's school group were all enthusiastically working on relining the long-stay ward, continuing their good work.

The helicopter landed down by the chorten in front of the village, and Gaga Passang, Di and I ran down to greet them. The walk up to the hospital was hard work for those not acclimatised, and it was nice to be able to offer them a cup of tea and fresh tomatoes on crackers in the kitchen. Di had made some ordinary tea, but, not a chance. Within minutes, one of the local women had appeared with a thermos of good old Sherpa tea, and another from the village brought chang.

As we sat chatting, I was a little surprised by their cameraman, who was rather intrusively filming us all, and it wasn't until June said, "Who is this guy?" that we realised he was in fact from the European film crew, and had just sneaked himself in with the crowd. Di, the bouncer, got him out pretty smartly. In fact, the film crew who were with Ed were quietly sitting in the corner merrily hoeing into some of Di's cake. They turned out to be really nice guys, and didn't seem to get in anyone's way at all.

Ed managed to check a few things out around the hospital, then briefly

greeted Peter's school group. Although they'd all been very excited to meet the man, most suddenly became overwhelmingly shy, and instead of greeting him put their heads down and burst into enthusiastic manual work. Still, a few managed a shy handshake. The group then helicoptered down to Namche. We wandered down that afternoon and stayed with them.

The next morning was the Himalayan Trust Sherpa Meeting, which was very well attended. It was interesting to see the local people defer to the Tengboche Rimpoche, greeting and serving him before Ed. I hadn't realised he was so important. Ed gave a speech about the future of the Trust, explaining what would be discussed at the September meeting in Auckland. We are delighted that Kami is among those Sherpas chosen to attend the Trust meeting in New Zealand this September. Wish we were going too!

That night we attended a party put on by the Tengboche Rimpoche at one of the Namche lodges. We were all seated along the front of the room, with the Sherpas sitting in vertical rows down the room, a bit like a wedding feast. The buffet meal was very good, but the party was quite subdued, probably because of the Rimpoche's presence as he sat high up beside Ed, and the fact that they didn't offer any alcohol until the meal was finished. Certainly not a typical Sherpa party!

During dinner, a group of trekkers ambled into the room, walked straight up to the head table, ignoring the Rimpoche, and settled in front of Zeke O'Connor. "I hear you're a bit of a legend around here," the young man said to Zeke. Larry and I burst into laughter with, "Oh yeah, he's a legend all right!" and all three of us pointed to our right, "but this is probably the man you're looking for." I really don't know how Ed stands it. They then squeezed the rest of us out of the way to sit beside Ed while they took photos of each other with him, then got him to autograph various items they had with them. Then they wandered around the private party, embarrassing some of the local people by sticking cameras in their faces. We thought that they were very rude, and I'm afraid I'd have told them to sod off out of there and let me finish my meal in peace.

Zeke really is fun to have around when Ed's about. The next day when we were waiting for the helicopter, a New Zealander bounded up to Zeke saying, "I'm an old Grammar boy too. I spent half of my schooldays looking up with pride at your picture hung up on the school hall wall. I'd know you anywhere. And I'd just like to shake your hand, Sir Edmund!"

Poor Zeke, almost a legend!

Most of the group flew off to Thami for a brief reception, while the Tengboche Rimpoche, Di and I waited back at Namche with the luggage. With the increase in altitude, the helicopter couldn't take too much of a load. We watched the aircraft fly up the valley, and it took only three minutes for it to land in Thami. Sure beats the three-hour walk.

The weather closed in a bit over the hour they were away, and it even began to snow lightly , but fortunately with high cloud. Di and I were quite nervous, having never been in a helicopter before, and we were grateful that the Rimpoche would be travelling with us. All that good karma wouldn't go astray.

The helicopter arrived, and we took off with a mixture of terror and exhilaration, which soon turned to delighted shouts of, "Hey Di, look at all those magnolia and rhododendron trees," and "Oh wow, look at that, wheeee!. . ."! which I suspect faintly amused our far more travelled companions.

We stopped for lunch at Lukla. Neither of us had been there because we'd walked in from Jiri. The down-valley health clinics stop at Chaurikharka. Lukla was a lot bigger than I'd thought, and the lodges seemed more like Kathmandu, with the wider range of goods available.

Next we flew to Pangkoma. As the helicopter circled the school, we passed a barn/animal house, and suddenly most of the shingles on its roof exploded up into the wind currents caused by the aircraft. It looked just like a movie of a nuclear bomb going off. Larry, Di and I saw it happen and initially were stunned and excited by it. It certainly was an amazing sight, and I'm ashamed to say we were mainly intrigued and excited and regretted not having our cameras at the ready. It was not until Peter and Ed seemed quite concerned that we realised someone could have been hurt, and that the owner had had his property damaged. We landed, half expecting some angry villager to race towards us, but everyone seemed happy and enthusiastic, as usual. Ed got one of the Sherpa Trust workers to find out whose barn we had totalled, and gave him $NZ40, a very adequate amount for repairs. The man took some convincing to take the money, and obviously held no grudge.

The Pangkoma school looked lovely, laid out with welcome signs and beautiful rhododendrons. Our group walked through the clapping, welcoming children, and arrived at the other end, covered in khaarta and garlands. We were then given snacks, chiyaa and/or beer to drink, while a group of teachers and school children sang a song for us. One teacher strummed a guitar while the other played a type of piano accordion. They had obviously made the song up themselves: "Welcome BaDaasahib". I don't think it'll hit the charts, but it was a very nice thought.

Towards the end of the reception, I wandered back to the helicopter to have a good look at it. Three of the Pangkoma woman had just come down to greet the pilot. They gave him khaarta, then tried very hard to give him beer to drink. I was greatly relieved to hear cries of "Khaadeina, khaadeina" as he assured them that he couldn't drink their beer, but he did have a couple of cups of tea. The helicopter couldn't take off with all of us, from where the pilot had landed, so we sheltered behind a mani wall while the pilot took off and turned around, landing in a nearby field on the edge of a steep hill. We managed not to destroy any more Pangkoma property as we headed off for Mani-Dingma.

Mani-Dingma seemed to be no one's favourite place, and as the pilot landed the helicopter on a handkerchief-sized area, the crowd stared rather gloomily at us, in the down-valley Nepali way. Quite a contrast to the excited waving and beaming smiles of the Sherpas.

We walked down to the school and were greeted with more enthusiasm there. I joined the procession through the clapping, smiling children, and it really was a thrill to be covered with khaarta and garlands of flowers. I was at the end, so probably got more than my share, since children who had two or three left just put them all on me.

Instead of sitting at my proper place at the head table, that is, right at the end, Zeke sat me down between June and himself, and I was able to experience the local people's mistaken belief that I was someone important too. It really was quite different from sitting at the end of the row. People were much more insistent about offering drinks and snacks (interestingly beer again, rather than chang), and the khaarta just kept coming and coming. Those more used to these things took theirs off after a while, but I lapped it all up and sat for the whole reception sweltering in so many khaarta that I think I could have been mistaken for Ed Hillary too!

Ed was then given a handful of petitions and, I gather, some unreasonable requests, since June leaned over to me and muttered that they might want to take their khaarta back now. One of the things I really respect Ed Hillary for is his approach to aid. He has not jumped in and tried to take things over for the local people, deciding what is best for them. All of his projects have been asked for and initiated by the local people. He has kept the support of the Himalayan Trust on a very personal and practical

PLACE OF HONOUR AT MANI-DINGMA.

level. Whenever possible, the aim is to hand the running of services to the local people, helping by training them in the required skills.

The meeting went very well, and as we took off the villagers had to run for cover from the enormous dust cloud we created, as we headed towards Kathmandu.

It was fascinating to see the changing patterns of colour, from black to reddish rock, and all the different shades of green — colours we hadn't seen for almost a year. Di and I glued our eyes to the windows and soaked up the scenery. Then the delight of *flat* land and warmth as we alighted from the aircraft in Kathmandu.

We'd expected to be freaked out by the noise, heat, pollution and traffic, but I just loved it. The air didn't seem too hard to breathe, and the noise (because I guess it was a change) was music to my ears. It was so exciting to be in a city again, with people and cars and things to do. It felt like an escape from our beautiful prison.

It was lovely to see the Trust staff again. They made comments such as, "Is it possible?" when seeing Diane 25 kg lighter.

With her weight loss, Di is not quite the Nepali sex symbol she was a year ago, but I still have to watch out for her. After one very long, hot day of wandering around the shops, we became separated for a while. A young man bounded up to Di and stroked his hands up and down her arm, saying, "I think you are a beautiful woman."

Di replied, "Go away. I am hot and tired and I just want you to leave me alone."

"What country do you come from, beautiful madam?"

"New Zealand. Go away."

"Oh, New Zealand. That is my *faaavorighte* country."

"If you don't go away now, I will kick you," said Di calmly.

"Kick, what is kick?"

Di demonstrated, and he very rapidly moved away and towards me. He opened his mouth to start his routine again, and I wondered if I could get him to say that Czechoslovakia was his *faaavorighte* country. But after receiving one of the famous Harding cool, hard stares, he thought better of it and walked away. Di is very popular in Kathmandu, but nobody seems to think I'm a beautiful woman around here!

We had dinner with Kim, one of our trekking guide friends, who has a rather Amazonian build. She said that recently a young Nepali man was trying to chat her up and she couldn't get rid of him. She finally said, "Now look, it just wouldn't work. You are a very small man. I am too big for you. We just wouldn't fit well together."

"Oh no, no, no, we would be *louverlee* together. Don't you know that all Nepali men love big, fat women!" It was not a winning line.

Wherever we walked we were offered, "Hash madam, opium?" or "Change money?" Our friend and I decided to change some of our American money on the black market. It was quite exciting and a bit scary really. When the next young man approached us with this offer, we said, "How much will you give us?" He wouldn't tell us and we were dragged down a small alleyway and up some stairs into a carpet shop. The doors were closed, and we were sat down, while he left the room. We were very glad that we'd done this together but were still concerned that we might be robbed or injured or worse. It would be very unlikely that we'd report such an incident to the police, and we suddenly felt rather silly and vulnerable.

An older man came in, and asked us how much money we had to change, and in what size of bills. He gruffly said, "I'll give you Rs50 for $US1". My friend said yes, but a Sherpa friend had said they were giving Rs52 now. I refused and said Rs53. He offered 51. I went down to 52. He seemed to get angry and offered 51.5. I stuck to 52 a few times, but my friend was going more and more pale, and was shaking my arm, muttering, "Take it and let's get out of here!" Not the best of bartering partners. I finally took Rs51.5, and the man pulled out his calculator and worked out how much we were to be paid. I took the calculator from him and checked. He pulled out an enormous wad of money from his pocket and paid me. Then he gave my friend the money, which she just put in her pocket. I made her count it out and he'd given her less than he should, so I demanded the rest. As we left, he told us to come back any time, with a great smile on his face, so I guess I didn't barter as well as I could have. We almost ran down the stairs, half expecting to be mugged by his companions, or arrested by a waiting police officer, but nothing happened except for a cheerful wave from the tout who had brought us down the alley. Better than the bank, which takes hours and only pays about Rs48!

I needed three appointments with the dentist to have five fillings done and one cracked tooth ground down. (It was my first experience with a dental dam.) Di saw him only once and had one filling done and a cracked tooth smoothed off.

I hope we don't meet any more bits of rock in our rice. The break from Khunde has been very much needed, especially for me. Petty things that had been bugging me for weeks seemed pretty unimportant and back in perspective once we hit the big city. We never want to live anywhere remote again!

We managed to resist the hash and opium, but fell victim to the dreaded vice of gambling. There are about five casinos in Kathmandu — obscene amongst all that poverty. Zeke took us out to dinner and talked us into trying the fruit machines, blackjack and finally roulette. What a miserable exercise that was! We consistently lost at everything. I certainly can't see the thrill in watching my hard-earned money disappear at a rapid rate. Zeke seemed to be perfectly happy to have lost a lot more than the average Nepali annual income. Our losses were a great deal less, but I still found it hard to keep a brave face about it. It's certainly cured me of any innate gambling streak I may have had, though I doubt I ever had one. Never again. Diane really surprised me the next morning, as I was still sulking about our losses, by saying what a fun evening it had been! Definitely not my scene.

After a week, Di was thoroughly sick of Kathmandu — the noise, the crowds, the pollution, the traffic and the rip-offs. She was very happy to return to Khunde. I could have coped with a bit more excitement, although the noise and crowds were getting to me too. We can't see how anyone could stand living permanently in Kathmandu. So neither of us were too sad to climb on to the helicopter to Shyangboche, though I would have preferred it to have been going to Auckland. We're not unhappy here, but these bouts of homesickness certainly get worse when friends visit then go home. I want to be going with them.

One thing that really hit me when I got back to Khunde was how used I had become to seeing children working and begging. It was only later that I thought that in our country the vast majority of these children would be at school or play. I've been reading a fascinating but rather depressing book about child labour in Nepal. Overall, only 36 per cent of children in Nepal ever go to school. Forty-four per cent of boys and only 28 per cent of girls! There is only a 30 per cent literacy rate. Other sources quote a 55 per cent literacy rate in men, as opposed to 25 per cent in women. There is still a very obvious and strong preference for boys and men in this country, particularly in the Hindu culture. A common Nepali saying is that "investment in a girl child is like watering a neighbour's field", referring to the fact that the girl is lost to the family as soon as she marries. I feel very lucky to have grown up in a family and culture that allowed me so many opportunities.

I was also fascinated by some other figures mentioned, which give a good indication of the state of this country. Just under 20 million people live in Nepal. The per capita income is $NZ152 per year, but this is not typical and is grossly inflated by some very rich people. Sixty-one per cent live below the poverty level. Of course cash income is not always the best indicator of poverty, especially since 91 per cent survive by subsistence farming. Nine point five per cent are unemployed, but 40 per cent are underemployed.

Seventy per cent of girls and women over 10 years of age are married. The mean age at marriage is 17, with 15 being the norm in the Terai (on the border with India). Forty per cent of women between the ages of 15 and 19 years have given birth to at least one child.

Sixty-three per cent of people do not have access to safe drinking water. Ninety-four per cent do not have access to sanitation!

Infant mortality is 8.5 per cent. Only 6 per cent of births are attended by any form of health personnel.

Sixty-nine per cent of people smoke — one of the highest rates in the world.

There is one nurse for every 4680 people, and only one doctor per 32,710! To make things worse for the remote areas, half of the doctors and health facilities are concentrated in the Kathmandu valley, where less than 5 per cent of the population lives!

Only 5.5 per cent of the national budget is spent on health. Per capita health expenditure is only $NZ3 each year, and again this is much less in the remote areas!

New Zealand isn't all that bad in comparison.

The break in Kathmandu was very effective, and I seem to have cast aside my recent depression about being here. Today we have been in Khunde for one year, and in Nepal for 14 months. The days are becoming more cloudy, but the rhododendrons are blossoming as the monsoon approaches. Thami Mani-Rhimbdu starts in thirteen days, and Dumje follows one month after that. It really is beautiful up here, and fortunately I've been busy.

Recently we saw two seriously ill trekkers with high-altitude cerebral oedema and pulmonary oedema. Both presented on the same day. One woman and her husband decided to walk two days in one, up the Gokyo Valley. This is very easy to do, since it climbs quite rapidly in a very short time. She became drowsy and then unconscious at Macchermo (4410 metres), and the Sherpas asked them to descend. The husband refused, and she stayed at that altitude for almost two days. Late one night a young Sherpani turned up asking for some acetazolamide. When I asked more about why it was needed, she said, "Oh don't worry, the sahib is probably dead by now anyway." We wrote down instructions of what to do, and told her to run immediately back to the trekkers and get them to carry the person to the hospital.

We waited all night, but no one came.

Late the next afternoon, an unconscious woman was carried in on a Sherpa's back. We found out later that the Sherpani had gone off to stay with her boyfriend for the night, and hadn't got to the group until lunchtime.

The unconscious woman had an oxygen saturation of 34 per cent. (At this altitude it should be above 80 per cent, and below 60 per cent we recommend emergency evacuation!) We had to keep her in the Gamow bag for 21 hours, until the helicopter came to rescue her. Her oxygen saturation would climb up to 60 per cent after a few hours in the bag, but within 15 minutes it would crash back down to the low forties. This was despite maximal doses of dexamethasone, nifedipine and acetazolamide! The oxygen helped temporarily, but we certainly didn't have enough to last out the night. Scary stuff.

When I explained to her husband, who spoke very little English, that his wife was very ill and might die overnight, he proceeded to get drunk. After a few hours he became aggressive and started pushing people around, insisting that it was not fair to make his wife sleep in an uncomfortable bag after trekking for so long. He kept trying to drag her out of the recompression chamber. One of his guides filled him up with rakshi until he collapsed unconscious on to a next-door bed.

While all this was happening, another trekker was carried in, confused and ataxic. He spent the night in our other Gamow bag. Neither of the patients were capable of sensible speech, and none of their companions spoke much English at all, so we managed with a lot of sign language.

The next morning, both patients were carried on stretchers to the airfield. Both deteriorated rapidly while waiting for the aircraft and we had to put them into Gamow bags again. The woman's husband still couldn't see what all the fuss was about, despite the fact that she had not regained consciousness. We gave them referral letters and instructed the companions to catch a taxi immediately to one of the Kathmandu hospitals.

A friend of ours saw the husband and wife a few days later in Kathmandu. She was walking about in an ataxic manner, and as they crossed the road, she collapsed into a heap. Her husband threw her into a taxi and whipped her off. Our friend checked all of the hospitals in Kathmandu and their embassy. She had not been taken to any clinic and has not been heard of since.

We have been told that a trekker was murdered in Puiyan last week. He and a Sherpa lodge owner apparently got into an argument over the bill, which turned into a physical fight, ending when the lodge-owner threw the German over a cliff. He survived for a while, and a passing "Good Samaritan" doctor got him to Lukla and treated him until he could be flown to Kathmandu. The trekker made it to Kathmandu, but died shortly afterwards. They were arguing over $NZ4.

There has been a protest at Lukla, where many of the village's women and children lay down on the airfield, not allowing the Asian Airlines helicopter to land! A few days later the owner of the airlines went up to Lukla to negotiate, and the rumour is that Asian Airlines will soon fly only an "emergency charter" once a week to Shyangboche, and will have three flights a week to Lukla. Another rumour is that they won't fly foreigners anymore, and it will become a service for locals only. However, the flights still seem to be coming into Shyangboche. I'd be surprised if Asian

Airlines would buckle under the pressure so easily, so we'll wait and see what happens.

A couple of months ago a "cretin" woman from Khumjung went to stay with relatives in Kathmandu for a few days. She took her three-year-old daughter, who is adorable and apparently of normal intelligence. A local woman befriended the Khumjung woman and spent time with her over a number of days, always bringing sweets and presents for the child. One day, she asked if she could take the daughter a few houses along to give her a drink. That was the last that the Khumjung woman has seen of her daughter. It was just awful. She walked hopelessly around different parts of Kathmandu, crying and looking everywhere for her baby, but the child has disappeared. We would hope that the child is too young for a brothel. Maybe she was abducted so she could be sold to a childless family. It's very upsetting. The poor woman, being a "cretin", is unlikely to ever have another child.

The forestry warden held a meeting at Pangboche a couple of weeks ago, and has announced that from the 1st of September, all lodges in the National Park are banned from burning firewood, and must use kerosene for cooking and heating. A kerosene depot will be set up at Deboche. This is a great step forward in attempting to arrest the deforestation of the area, but the warden certainly is not a popular man. We have been shocked by the anger and short-sightedness of many of the locals. Most say that it will be hard for them to be caught and that they will continue to burn firewood. If they see a park ranger coming towards the village, they'll just quickly put on the kerosene stove. We have tried to persuade them that trekkers won't mind paying a little extra for their meals to cover the cost of kerosene and purchase of stoves and heaters. And that, in fact, they can increase their profit by just adding a few rupees to each item on the menu, but people seem very resistant to the change. Even Kami and Mingma, who voice positive feelings about the regulation, are very sceptical about how it can be policed. They also comment that wardens come and go quite frequently, and probably the next one will be too lazy to care. So the change may not be as effective as hoped for. We'll just have to see.

CHAPTER

19

Last month Kami and I headed up-valley and did a morning clinic at Phortse and an afternoon clinic at Pangboche. Di and our porter went the shorter way around and met us at Pangboche.

I had made up a notice for trekkers, advising them about altitude sickness and suggesting guidelines for ascent. At every lodge we came to, we would stop and post these up on the wall. I'm also involved in an iodine study, and we surveyed most people we met along the way, asking them what type of salt they use, testing the salt for iodine content, and examining them for goitres. As you can imagine, what with Sherpa hospitality, it made for very slow progress. Every lodge-owner would insist on us having chiyaa or even, in one place, a bottle of beer! Suddenly platefuls of dhaal bhaat, noodles or potato pancake would be placed in front of us, with much insistence of "shey, shey, shey" to polish it off. This became harder and harder as the day went on. Finally we waddled our way into Pangboche, very late. Fortunately, the clinics were quiet, with only a few simple cases.

Then it was time for us to start our holiday. We had arranged for two New Zealand doctors to cover us for two weeks. They were supposed to have turned up a week before, but Mingma and Kami had convinced us that they must have just been held up for a few days and were sure to appear soon, so we should go on our holiday anyway. That night our Deboche health worker said she had met these doctors when they stayed in her lodge. They had told her that they were going to cover the hospital for two weeks and were on their way down there. We assumed that they'd got to Namche early and had zipped up the Everest Valley before seeing us. I wasn't entirely happy leaving the hospital in the hands of people I hadn't actually met, but we decided it would probably be OK, and continued with our original plan.

Kami decided to go back to the hospital to check out the covering doctors, since I'd voiced concerns about them. I wondered what kind of people they were if they were happy to turn up a week late. Kami was to catch us up at Lobuche in a couple of days. Di, our porter and I headed off up to Pheriche, usually an easy two-hour walk, but slowed considerably by my salt survey and altitude notice postings. The porter doesn't speak much English, so was no help in interpreting. We managed with our limited Sherpa vocabulary of "la tuk", (literally "pass poison", meaning altitude sickness), "tsa" for salt, and a great deal of sign language. We made a very waterlogged entrance to Pheriche some four hours later.

We spent two delightful days at Pheriche, which is a windy, very cold place, but was brightened by being able to spend time with the Pheriche doctor, Dan, and his wife Dee. Dan is one of the doctors who works at the Himalayan Rescue Association Health Post, which is open for two months twice a year and deals mainly with trekkers who have altitude sickness.

On our second day in Pheriche, Dan and I were called to see a sick zum (female crossbreed of a yak and a cow). She was heavily pregnant with a calf, and had been well until the previous morning, when she just went down. I wondered whether zums got toxaemia in pregnancy. When we saw her, she was shocked, short of breath, had swollen forelimbs, but also subcutaneous emphysema over her entire chest wall. Running your hands along her chest felt very like the bubbled plastic that's used for posting fragile items. She looked pretty sick to me, and I was sure she would soon be dead. I said this to Dan and suggested that maybe we could do a quick Caesarean section, so the farmer would at least have one animal. But we couldn't feel any foetal movements, and the farmer told us that he thought the calf had died sometime yesterday.

Dan had seen this before in humans, and felt that she had gas gangrene. This is a very nasty infection caused by a bug called Clostridium perfringens, which usually enters through a cut or wound. We couldn't find any wound, but it's a bit hard on such a hairy animal. Normally, you'd open up the skin and let the bubbles out, just like lancing a pus-filled wound, but we could hardly open her whole chest wall. We raced off to get some penicillin, which could possibly help. Not sure of zum doses, we

SHERPA MEMORIALS
ABOVE DUGLA.

thought too much couldn't do harm, and drew up 10 million units, which is all we had. By the time we got back, the poor animal was dead. In fact, it was just as well she died before rather than after our injection, or else we would have been blamed for her death.

This is a big loss for the villager. A zum costs about $NZ240, and he has also lost the potential income from the calf that died. To make things worse, we told him that he mustn't eat the meat. We weren't too sure about the transmission of Clostridium, but explained that the bug that killed his zum could kill people too. He was very upset with us, and we doubted that he'd take our advice, so we then said that if he insisted on eating the meat, he must be very careful not to cut himself while butchering the animal, and the meat must be very well cooked. It is common to hang the raw meat over the fire for weeks or months, until it's slowly smoked, but we told him it had to be boiled very well first. We heard later that he did the traditional thing of burying the beast for a few days, then, butchered it and has kept it for eating. We haven't heard any bad news yet, so the family must be all right.

The next day we headed off to Lobuche. Di had not been any higher than Pheriche before, so it was great to see her enjoy the new scenery. Halfway to Lobuche, on the top of the Dugla hill, a long row of chortens are set out, as memorials to Sherpas who have died trying to climb Mt Everest. Right at the end of the row is a cremation spot, where the body, if it is found, is disposed of. It is one of my favourite places in the Khumbu, with a very peaceful, good spiritual feel to it. The site has beautiful views of the Khumbu, and is delightful with its rows of cairns (piles of small rocks). We could also see Pumori, which is a beautiful symmetrical 8000-metre peak beside Everest. And there was Kallar Pattar, our first goal, which in comparison to Pumori looked nothing at all.

We waited for Kami in his cousin's lodge at Lobuche. There was a snow storm outside, and we huddled around the fire with a number of other trekkers. Unfortunately, we had to share our space with a loud-mouthed trekker who'd ridden his mountain bike from Lukla to Phunki Thanka, then walked on up. The only times he stopped talking about himself were when he would cheerfully smoke his hashish cigarettes in our faces, or when he would play his short-wave radio, changing the station on average every 30 seconds. He seemed oblivious to the fact that soon almost all of the trekkers, ourselves included, had decided to stand and shiver out in the snow, rather than be in his company. I know, I know, we're all wimps. Most of us tried the normal subtle body language, such as plugging our fingers in our ears, coughing and waving the smoke from our faces, opening doors and windows, but none of us could actually bring ourselves to tell him to shut up and go outside. So much for assertiveness training. Anyway, everyone left him to it, crawling into their sleeping bags at about 6 pm, to read books and shelter from his company.

Kami didn't arrive until early the next morning, having been held up by the snow storm. He also brought the bad news that the New Zealand doctors *still* hadn't turned up to cover the hospital. Mingma was coping well, with no disasters so far, but it really was a worry. We very much wanted to visit Jan and Rob at Base Camp, and decided we'd do that, then forego the rest of our trip and get back to the hospital.

The obnoxious trekker decided that it was snowing too hard that day and he would stay another day at the lodge. As soon as he announced this, the entire lodge decided that a bit of snow and cold was preferable, and we all headed off in various directions to the next village. We arrived at Gorak Shep a couple of hours later, and huddled around the fire most of the day. In the early evening Di happened to wander outside, and called us all out. Everest had become a brilliant glowing red triangle, as the clouds had parted briefly to let the sunset reflect on it. It was a truly amazing sight. By the time I'd stopped gasping and gaping and run to get my camera, the hue had faded to a cool orange, so I missed the shot of the century, but at least we got to see it.

The next morning, Di, Kami, our porter and I wandered up Kalla Pattar. It's quite a walk, and took us three hours to get to the top (5545 m). Halfway up we watched the sun rising behind Everest, which again turned it into a beautiful luminous triangle. The weather was fantastic, and we sat at the top delighting in the cloudless clear view of Everest, Base Camp, the Ice Fall, Pumori, Ama Dablam, and all of our other favourite Khumbu mountains. Unfortunately, I developed an altitude headache and had to go down. I paid for being silly and staying up too long, and spent a couple of miserable hours with a throbbing, please-shoot-a-bullet-through-my-head-and-put-me-out-of-my-misery, nauseating, migrainous headache. But fortunately it settled down, and I was able to join the others, relaxing in front of the lodge in armchairs, watching the fat Tibetan snow cocks

THE BASE CAMP, THE ICEFALL AND MOUNT EVEREST FROM THE TOP OF KALLA PATTAR.

(sacred and unable to be eaten) bumbling about in the sun.

The next morning we headed off for Base Camp. It was really exciting to be covering new territory, but we were very pleased to have Kami with us as a guide, since the trail was difficult to follow. Just before the rocky moraine started we came across a large rock with memorials to people who had died climbing Everest. Included was a small mani stone "In memory of our friend and brother Gary Ball". That did bring a wee tear to our eyes. Although Gary died at Dhalagari in West Nepal, it seemed very appropriate to have a memorial for him at Everest.

We climbed up and down the moraine for a while, and then came across amazing three-foot spears of ice, just standing up out of the gravel, all over the place. A little further on we came across the ice seraks and flowing hills of ice. It looked like a Disneyland backdrop, and I kept expecting a polar bear to come wandering out from one of the ice hills.

After three-and-a-half hours of this awe-inspiring scenery, we reached Base Camp. It was larger than I'd expected, with many tents pitched amongst the rocks. We found the New Zealand camp, and were relieved to see some familiar faces greeting us enthusiastically.

Ed Viesturs is working for Rob Hall as a guide. He is an American veterinary surgeon who has spent the last three years full-time as a mountain guide and has summitted Everest twice without oxygen. He felt that gas gangrene was the most likely diagnosis of the zum we had attended, but also informed me that cows can get subcutaneous emphysema around their chest from descending too rapidly from high altitude. This, however, is quite innocuous and settles rapidly on its own. You just never know when you might need to know about rapid-descent oedema in cows!

Oscar Kihlborg and his climbing partner, Mickey Reutersward, are two mad-cap Swedish guys who run adventure tours, produce films and books, and do crazy things like swimming amongst sharks during a feeding frenzy, or paraponting over the Alps. This year, Rob, Ed, Oscar and Mickey hope to be the first to summit Everest and Lhotse in the same season. Rob will then go to Pakistan and have a go at K2.

The mess tent was very luxurious and warm. Oscar and Mickey filled us up with fresh Swedish chocolate, as we handed out the ANZAC biscuits Di had baked the week before. The room was full of delightful comestibles that we hadn't seen for a long time: Sanitarium Toasted Muesli, real crunchy peanut butter, good old Vegemite, smoked oysters, salted peanuts and cashews. Jan explained that they needed really tasty food, since it's very hard to maintain weight at this altitude, and people tend to lose their appetite. No such luck with us, and we gorged ourselves on all of the delights!

The rest of the group were interesting. Although they are the New Zealand team, the only Kiwis are Rob, the expedition leader, and Jan Arnold, the team doctor. There were six clients, each of whom paid $NZ156,000 for the privilege of attempting to summit the highest mountain in the world. Now we really are talking about quite an élite class who has that kind of disposable income. I had thought briefly that I wouldn't mind having a crack at Everest myself, but worked out that even if I could save $NZ250 each week, it would take me 12 years to save the required fee, which by that time would probably have gone up anyway. I was interested to find out a little about the kind of people who could do it.

One man is a staggeringly good-looking Norwegian, in his mid-thirties, who is quite a national hero. He has skied to both the North and South Pole, and now wants to complete the "third pole", that is, Everest. He has not climbed seriously before! The oldest, in his late fifties, is the strongest climber, with many summits to his credit already. He is a German and is managing director of a furnishing company. Another German looks to be in his late forties or early fifties. I don't know what he does for a living, but he's done a lot of interesting climbing and trekking in the past. One of the Americans is a big-wig for a company that sells recreational vehicles, such as snow mobiles and jet skis, and also deals in farming equipment. Then there's a plastic surgeon from Texas, and another baby-faced American, in his early twenties, whose Dad paid for the trip.

Jan told me a horror story of having to look after a member of one of the other teams, who had developed high-altitude pulmonary oedema, then pneumonia, and then developed a complete bowel obstruction. She

THE NEW ZEALAND
MESS TENT AT EVEREST
BASE CAMP.

is the only doctor at Base Camp, and spent 60 long hours caring for this man in their Sherpa kitchen, which she converted into an intensive care ward. He had tubes everywhere — an intravenous line, nasogastric tube, catheter and oxygen. Rob spent $NZ2000 on phone calls trying to get some form of rescue for the man. The army kept saying that they had more important priorities, and wouldn't come up.

Finally, after two days of trying, the Asian Airlines 28-seater Russian helicopter landed at Base Camp, complete with attendant doctor and embassy staff. I'd have loved to have seen that great monster landing at Base Camp! The patient was flown straight from Kathmandu to a hospital in Singapore. Very wise too. I certainly wouldn't have emergency surgery in Nepal. After the patient had left, the lama had to be called up from Pangboche, to perform various pujas to bless the kitchen before any of the staff would start work again!

Base Camp is at 5350 metres, which is the highest altitude we've slept at. I was worried that it would be cold and miserable, and I'd spend all night tossing and turning, unable to sleep. In fact, we were very lucky. We stayed for two nights, and had the best, warmest weather they can remember up there. We ate very well. Jan and Rob had a solar-powered stereo, so we had great music and a generator to run lights. It was a very comfortable and exciting time. Just getting the chance to rub shoulders with a group of adventurers was quite an experience.

I went up to the icefall three times, and went on to it as far as you could go without needing crampons. That was very exciting for me, and I spent many long hours there staring up and dreaming of being able to make my way across the ropes and ladders, over the crevasses, up to Camp One. Base Camp is never quiet, being situated on a glacier, and it was exciting to hear and feel the earth creak, groan and move beneath us, as more crevasses formed and rocks fell down the surrounding cliffs. We'd often hear an avalanche in the distance and, on our last day, got to see a small one nearby.

When we arrived we had seen a group of people climbing up the icefall. We later discovered that one of the commercial expeditions had allowed 10 trekkers (with *no* climbing experience) to put on crampons and climb almost up to Camp One! This was for the mere additional fee of $NZ10,000 each! The group leader had apparently gone to the Ministry of Tourism a few weeks before, asking for permission to do this, and had been forbidden outright. The icefall is considered by many to be the most dangerous part of the climb to summit Everest. The leader ended up having a screaming match with the official down there, then came up here and just did it anyway. When he returned from the icefall, the Nepali Liaison Officer was waiting angrily for him. High drama at Base Camp. The group leader tried to bribe the liaison officer to no avail, and could well have had his Everest expedition stopped and been fined heavily. Fortunately for him, the liaison officer asked Rob Hall what he thought he should do, and Rob told him he thought that the guy had learnt his lesson, and was genuinely sorry, and would never do it again, so maybe he shouldn't report the incident to the officials. So he got off. Last we heard, he was planning to send another group of 10 trekkers up, and Rob had wiped his hands of him! What a cheek!

On the morning we left, I was able to follow the Japanese team up to the icefall, and watch them put on their crampons and make their way up for their final summit bid. As they were getting ready, one of the Sherpas called out, "Maati jaanu hunchha, didi?" to me ("Do you want to come up, sister?") I replied, "Maybe another day," and we all laughed and waved each other off, with me shouting good luck in Nepali. I don't know how to say it in Japanese. It was exhilarating to watch the group of men climbing over the ladders and up, until they became little ant-spots at the top. Part of me really did want to go up with them.

JAPANESE CLIMBERS
PUTTING ON
CRAMPONS TO START
THEIR ATTEMPT TO
SUMMIT EVEREST.

It was certainly time to leave. Jan and Rob really made us welcome, but the clients were starting to become tense and introspective in preparation for their climb. Understandably, visitors were not welcome, especially as the climbers became more and more paranoid about the bugs and illnesses we might bring with us. The Pheriche doctor and his wife arrived the day after us, and although it was great to see them, we felt sorry for them in that it was fairly obvious that the clients found the presence of onlookers a bit of a strain. Dan very kindly offered to go down to the hospital and cover for us, so we could continue our trek. We were very grateful. Anyway, Kami had heard that the New Zealand doctors had been seen in Gokyo a few days ago, and were still telling everyone that they were going to cover the Khunde Hospital for two weeks, so should already be at the hospital.

Just before we were about to leave, Rob and Jan very kindly offered us both a free phone call home on their satellite telephone. This really was extraordinarily generous of them, since it costs them $NZ40 a minute!

Di's dad had moved recently, and we didn't know the phone number, but she thought she'd ring her brother instead. For one panicked moment, she couldn't remember the number, but we sat down calmly and had a few goes at writing it down until she got it right.

I got to ring first. It was 8 am, so I thought it unlikely that Mum or Dad would be home at about 1.30 on a Wednesday afternoon. I thought that Mum had needlework class, and that Dad worked at his geriatric hospital that day. So I wrote down a quick paragraph to recite into the answer phone. I rang, expecting three rings, and then to hear my own recorded answerphone message from before we left. But the phone rang a fourth, and then a fifth time, and my heart sank, thinking that Mum and Dad had left the machine off when they'd gone out. Then I heard Dad's voice. It was initially such a delight, and then became panicked horror. The reception was not good, he couldn't hear me well, and seemed to have decided that this was someone playing a cruel joke on him. As he irritably muttered, "And just who do you think you are?" I could feel that he was about to hang up on me, as I desperately shrieked, "Dad, Dad, it's me, Liz, your daughter, *please* don't hang up!" At last the penny dropped and there was a delighted cry at the other end and a hasty call for Mum to run down to the other extension. They were able to give us the marvellous news that the parcel our friends had posted three months ago had arrived! It was so good to hear their voices! They briefly talked to Di, then we said goodbye. Two minutes and forty-five seconds.

I was so excited I raced out of the tent, enthusiastically hugged Jan and Rob, then bounced up and down a few times, calmed down, and finally went to be with Di while she made her call.

Di got hold of her sister-in-law, who took a little while to register that this really was Diane, and, yes, she was ringing from Everest Base Camp. As fantastic luck would have it, Di's dad happened to be there visiting, and Di got to talk to him too. Unfortunately, he couldn't hear a lot of what she was saying, and when she asked him to put her on to someone who could hear her, he hung up! Three minutes and fifteen seconds. Ah well, at least he knew that she called, and Di got to speak to him. That was just great. Di had a wee happy weep.

It really was so kind of Rob and Jan. Our six-minute thrill cost them $NZ240!

After many farewell hugs and good-luck handshakes, we happily wandered back through the moraine, down through Gorak Shep, and on to Lobuche. I stopped off at the "Pyramid", which is an Italian physiology research station. It is made completely of glass covered by solar panels, and is shaped like a pyramid, looking rather as if a space ship has just landed in the Khumbu. One of the Rai men was sick, so I saw him, then had a look inside. What luxury! They had a microwave, television and video, all solar powered. The two  laboratories had excercycles and computers, and looked just like a plush office at home. Two bathrooms, with a flush toilet and shower, that you'd be proud to show off in New Zealand. And the bedrooms. Double bunks with luxurious mattresses, maybe a foot thick, just like at home. Oh, the ecstasy! I was very impressed, and not a little jealous. When I told Di about it, she said that she was glad she hadn't come, since she probably would have just cried.

We had lunch at Lobuche, then left the Everest Valley trail, wandering up around a hillside and beside a large ice lake, near Dugla, until we finally reached a very small place called Dzonglha, our home for the night. It was about 5 pm when we arrived, and it was raining quite heavily. I had got cold and dehydrated, and Di had to help me up the last hill. I don't remember much, but she says I was confused and ataxic. It was pretty scary for her, but she got me warmed up in the lodge and poured about two litres of sweet tea into me, and I came back to normal after a short while. The only thing I remember about it is deciding that I had high-altitude cerebral oedema, and why was Di pushing me uphill, and I was probably going to die, so why didn't she just leave me alone and stop bothering me. She said that I was quite gruff with her.

The lodge at Dzonglha was very simple — dark and smoky with no chimney, and only two single beds (two minuscule squabs over very lumpy rocks). The woman who runs it lives there by herself, which must be very lonely. We cooked our dehydrated meal over a kerosene cooker, discovering that the manufacturers obviously couldn't count, and their meal for four would hardly feed two anorexics on a diet. Talk about "Lean Cuisine"! Fortunately, the woman could supplement this with a gratefully accepted bowl of boiled riggis. Di and I slept on the rock bed, gasping with the smoke, while Kami and our porter slept in the tent on our Thermarests. For once, I think they got the better deal.

We continued our salt survey, and I discovered that our hostess had a goitre. We decided that the lodge was too dark and smoky for anyone to be able to read one of our altitude-sickness posters.

We headed off to cross the Cho La, which is the pass between the Everest and Gokyo Valleys. This was certainly the highlight of the trip for me, and we were blessed with a perfect, cloudless day. We walked up, up and up, for about three hours, until we got on to the pass. The last bit was quite exciting, with a very steep rock face, so required a bit of climbing. It was great, though Di didn't enjoy it so much and called me a few names at the top, muttering that she would never have come if she'd known what it would be like and that the only reason she wasn't going back was that it was worse than going forward.

Well, she was wrong about that, but what a blast it was! We made our way up a very steep, slippery snow hill, and then walked along the flat snow on top of the pass for about 20 minutes. It was so beautiful. We told our porter many times to put on his sunglasses, but he, in typical teenage, know-it-all fashion refused, and we gave up.

When we got to the end of the pass, we saw that the hardest part was still to come. It really was scary. The drop was sheer, and the trail consisted of loose rocks and slippery ice. We just had ordinary tramping boots on, no ropes or crampons. Still, we made it down after an hour of adrenaline and sweat, spending a lot of time on our behinds, clinging rather desperately to each other.

It was such a buzz when we got to the bottom and looked up at where we'd been!

We then wandered up and down and up and down, and then down a very long hill, to arrive at Dragnag three hours later. Although it was only 1.30 pm, we were all very tired and were looking forward to staying there for the night.

LOOKING DOWN THE VALLEY TOWARDS DZONGLHA.

Unfortunately, both of the lodges were closed. A very kind family gave us chiyaa and boiled riggis, and at 2.30 we headed off for Gokyo. While we'd been relaxing in the sun having lunch and chatting to our hosts, an earnest couple of Germans had stomped up to us and aggressively demanded "Gokyo". We pointed the way, and they grunted at us and strode on, thrusting their two walking poles each ahead of them. We laughed at the thought that they weren't having the kind of holiday we had in mind, and forgot them.

We wandered for about an hour up and down the moraine, admiring the glacial lakes. We'd occasionally get lost and have to back-track. Because the glacier changes each year, some of the cairns marking the way are old ones and no longer valid. At one point we came across "Das Klickers" striding angrily towards us, back towards Dragnag. We asked them if they were lost, and were greeted with a frosty glare of "No". We hesitantly asked them if they might be heading for Gokyo, and received an aggressive, "Of course!" We explained that they must have become lost, as they were heading completely the wrong way. We showed them Gokyo Ri, in the distance, and headed them in the right direction, receiving a grunt, and "these crazy people with their cairns" as thanks.

We came out of the moraine just above the first lake and ambled tiredly past the other two lakes, arriving at Gokyo about 5 pm. The lakes are a beautiful, jade-green colour, and the place looked wonderful.

We decided to spoil ourselves and stay at the Gokyo Resort, which is expensive but luxurious — by Nepali standards anyway. I was extremely annoyed to discover that the New Zealand doctors had only just left Gokyo that morning, and should have arrived at Khunde just as the Pheriche doctor got there to cover. Infuriating.

Kami and I raced around the other lodges, sticking up notices, doing the salt survey, and being filled with chiyaa and chang, while Di and our porter warmed up around the wood burner. By the time I got back, the word had got around that the Khunde doctor was in town, and I saw a queue of trekkers, all wanting freebie consultations. At that stage I was too tired to resist, and it just seemed easier to get it over with.

We spoilt ourselves with a delicious vegetable and chilli pizza and a bottle of San Miguel beer. We'd asked Kami if we could have a private room, since we were a bit sick of dormitories, and he said we'd just have to wait a while, so they could clean the room out. A couple of the other trekkers snarled that they'd asked for private rooms and the lodge owner had said they were all full, so we thought perhaps someone had moved to another lodge. It wasn't until the next morning when we got up and found the family sleeping in the kitchen that we realised they had moved out of their own bedroom to accommodate us!

The next day we just rested, and had a lovely time sitting in the solarium reading books. Our porter, in contrast, was miserable with snow blindness from not wearing his sunglasses, but this wore off after a day. We planned to climb Gokyo Ri the next day, and go up to the fifth lake the following one.

Next morning we got up at 5.30 am, and wandered over to the lake to climb Gokyo Ri. Already we could see that it was going to be a beautiful day. We had to cross a 25-metre row of stepping stones across the lake to get to the bottom of the hill. They were all iced over and very slippery. Unfortunately, Di slipped and fell into the lake. She cut her hand, sustained several bruises, and pulled a muscle in her thigh. And the water was very cold. She understandably burst into tears. Seeing her crying, I burst into tears too, and would also have fallen into the lake if she hadn't gallantly walked through the water and held my hand to help me back to the side. We both stood there for an instant, hugging each other and sobbing on to each other's shoulders, all pretence at being tough adventurers gone.

We wandered back, Di changed into warm dry clothes, and we had breakfast, fooling ourselves that soon we'd feel much better, would go up to the fifth lake, and do Gokyo Ri tomorrow. But really, we'd just had enough. We'd had a great time, but were sick of it all now. I certainly didn't want to climb up Gokyo Ri, having done it before, but felt that I didn't want to spoil Di's chance of seeing the views from there. Di didn't want to do it, but felt that I expected it of her and would be disappointed if we didn't go, so had feigned enthusiasm. It was with considerable mutual relief that we both decided to go home.

It is odd how memory plays tricks on you. I could have sworn it was just about completely flat, or gently downhill, to Khunde. Well, it certainly wasn't flat, as Di unnecessarily pointed out to me a number of times. It was quite a hard day. We left Gokyo at 9.30 am and arrived at Khunde at 6.30 pm, delighted to be home.

I was even more delighted to find the Pheriche doctor and his wife there, and to discover that those blasted New Zealand doctors had turned up at last but, as soon as Dan had arrived to cover, had disappeared off to Tengboche. I really cannot believe those guys! Many people write to me begging to work briefly at the hospital, and I spend a great deal of my time sending off kind refusal letters. Finally we agree to have someone stay, and they don't turn up!

The next day, we heard the great news that *all* of Rob Hall's group summitted Everest! I think this is a record. Never before has everyone in a team who has tried to summit Everest actually made it. It's a real credit to Rob's organisational and guiding skills.

Three of the Japanese team and eight of their Sherpas summitted. One American team sat on the South Col for four nights waiting for the wind to drop! Unheard of! One of their guides had to be flown out with frostbite. Only two of the seven clients, plus three guides and five Sherpas summitted.

Good on them all! Before I came to Nepal, I didn't think too much of mountaineering feats, but having lived amongst the mountains and seen the icefall and Everest, and understood more about what is involved, I really have great respect and admiration for those who have summitted.

The New Zealand doctors rather sheepishly turned up a few days later to make amends. They had not received my last letter, and had ended up changing some of their travelling plans, so the mess-up was sort of explained, though we really couldn't whole-heartedly forgive them and felt that we were being more polite than friendly. They seemed to be nice kids, but very young and maybe not terrifically responsible. Still, good on them for dropping by. It would have been much easier to just pass by and forget the whole thing.

The really silly thing is that we had passed each other in Phortse, on the first day of our holiday. Kami and I were putting up our altitude-sickness posters when we came across a young couple, both skimpily dressed in minuscule shorts. Kami was quite embarrassed, and we commented to each other about how inappropriately they were dressed, especially being in such a traditional village. We gave them a fairly cool "hello" and wandered on. They had seen my New Zealand-brand hat, and would normally have stopped to have a chat, but were hungry and looking for somewhere to have lunch. When they arrived at the lodge they saw my notice, dated for that day, and realised who we were, but by that time they thought we'd gone.

They spent their time at the hospital, still in those tiny shorts, holding hands, hugging and cuddling like two kids on their honeymoon. Any demonstration of affection between the sexes is absolutely forbidden and considered to be quite shocking in this country. Men can get away with knee-length shorts, but a woman wearing shorts here would be comparable to me turning up for work topless. The guys were quite shocked by their appearance and behaviour, though of course, in typical Sherpa fashion, didn't let on at all. I had to keep reminding myself that this kind of thing is quite normal in New Zealand, although it still felt strange to me. I became relieved that they hadn't turned up on time, after all.

Monsoon has come early, and most of the days are cloudy now. The rhododendrons and other wild flowers are looking beautiful, and the area has turned green. Baby yaks and zupchoks frolic happily around the village. The villagers are hard at work spreading their leaves and manure on the fields and blocking them off from the animals. The riggis seem to be growing well.

Water is still a problem, and we continue to be woken at 4 am to the sound of the young men beating their jerrycan "drums" and singing loudly while they wait for their turn to fill their containers with water. One good reason to look forward to rain.

I have realised that the problem with being here is not so much being away from our friends and family, or living in another culture. It is more that there just isn't enough work here to keep me interested. The job seems to be one in which anything in the world could happen, but it rarely does. We have an enormous amount of spare time on our hands, but there's just so much walking, reading, photography or writing that you can do, and we are always dreaming up ways of entertaining ourselves. (Diane is at this moment filling in the old rubbish pit, for a bit of excitement.) Holidays are great, but two years is too long to be mucking around. I really look forward to getting my teeth into some hard work. I do believe that if we were seeing a lot more patients, with far more challenging conditions, I would be much happier here.

It's been a slow season for the shop and lodge owners. Trekkers were 40 per cent down this year! I was also interested to hear that 80 per cent of trekkers who come to the Sagamartha National Park (the entrance to the

Khumbu) are university educated. I wonder if this is true for most travellers, or does Nepal attract this particular group of people?

Mani-Rhimbdu went very well this year. It was the first time that Thami had hydroelectric power! The foreign company decided to provide lights for the festival, as a once only, to test the project and let the local people see that it is a possibility. Power for the district still seems a long way off, and the connection to the Thami monastery has already been stopped. It almost didn't happen, and caused quite a few grey hairs for the electrical technicians.

The day before the festival, they discovered that the Nepali contractors who had buried the line had left one join unconnected. They spent the entire day checking every join, and finally found it, dug it up and connected it. They arrived at Kami's lodge in high spirits and celebrated most of the night. The next day, blessing day, was all gloom and doom. There was another disconnected join. The Thami Rimpoche was furious, and they spent another day searching for it. Fortunately it was all sorted out, and fluorescent lights were set up in the centre of the dance floor. I thought that it took something away from the aesthetics of the dancing, but the Sherpas were delighted to have lighting for the all-night party that came after the monks' dancing. The locals are very happy to see that the power can work.

As an aside, one of the foreign engineers recently bought a horse from a local untouchable man, for the exorbitant price of $NZ1400. Horses don't seem to do well at this altitude, and the poor animal died after 35 days, having cost our friend $NZ40 a day for the privilege of saving his legs for a little over a month. The Sherpas think it's a great joke!

THAMI BRIDGE.

Kami and his wife Da Doma were run off their feet catering to all the trekkers staying at their lodge. One morning they fed 27 people for breakfast. People were sleeping everywhere, even on the floor. Next year Kami should have the dormitory downstairs ready, so hopefully won't have to turn so many people away for Mani-Rhimbdu.

Di and I enjoyed the festival. It was nice to have already seen it and taken photos, so we could relax, and go home when we'd had enough, instead of feeling that we mustn't miss a thing. We didn't wear our ingis, and felt far more like ourselves. We were still treated as respected locals, and had tea with the Rimpoche and later were invited to dine with him.

There were a lot more trekkers this year, but most seemed to be nice people who didn't try to take over the place. However, there was one very aggressive European woman who was photographing for a choreographer, and really was a nuisance and an embarrassment. She kept pushing everyone out of the way, and coming up to the local kids shouting, "Move!" as she kicked them aside to get her shot. Diane had some fairly severe words with her, and explained in no uncertain terms that this was the locals' festival, she was here as a privileged guest, and she should settle down or leave. Diane can be quite fierce when standing up for others, and she certainly managed to quieten the woman down.

We were delighted to discover that mad-as-an-ice-axe-Gertrude did not attend Mani-Rhimbdu this year. Kami had issued strict instructions that she was not to stay at his lodge if she turned up. She has apparently been deported to her own country. This is probably a result of her meeting up with the Gurkha officers at last year's marathon. After rescuing the lodge owner from her ice-axe attack they swore they would get her deported.

We met a professor of womens studies from America, who told me about a Nepali woman doctor who was trained in Russia. She is a staunch Communist and radical political feminist. Not a common thing in Nepal. She and her husband — also a doctor — spend much of their time fighting "girl-trafficking", and run halfway houses for HIV positive women in Kathmandu. Most of these women and girls come from the 10,000 who are sold to the brothels in India each year. India has compulsory HIV testing for prostitutes, and as soon as the women or girls become positive they are dumped

WITHOUT A SKILL, SUCH AS SPINNING WOOL, THIS GIRL COULD WELL HAVE ENDED UP IN PROSTITUTION.

across the border. Their families are usually not interested in caring for them, and they have few job skills, so often end up working in the carpet

217

WEAVING IS ONE OF THE SKILLS TAUGHT AT THE HALFWAY HOUSES.

factories or returning to prostitution. The women in the halfway houses are taught other job skills, such as sewing, knitting, reading and book-keeping, and are given somewhere free and safe to live.

The term "girl-trafficking" is quite accurate. Most girls who are sold to the brothels in India and Thailand are aged 10-14. There is a certain group of villagers who are known as the prostitute caste. It is probably the only village in Nepal where the birth of a girl is celebrated and welcomed. At the age of 10 she will be sold to a brothel for $NZ600-$1600 — a relative fortune.

She will spend a few months being "broken-in", usually involving considerable violence and abuse, and then sent on to the brothel. Once there she will be locked in a room, day and night, for months on end. Two meagre meals a day will be brought to her and she will be provided with a bucket as a toilet, which is emptied from time to time. A number of men will come to her room, maybe six to 10 a day. She is beaten by the owner if she "takes too long" with any one customer. She receives no pay, and never leaves the room. Every few months, her father or one of her brothers will come and collect her small salary. This could be her life for the next 20 or 30 years, until she is considered to be too old and is fired. Becoming HIV positive is a form of escape.

Some women can return to their village, and may be welcomed by the family because they have brought a lot of money to them, but many others are not so "lucky", and have an even more grim future ahead of them.

The carpet factories employ 300,000 people in Kathmandu, and half of these are children aged 14 and under. These people work an average of 16 hours a day, in cramped, hot, poorly lit, unsanitary conditions, with little ventilation. Some are paid about $NZ0.80 a day. Some children are not paid anything at all. They are beaten and sexually abused by the foremen and owners. The carpet factories are well-known recruitment centres for "girl-trafficking".

Quite a number of those "employed" are bonded labour. A tout will go to a remote village and lend money to a family in difficulty. He will charge exorbitant interest rates, which the family, of course, cannot keep up with. As compensation, he will often take one of the children to work for free in his carpet factory, or may sell the child to another factory or brothel. He will take the child's wages as part payment on the debt. In the meantime, the debt grows, and other family members may be recruited to help pay it off. And on and on it goes. It is a very profitable business for the tout. There is also a caste called the Kamaiya, who are bonded labourers. These people inherit the debts of their predecessors, and may be working as slaves for families or businesses all their life, paying off debts accrued by long-dead great-great-grandparents. Many work as slaves for private families, but some are also sent to provide an income for others in the carpet factories or brothels.

The Sherpas, in general, are not victims in this system of abuse. Most Sherpa children who work in the brothels or carpet factories have run away from their families, lured by tales of excitement in the "big city".

The richer families do keep servants, who are really just short-term slaves. If a Sherpa has contacts with a trekking agency, a poor down-valley Nepali may come and ask for a job as a porter. The Sherpa will "employ" him or her as an unpaid servant for a couple of years or so, with the promise that he or she will eventually be given work with the agency.

Our mail-runner worked for Ed's sirdar for free for two years before he was put forward for the Trust job. This man collects the mail from the Himalayan Trust office in Kathmandu, catches the bus to Jiri, walks five days up to the hospital, "rests" a day, then takes our mail back to Jiri, and on to Kathmandu. He completes the entire circuit every 12-13 days. It was only after eight years of doing this job that one of the doctors discovered that he would spend his turn-around day working for the sirdar's family for free, cooking and carrying water and wood, as a form of bonded labour in gratitude for the job! This was of course stopped immediately, but gives an idea of how people can be abused for many years. In fact it is our Western perspective that sees this as abuse — the local people feel that this was fair enough. The Trust pays the mail-runner well, and he certainly feels that the two years of slave labour were well worth it and that he really is one of the lucky ones.

On the way home from watching Mani-Rhimbdu at Thami we dropped in at the Thamo Nunnery, which is becoming the Thamo clinic, since we usually see more people there than at Thami. They always spoil us with milk coffee and Kathmandu toast and marmalade (with the butter on top). It is always very special to visit the Tibetan nuns. They have so little, yet always seem happy and so emotionally rich. Despite it being a very scruffy little gompa, it seems to have so much more spirituality than the grandiose rich monasteries the local monks live in.

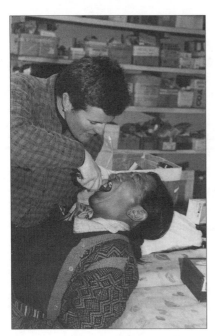

It is marvellous having the 286 computer here, but I recently had an upset with it, and had to send the hard drive on our mail runner's back to be "fixed" in Kathmandu. A couple of weeks ago, I thought I'd do a bit of spring cleaning on the computer. (This is one of the things people do when they are *really* bored.) I tidied away merrily, chopping and changing files and moving them neatly into various directories, all looking very smart. Then I got annoyed at the computer files that came with it, things like AUTOEXEC.BAT, CHKLIST.CPS and CON-FIG.SYS. What messy, nasty little files they looked, with unattractive names and all those silly symbols and markings that I didn't understand. So I thought I'd get them out of the way too, and copied them into a directory that I named "Computer". I tried to delete AUTO-EXEC.BAT from the main bit and the computer wouldn't let me. I thought, "Hmm . . . these files might be important," and since the computer wouldn't delete one of them, I thought I'd better leave it there, messy as it was. So I went on to the next one, CONFIG.SYS, and it happily deleted itself. So I thought, "Great, this computer is foolproof and has some fail-safe mechanism that won't let me delete anything important," so I proceeded to wipe all the rest of the files.

Later I sat there smugly looking at my almost-clean screen, and tried again to get rid of that wretched AUTOEXEC.BAT, but it just wouldn't go away. I then shut off the computer, and proudly announced to Diane that I'd done some tidying up, with the satisfaction of someone who's finally cleaned out a bedroom that for years has just had the door pulled shut to hide the mess.

Well, this fool was obviously too clever for the computer's fail-safe mechanism. Next morning, the tears and howls of frustration and grief could have been heard in Kathmandu. The computer wouldn't let me in. Completely barred, despite all the tricks I tried and the pleading I did with it. I ended up curled in the foetal position, all cried out, staring hopelessly at Diane while she had a go with the machine. Finally, taking over the situation in her own practical way, she packed the hard drive up, made me sit down and write a note to the computer people telling them exactly what I'd done, and organised our mail runner to zap down to Lukla with it and jump on the next plane to Kathmandu. It arrived back four days later, all fixed. So it turned out all right in the end, though the locals think it's a great joke that the memsahib broke the computer, and keep telling me I should stop hitting it with a hammer, or throwing it around the room, which seems to be the popular view of how I broke it. Anyway, no more spring cleaning for me!

On Black Friday last month Khunde/Khumjung held their O-Sho procession to bless the fields. It did not rain the next day, which people feel is a bad sign for the riggi crops. I hope they're wrong. After the trekker death last Black Friday, we decided not to tell anyone what day it was this time.

Unfortunately, there was an argument during this year's O-Sho. It was over the Italian man who died of altitude sickness recently in the Gokyo Valley. Two Khumjung families both have lodges in the village in which he died, and the families are quite jealous of each other's success. One family accused the other of stealing the dead man's belongings. This seems unlikely since none of this family were in the village at the time, but abuse was shouted for most of the procession.

The next day the fighting continued, until one wife and sister attacked the other family's two daughters, in the middle of Namche market. The whole crowd cheered them on. When they started hurling rocks at each other, the headmaster raced in and pulled them apart. While he was restraining one of the daughters (who is seven months pregnant), the 10-year-old grandson from the other family repeatedly kicked her in the stomach! Fortunately, the baby seems fine. The whole incident made me feel a bit sick, but has delighted the local people, with

NAMCHE MARKET.

the story getting better and better with each telling. Kami warned us that this wouldn't be the end of it, and the fighting would probably start again at Dumje!

There is also another battle, which may re-emerge during the Dumje week. The new nawas (villagers who make sure animals are kept out of people's fields) have been chosen, and recently had a meeting to decide on the dates that the animals should leave and be allowed to return to the village. This is to protect the potato crops from being eaten by stock. Every villager who wants to abide by their ruling, and thus receive their protection, had to bring a jug of chang or the equivalent sum in money. As you can imagine, with all that free alcohol about, the village was full of drunkards staggering about.

One couple started accusing another man of stealing, and the heated shouts of abuse soon turned to pushes, then punches, then rocks being thrown. The couple who started the argument fared worst, with the old woman being thrown through a rock wall into someone's field, and the man receiving a nasty laceration across his forehead, looking very dramatic with blood pouring down his face. The other man, unhurt, strutted about the village, enraging his opponents by bragging about what a good fighter he still is. The woman grabbed a bag and collected the rocks used in the battle (as evidence!), then they both trotted down to the Namche police to file a complaint. Next day, the police came up and took our "hero" away. But in the end, nothing happened, not even a fine. So the older couple are still looking to get even!

At last we have been able to start our health classes for the school children. Last Tuesday we taught Class Five (aged 9-13) about iodine deficiency, goitres, cretinism, and iodised salt. They all brought a sample of salt from home, and enjoyed being able to test it for iodine content. On Thursday we taught Class Nine (aged 15-20) about first aid management of cuts. The children seemed very keen and interested. We plan to teach Class Five mainly health issues, such as hygiene, not smoking, moderate alcohol use, and some fairly tame sex education. Class Nine will mainly learn about first aid, though we'll just see what seems to interest the children. Kami and I will play it by ear.

Sometimes I think we are just a bit slow. For 13 months we have been complaining about Pus, the wretched hospital cat, and particularly about his ability to open doors but not close them. It really was a problem in winter. We'd come out to the flat to find that the blasted animal had opened the door and was happily asleep on our bed. Meanwhile, the flat was freezing cold and snow had blown into the lounge. We had to lock the kitchen door at mealtimes to stop Pus coming in and hassling us all while we ate.

Finally it has dawned on us that he can't turn a round door knob, and we have attached these to the kitchen and flat doors. Life is much more peaceful, though we still hear the occasional thump as the cat throws himself at the door handle, and admit to a wee snigger at his lack of success. Now if we could only get him to stop climbing in the windows. When he's inside, he'll sneakily prise the latch open and push the window out a little. If we don't notice, he can later reach his paw around and open the window from the outside, so can get inside in the middle of the night. We have put a netting frame over one of the flat windows, which can now be left open all the time. Occasionally we'll hear a bit of scrabbling at the netting in the middle of the night, but the cat still stays outside. We just hope he doesn't catch on about turning the round door handles!

There was another trekker death just before Mani-Rhimbdu. Again we only heard about it after the woman had died, which is very upsetting and frustrating, since she was only at Tengboche! She was an elderly woman who became short of breath and unwell at Pangboche. Someone walked back with her to Tengboche, and said that she took *five hours* to get from Deboche to Tengboche (usually a 20 to 30 minute walk)! She was apparently a very large person, and none of the Sherpas were prepared to carry her. They say that there was no way that she would have fitted into a Gamow bag.

Her trekking group left her alone in a lodge. She spoke no English and could not communicate with anyone. The local people were apparently very kind to her, but decided that she was too big to move. No one thought of coming to get us. She died alone, with no friends about, and no one who could even speak to her. It seems such a cruel and unnecessary way to die, and makes me very angry! We have since heard that two days later her trekking group was told that she had died, but decided to continue with their holiday anyway! I suppose that once she's dead there's not much for them to do, but it still seemed a bit callous to us.

The two new health workers seem to be working out very well. They are keeping good records and stay in contact with us regularly. One saw over 100 patients in the last three weeks at his Monzo Clinic. The other saw 56 Phortse people last month, and dealt very well with another diarrhoea epidemic.

We have unfortunately had a lot of verbal complaints, and now a written one, from a down-valley village about their health worker. Some are justified and of quite a serious nature, such as turning up to work drunk and only giving Depo Provera to women who provide bribes. We will be giving her a final warning to mend her ways or else we will be looking for a new health worker in the near future.

We are delighted that our replacements have been chosen. We wonder about the value of such a long initial time in Kathmandu. We ended up hating the place by the time we left. Certainly some things are important, such as Norplant training (in order to get the certificate). The technique itself could be taught to a doctor in half an hour. However, certification takes at least a week. It is also important for the newly appointed Khunde doctors to visit the Kathmandu hospitals (if only to convince them that if they become seriously ill themselves they should leave the country). In fact, it is important for them to be able to see where their patients can be referred to.

We felt that lessons in Nepali were of limited benefit. Most people speak Sherpa up here. When we do have to negotiate with Nepali officials, getting the message straight is too important to work without trusted interpreters. A few common and medical Nepali and Sherpa terms would have been of more use than struggling on with conversational Nepali which we have never used. We could have done with more Sherpa culture, and it would have been an advantage to learn a few Sherpa songs and dances before we came up. I really don't think that all this would take more than two or three weeks.

Vaccination day is still proving to be popular. We have beaten our own record, and saw 113 patients last Sunday! We seem to have vaccinated all of the interested people in Phortse and Khumjung, but now the Thami/Thamo villagers and many people from Lukla/Phakding and Monzo are coming up. Still no one from Pangboche. Four children contracted measles in that village a few weeks ago and, sadly, one died.

We vaccinated 50 children and gave 32 adults tetanus toxoid. There'll be a few more today, and then we'll have to throw away all of the rest of the vaccines, since the "coolie" bin won't keep them at the right temperature for more than two days. It will be great when we finally get a kerosene fridge for the hospital, so all these vaccines don't have to be wasted. At the same time, we always run short of BCG and measles vaccine, so a fridge would allow us to obtain a lot more, store them safely, and always have them available.

Officially we are only supposed to give tetanus toxoid to women of child-bearing age, but every month we throw out so much of the stuff that I have decided to give tetanus toxoid courses to adult men as well, since they are just as much at risk from the disease. Less vaccines are being wasted, and the women seem to enjoy their menfolk having a taste of what vaccinations are like.

*I*t has been a very dry monsoon, with clear skies in the early morning, and rain mostly at night. I'm sure it's much hotter than last year with temperatures getting up to 20°C at times. The local people say that the weather is very good for the riggis but bad for grass growth, and some predict a very cold winter as a consequence. The grass has all gone yellow at Pheriche, and many of the monsoon rivers up-valley are still dry! The riggis are already being harvested from just below Sanassa, and will be taken from Khunde in August. This is very early, as it usually happens in September. So the weather is really confusing this year.

The boredom of this monsoon was broken up for us by a visit from Diane McKinnon. She and her husband John were the first Khunde couple way back in 1966. Diane runs two or three treks in Nepal each year, so has a long history with the place. She brought a group of 20 New Zealanders, with Bill Sykes, a botanist, to look at the very beautiful Himalayan wild flowers in the area.

For a break from the hospital, I decided to join them on their trek, and had a great time. To catch the good views before the cloud cover took over, we were greeted with tea in bed at 4.30 am each morning, which is certainly not what I'm used to! But it's amazing what you can cope with when you're sleeping in a tent and have gone to bed at 6.30 pm.

To my great shame, I know nothing about flowers, and was fascinated to hear the group "oohing and aahing" over different plants, with cries of, "Oh just look at that *Thermopsis barbata*, and there's a *Gueldenstaedtia himalaica*. Wait a minute, I think I can see an *Androsace sarmentosa*!" They rattled off these long and difficult Latin names as if they were saying, "Oh look, there's a pretty bird/cat/dog"! Some would shake with the

225

excitement of a new find, and I was staggered to see such passion about plain old gardening.

It was a whole new world to me, but after a while I became caught up in the excitement too, and soon the names didn't all sound so foreign and difficult to me. After a week, I found myself exclaiming, "Now that must be a primula of some sort, Bill, which one is it? Ah yes, *sikkimensis*, of course, I should have known!"

BILL SYKES.

Most of the group were in their sixties, but we soon found things in common, and they were a really interesting group. One woman in her sixties had recently done a bungy jump at Queenstown (it's free if you're over 60) while her 85-year-old mother watched and cheered her on. Another couple really impressed us. Good old farmers from Gore. They had only been to the North Island twice in their lives, and this was their first ever overseas trip! They coped so well with all the differences and hardships camping in a Third World country. We came to like and admire them very much.

We made particular friends with one woman who teaches English as a second language back home. We were also delighted to get to know a Hong Kong Chinese woman who is a District Court Judge in Wellington. She was great company and a lot of fun. One man was a surgeon who had worked with my dad in my home town of Dargaville, before I was born! Two other members of the group knew my mother through their work in marriage guidance, so it seemed a very small world.

We came across a lot of other trekkers on our travels. Most are good people, but the occasional one would be very condescending to the local people and obsessed with "how dirty everything is here". Too many Westerners confuse lack of educational opportunities and minimal English language with low intelligence, and seem to feel that people who live in very basic facilities with poor hygiene do so because they like it that way. They don't realise that the person they are talking down to probably speaks Sherpa, Nepali, English, and possibly some Tibetan, French, German and/or Japanese. If clean running water and flush toilets were available, people would be delighted to use them!

I don't think Gokyo likes me! All three times I've been there, I've had to leave before I was ready. The first time was last October, when Di called me back for a delivery, and I walked seven hours through the dark to find that it had all happened a long time before I got there. The second time was the trek with Diane in April, when she fell into the lake and rapidly lost interest in the place.

This trek, we had just settled into our tents below the third Gokyo lake when I received a message from Di to come back to the hospital as soon as I could for a 10-year-old girl who had fallen and sustained a right supracondylar fracture. This is a break just above the elbow, and can be nasty because the radial pulse can be cut off, resulting in an ischaemic, dead arm. I decided that walking back in the dark was definitely a once-in-a-lifetime experience, and set off at 6 am the next morning with the local boy who had brought the message up. We didn't run, but kept a steady pace and didn't stop at all, making it to the hospital in *under five hours*! (Actually, four hours and 58 minutes.)

We put the girl out with ketamine and I yanked and pulled and twisted again and again, with little improvement. We took two intraoperative X-rays, and even had to put her under a second time. Finally I was able to move the bones so that about 50 per cent of them were in contact, instead of being completely separated, and we could feel a radial pulse, but only with her arm at about 150 degrees — useless really, since the bones were likely to pop out of alignment again very easily. It's so frustrating not having the skills to do things properly. We ended up sending her off to Kathmandu for internal fixation/pinning, but I doubt she'll ever have a normal arm again.

While I was back at the hospital, Di and I looked through some New Zealand magazines that Di McKinnon had kindly brought over. Things like the *Womens Weekly*, *Metro* and *North and South*. We were utterly shocked by the near nudity of the photographs. Women with short skirts and men with no shirts on. We have become used to people being covered from neck to toe, and neither of us have seen much bare body for over a year. Mingma was obviously quite titillated by the magazines, and would sneak off privately to look through them. Kami opened one magazine to a photo of a rock group, naked, but with their genitals hidden behind their guitars. He was horrified, said that the magazine should be banned, and refused to look at any of the others. How will we cope when we get home? It is confusing to perceive our own culture as weird and debased.

Incidentally, we have read in the *Newsweek* that ketamine, called "Special K", has become a favourite recreational drug in night-clubs in

New York. It is said to cause disorientation and confusion, which doesn't sound that appealing to me, especially in a foreign night-club.

The next day I wandered up the hill, met the group at Phortse, and we continued up to Dingboche. At Dingboche, one of the Sherpas on the trek came running up to me saying that a man was looking for me with a message that I had to return to the hospital urgently! I sent messages of my own all over the local area, to Pheriche, Dingboche and Osho, saying where I was and requesting the man to come and talk to me. No one turned up, and I agonised, but decided that it wasn't worth racing back on a rumour. I did not sleep well that night and felt quite uncomfortable and guilty for the next couple of days until Di met us in Deboche. She knew nothing about a messenger from the hospital, and they certainly hadn't called me. So it was just as well I didn't bolt down again!

Another reason I am glad that I did not race back down was that I had the chance to visit our dear friend Gaga Doma. A few weeks ago, her son got into yet another of his drunken rages, beat her, and threw her out of her own house! This is not the first time this has happened, and we are delighted that she has moved up to Pheriche to live with her son's ex-wife. We miss her, but know she will be cared for much better up there. Interestingly, she came to the hospital before she left to get some acetazolamide to prevent altitude sickness, which she has had in the past walking up to Pheriche in one day.

It was great to see her again. We sat holding hands tearfully for about two hours' getting by with lots of sign language and the occasional translation from her grandson. "I will die in Pheriche," she said, and we both feel it is a good thing that she will not return to Khunde, though we miss her.

I had an odd experience at Dingboche. I was lying in my tent alone in the middle of the night, unable to sleep. A movement caught my eye and my mother came into the tent. She was wearing her nightie and looked straight ahead, not at me. I said, "Hi, Mum," but she ignored me and floated on out through the other end of the tent. It wasn't until she'd gone that I realised that this was an apparition of some sort. This was something quite unusual that I'd never experienced before. I was not frightened because my mother would never do me harm. I just thought it was an odd thing to happen.

I rather sheepishly told Di about it when we met up at Deboche, and she became very concerned. She reminded me of tales from other people she'd read about. She felt that maybe my mother had died and her spirit had come to say goodbye before it disappeared. I didn't feel a sense that my mother was dead, but became very distressed as I mentioned the event to others in the group, who seemed to agree with Di's theory. I preferred to think that it was the altitude playing tricks on my mind, but it was a sickening feeling realising that a reply to letter sent home as soon as we got back to the hospital would take six weeks. I tried to put the whole thing out of my mind.

Di had had a difficult time at Khunde while I was away, but coped admirably on her own. A Khumjung man had been carried up after a stroke which had left him paralysed down the left side of his body and the right side of his face. His blood pressure was high. Di found the notes of another patient we have with a similar problem, and put this man on the same regime. Worked just fine!

She also had an urgent call in the middle of the night to visit a woman in Thamo (two hours' fast daylight walk away) in her first labour. The husband had seen a foot sticking out, and had come to get the doctor. Footling breeches do not do well, and the baby delivered himself an hour later, dead, before Di could get organised to do anything. The mother is fine. It wouldn't have mattered whether I had been there or not, but was a hard time for Di on her own.

When the trek returned to Khunde, Di and I put on a chang party for the whole village and the trekking group. This was more like a regular party, where we provided music, chang and juice and people just boogied down. It was a great success, and everyone Sherpa, Nepali, line and disco danced until the wee small hours.

A MANI STONE AT GHAT.

The day after the group left, Kami and I walked down to Lukla, ran two Norplant and medical clinics there, and then another at Monzo on the way back. Over the three days we saw 160 patients, and I inserted 32 Norplant devices, so it was certainly worth our while going down there.

On the way back, just above the Shyangboche airfield, I was greeted by a tearful Diane. She seemed to be devastated and unable to tell me what was wrong for a few minutes. Finally she told me the bad news. Longin, the hospital dog, had died the day before. At first, all I could feel was incredible relief that it wasn't my mother. I felt angry at Diane for giving me such a fright, and dismissed the dog's death as something unimportant. Until that night, when I woke to realise that Longin's snuffling and snores were missing, and it finally sunk in that she was gone. I cried most of the night, and felt guilty at my initial relief.

LONGIN, THE HOSPITAL DOG.

Longin had developed vomiting and gone off her food, and had lain by our bed most of the night groaning until, at 6 am. She had taken her last breath as Di was gently patting her. We assume that somebody poisoned her. We have both been very upset about it, and miss her a lot. We won't get another dog, since it would be too hard on a puppy, and us, to say good-bye after only about seven months. We still find ourselves absent-mindedly calling Longin for a walk or taking our leftovers out to her, suddenly realising she's gone and bursting into tears. But I guess we'll get used to it soon. Longin's passing makes me miss my own dog, Matt, even more, and I can't wait to see him again, though I am very pleased we did not bring him up here.

The locals are quite shocked by the extent of our grieving. They have been very kind, saying things like, "Longin was a good dog. She will be reincarnated to a human next time." But they really can't see what all the fuss is about. I just hope she doesn't come back as a Hindu Nepali woman.

Press release for *House and Garden* Magazine: The Khunde Hospital flat has had a face lift! Now, instead of the dreary, dirty white walls, which haven't seen a lick of paint since at least 1978, the place is vibrant with colour. As you wander into the lounge, you are positively hit by the four bright canary yellow doors and beams leading off to adjoining rooms. This is quietened by soft pink walls, white ceiling and mottled brown curtains. Walking to the left, the bathroom is ablaze with deep "tinned guava" pink, tastefully contrasted by one wall and fixtures in "smurf" blue — an absolute delight! Back through the yellow and pink lounge, past the newly varnished bookcases covering two walls, and through to the main bedroom, which is a dark salmon pink, matched perfectly by its maroon and black duvet cover and beige and pink floral curtains. Then back through yet another canary-yellow door into the soft pink walls of the spare room, with its blue and white striped curtains. It is certainly a sight to behold! Next project, the new office!

There certainly is nothing like the death of a friend to get you busily working on mind-occupying activities. Di has organised us all to put up spouting along the front of the hospital and Kami's flat. So that should stop the constant dripping from melting snow while we change the next lot of Tibetans' frostbite dressings in the winter. The water is now running into a tank, so is supplementing the water supply for the village. Who knows, some of the villagers may follow suit and be able to collect their own water during the monsoon and winter.

We have also gone through the patients' clothing box, and are actively handing out the summer clothing, some of which looks as if it's been there for many years.

Dumje went well, with only a few minor scuffles. There continues to be a real problem with the rich Kathmandu Sherpas breezing in and showing off their wealth, creating jealousy and bad feeling from the local people. They put on excellent parties with beer, foreign whisky, prawn chips and other snacks, and gave twice as much rice as is normal. This was interpreted by some as trying to show up others, and a few punch-ups resulted.

Mingma also put on some good parties, although Di and I unintentionally started an argument at one of these. One of our friends was explaining the different names for tea to us, in our effort to avoid being given the Tibetan salt tea (which we both hate with a passion). Usually people give us sweet tea, which is very milky and weak with a large amount of sugar in it. If there is no milk, a raw egg is broken into the glass and whisked around. It is an acquired taste but preferable to the only other option of salt tea. This tastes a bit like lanolin soup. To top it off, a large glob of yak butter, preferably rancid, is placed on top of the salty brew. The more important you are considered to be, the larger the glob and more rancid the butter is. June Hillary told us the secret is to blow as you sip, which keeps the butter glob away from your lips. We have never been able to perfect the technique.

One of the locals took offence that our friend was teaching us words for tea in Nepali, and insisted that we learn the Sherpa words. This moved on to a pushing and shoving argument about which language was better, which lasted on and off for a number of days. Because most of the Nepalis who live up here are unhappy to be up in the cold and away from their Hindu culture, they tend not to mix in well. They are often people in positions of governmental power and are understandably unpopular. This is a very racist society, where the Hindu Nepalis believe that Sherpas are low caste and promiscuous (because of pre-marital sex), and the Sherpas consider the Hindu Nepalis to be weak, histrionic and lazy. Each knows that they are better than the other. Many Sherpas resent that their children are taught in Nepali and refuse to speak it themselves.

Khunde had what I assume is its first Gay Pride parade on the 26th of June! Di and I donned various rainbow articles and circumnavigated the village

YAK IN DRAG.

in a clockwise direction, to celebrate 25 years since the Stonewall riots. Longin also wore a small rainbow flag wrapped around her large tummy. It was a quiet event. A few villagers took a break from weeding their potato fields to say "Namaste" or "Kani peyo?" (where are you going?), obviously in support of the cause. A couple of the children shook our hands or waved hello. We took a break to help chase a yak out of someone's potato field. One dog growled at us, but we ignored his heckling. I did a wee line dance at the bottom of the village, and pretended that I was on a float in the New York parade at the Gay Games.

School Leaving Certificate results are out, and a girl came top of Nepal. Maybe that will encourage some parents to push their girl children's education along with the boys. Khumjung School did very well. Seven out of the 12 students who sat passed their School Leaving Certificate. The girl who came top of Class Ten obtained a first division pass. Five boys (including Tsumje's brother, who experienced a psychotic illness just before the exams) received a second division pass. Overall, 32 per cent of students in Nepal passed the School Leaving Certificate. This didn't sound very good to Di and me, but Kami says this is excellent, since usually the exam has only about a 27 per cent pass rate.

Two horses have been killed in the past couple of weeks at

Shyangboche. By the type of injury, it is certain that a snow leopard is the culprit! I'm sorry for the horses, but am delighted that this animal is not yet extinct.

I think one of the most frustrating types of problem I see up here are the "more than routine" eye diseases. Many people get conjunctivitis, and even more have allergic eye problems related to smoke, pollen and grasses. However, we see a lot of people with progressively reduced vision or other conditions, which are certainly beyond my general practice training. Although we can refer them to the eye clinic in Kathmandu (which is not bad), most of these people seem to be elderly and/or poor, and won't or can't go that far. So nothing happens. It is one area where I wish I had more skills.

There must be romance in the air. Just in this last week, there have been three Khumjung/Namche zendis (weddings), and three Khunde engagements.

With all the new lodges and building, Khunde is really beginning to look flash. Now 29 of the 66 Khunde houses have a tin roof.

The 5.2-kg baby whose mother required symphisiotomy turned one year old last week. And what a healthy, happy, intelligent wee boy he is too!

The wife of one of our health workers was severely beaten a few days ago. The Lands and Survey people are coming to the village soon, but will only measure land that is fenced. Our health worker's wife tried to make a fence, and had an argument with the neighbours about the boundary line. The neighbours held her down and repeatedly kicked and punched her all over the body, even after she had been knocked unconscious. When I saw her, she had bruising over almost all her body, and two large black eyes, but no apparent serious head injury.

We are hearing tales all around the Khumbu of disputes between neighbours about property boundaries. What with that and the required bribes, the Lands and Survey people are causing an enormous amount of worry, argument and misery around the place.

Recently there was a large meeting at Shyangboche. Some Namche people have told the Lands and Survey officials that Shyangboche belongs to them. However, most people consider it to be part of Khunde/Khumjung. With the regular helicopter service and the recent growth in Shyangboche, this is a serious issue, and the arguments continue.

It is now the anniversary of the Gen Lama's death (Tibetans celebrate

anniversaries after 11 months because of their different calendar) and there is great excitement about the place. Some of his bones remained intact after he was cremated, and these were blessed, carefully wrapped in khaarta, and stored in the gompa. When they were unwrapped some Tibetan writing had been inscribed on the bones.

We were fortunate enough to be shown these, and I was able to photograph the remains. On a saucer sat a trochanter (the ball-shaped top of the thigh bone which fits into the hip/pelvis) and two other pieces of bone. There was pale, cream-coloured writing on them, which didn't look like any pen or paint I could think of. It said "Om Mani Padme Hom", which is a very common Buddhist prayer. The married nun who looks after the gompa was even more excited as she showed us the intact Gen Lama's skull, which "has dark writing all over it!" This, unfortunately, turned out to be the normal black suture lines that exist between the different bones that make up the skull, but I didn't tell her. Everyone seems so delighted by the find. And we certainly can't seem to explain away the writing on the other bones so easily.

The Gen Lama's remains were placed inside the chorten that he had been cremated in and closed in. This was done with great ceremony by the more important monks in the area. Local people came from far away to bring khaarta to the Gen Lama and be blessed by his remains.

I am now the only member of the Khunde Hospital staff who has the odd tipple. Mingma, Tsumje and Diane are non-drinkers from way back. Kami has recently signed a pact with a Sherpa helicopter pilot, another Kathmandu businessman, and the Thami Rimpoche, that none of them will drink alcohol for the next two years. Anyone who breaks the pact will have to forfeit $NZ400. The Thami Rimpoche's wife was so delighted with the arrangement that she visited Kami the next morning with khaarta and chiyaa. Kami does not have a drinking problem, but has joined in to help the others out and provide a good role model. There are a few people around here we'd like to add to the list! I hope the scheme works out for them.

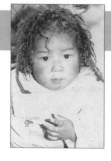

*D*i and I had a very upsetting time three weeks ago. Only 12 days after Longin died, the National Park workers had another of their regular bouts of dog-killing. This service is provided to rid the area of the many stray, unwanted dogs who often suffer from lack of food and love, bark all night and can be quite vicious. Contraception is virtually non-existent for animals here. We do offer Depo Provera to people's pets, but the idea has not caught on (especially after one of the local dogs died the day after its first shot). Because of the Buddhist beliefs, puppies are deserted rather than put down, and left for the National Park men to poison. I guess it's OK for a Buddhist to let an animal suffer and/or die by neglect, but it mustn't be killed directly.

When the National Park men came to Namche, they killed 28 dogs in one day. However, the local people commented that the vicious troublesome ones still seemed to remain.

When we heard that the National Park men were coming to Khunde the next day, we raced around the village telling people to tie their dogs up and/or put collars on them. There is an intellectually handicapped woman who lives at the bottom of the village, married to a Tibetan butcher, one of the untouchable caste, and not liked by the villagers. She owns two dogs, one snappy old bitch, and a delightful puppy we call "Crazy Dog", who bounds up to greet us on our daily walks and is a bundle of enthusiasm and fun. We didn't trust her to keep the dogs tied up, so tied a green rag as a collar around Crazy Dog's neck, so the National Park men would know she belonged to someone, and would not poison her.

There are three nasty dogs who live up by the gompa, and another one in the village, who will growl at and attack people, and we were relieved that the National Park men would put these unfortunate animals down.

I busied myself in the clinic and tried not to think about what was going on in the village. Soon, however, there was a great commotion at the mani stone just below the hospital entrance. A woman was clinging on to her lovely old dog, who was puffing away, with frothy saliva dribbling from its mouth. She and the Nepali dog killers were screaming at each other. Her wonderful old dog, who does nothing but sit quietly on a rock at the front of the house all day, had been fed the poisoned meat. The woman was understandably very upset, and insisted that she be able to hold and pat the dog until he died. The Nepali man was becoming hysterical because he said that the poison is very toxic and that if she got any on her she would die too. And he wasn't taking responsibility for that!

I felt enormous respect for the woman for standing up to him and the rest of the village, who stood around like ghouls, laughing at her sentimental behaviour. However, I was concerned at the thought of her frothing at the mouth, dying before our eyes from the poison. I asked if there was an antidote for the poison, but the Nepali officials knew of none and said that the dog would be dead in a few minutes. No, they had no idea of what kind of poison it was, just "dog poison" they said, looking at me as if I was an idiot. The dog by this stage was partially paralysed and couldn't walk, and its owner carried him home and held it until it died soon after.

It was very upsetting, and I tearfully returned to the clinic to see an untouchable man from Namche. He had a contusion on his fingernail from when his own dog had accidentally bitten him. His dog had been tied up just outside their house, yet the National Park men had come on to his property and poisoned it. The untouchable man saw them do it and raced out to stop them, but was too late. He forced about four jugs of water into the dog's mouth, and pushed its stomach to make the dog vomit. That's why the dog bit his finger, but fortunately did not break the skin. The dog survived! The higher caste National Park men probably poisoned the dog because it belonged to an untouchable. The whole episode made me feel sick, and extremely angry.

I became even angrier when I asked Mingma if he knew about feeding an animal water and making it vomit to save it from the poison. "Oh yes, he said, "it sometimes works." He'd been standing right next to me when I was asking if there was any way we could help the woman's dog, but hadn't bothered to tell me!

I then felt terrible thinking that I could have at least tried giving her dog Ipecacuanha (a syrup that induces vomiting), but hadn't thought of it at the time. I went off to sit by Longin's grave and howled my eyes out as I watched the woman bury her dog in her potato field.

Meanwhile, the National Park men continued around the village followed by every child in the area, and a few ghoulish adults delighted by the excitement. Our same health worker watched on with gleeful delight as they killed the vicious dog from the village. They were, however, unable to catch the three gompa dogs. The local people just made me feel sick, and I thought how much I hated them all, and being here.

I recovered a bit and thought I'd better check on the two dogs we have become especially fond of since Longin's death. First I went to see Setuk, who was unharmed and tied up behind one of our friend's houses. I was patting and talking away to her, when I looked down and saw the National Park assassins and their ghouls walking on to the untouchable's property at the bottom of the village, way off the main trail. Feeling sick, I ran towards the house in the hope of stopping them. But I was too late. Crazy Dog had raced out enthusiastically to meet his new "friends", who had even given him some fresh meat to eat. By the time I was able to run down the path to the house, those murdering bastards were on their way out. Crazy Dog was dead. His owner just looked confused and sad, and the local people laughed at the untouchable's misfortune.

I wanted to scream at them all. I wanted to punch the National Park men, and make them eat some of their poisoned meat. The incompetent bastards! Out of the three dogs they killed in Khunde, two were much-loved, harmless pets. But they wouldn't have understood my concerns at all, and, instead, I ran off and cried my eyes out.

I calmed down and went back to see Diane, who had been venting her anger and frustration about the woman's dog by painting the ceiling of the short-stay ward. When I told her about Crazy Dog, we both howled our eyes out again, then proceeded to get drunk on two bottles of San Miguel beer. We decided that we hated all Nepalis, and that our Sherpa friends were nothing but a pack of cruel-hearted ghouls. We couldn't wait to get home. We later went for a walk, stomping around the village, angrily kicking down people's rock walls. Pure childish vandalism, but deeply satisfying at the time.

Later, at tea, our health worker made the mistake of joking about the day's activities, which he had thoroughly enjoyed. He was bombarded by snarls of "incompetent bastards", "we should have punched their lights out" and "I'd like to bloody put them down myself", and was obviously quite shocked at our reaction to the death of a few animals.

I have since written to the Park Warden, who was able to tell me that the poison they use is "stretchin sulphate". I assume he means strychnine. The books say that strychnine poisoning should be treated with intravenous diazepam, to stop convulsions, followed by gastric lavage with diluted potassium permanganate. That's fine for humans, but I don't fancy trying to put an intravenous line or a stomach tube into a dog, who may be able to pass the poison on to me.

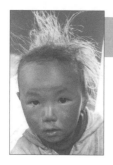

Today my sister Joy is to be married to Doug. We wish you all the best in the whole world, and today will circumnavigate the village in a clockwise direction and spin all the prayer wheels in front of the mani house, in your honour! It's hard to be away from the family on such a celebration.

People have finished cutting and drying their grass, and have almost completed digging the riggis. Just as well, since the nawas are not doing a very good job of keeping the Namche animals out of the village. At first they enthusiastically chased the livestock out, but then some Namche boys came up and threatened to beat them up. So the animals are being left to wander about on their own.

People are saying that maybe there won't be a nawa system for much longer. There does seem to be a rough crowd of young men from Namche who are bullying their way about the place.

The generators have been playing up recently, conking out every few minutes, so letter writing is a bit of a hassle. Diane has been getting very fit racing around to the shed to restart the blasted monster, while my blood pressure rises a few points every time the generator stops and I lose the last little bit I've typed in.

What a difference the knowledge that our replacements have been chosen has made to our feelings about being here. Just as an unfortunate combination of unpleasant events occurred around the beginning of this year to make us feel unhappy and dissatisfied with our Khunde experience, the news of our replacements and our booked flight home (in 175 days but who's counting?) has really lifted our spirits. Now that our time here is finite and shortening with every week, we are realising how special the people and experience here is, and have rediscovered an appreciation of the place. Recent niggles and difficulties we have had with the staff seem to have reverted to their proper petty status, rather than taking over our perceptions of the place.

We are experiencing the last of the monsoon, and look forward to the great views in a few weeks.

On the 18th of July, the village of Dingboche became deserted. It is believed that for the three months following this date (which is the beginning of a three-day fasting festival) any smoke in the village will make the gods angry. So all of its inhabitants pack up and go and live elsewhere until autumn. Most up-valley people also own a house further down, because it's too cold to live up there in the winter anyway. Khunde and Phortse have a similar rule about not bringing firewood into the village and prohibiting building, over a two-month period. One of the very rich local men is building an addition to his house, and some Khunde people are quite upset about his irreligious and untraditional behaviour.

We've been very busy recently, travelling around the area doing Norplant and health clinics. On the 10th of August, Mingma, Di and I walked over to Phortse to attend the official opening of the Phortse Health Clinic. This has been built by Papa Tony, an Englishman who has "adopted" the village, and Eton College, but will be operated by our health worker.

We arrived a little late, thanks to six housecalls on the way! We were surprised to discover that we were the guests of honour and everyone had waited for us. The school children were all lined up in rows, and we were greeted with claps, cheers and khaarta, in the same way that Ed, June, Zeke and Larry were on their visit! Two Eton masters, the headmaster, Mingma, Di and I were seated at the head table and plied with copious cups of chiyaa, surrounded by what appeared to be the entire village, plus 16 Eton schoolboys. Two Tengboche monks performed a good luck puja, and we all threw rice at the appropriate times. Then came the speeches. I found that I also had to say a little bit. Di and I were then asked to pull down the curtain dramatically, which revealed a plaque saying that the Phortse Health Clinic had been built by "Papa Tony" and Eton College. It was all done with great pomp and ceremony with hundreds of photos flashing off in our faces.

The clinic is very nice. It has a small waiting room. The surgery has an examination table in the middle of the room, another large table, a set of shelves for storage, and a stainless-steel sink and bench (with a drain, but no running water). It has green-and-white striped lino on the floor. The clinic is painted white with a red-and-yellow door and window frames. The curtains are a patterned brown. There are two large windows in the front, but unfortunately no skylight. It was very dark and hot with the curtains drawn for privacy, but when we opened the windows for a bit of fresh air, we found that the local people started trying to climb in that way, instead of waiting in the outside room!

We ran a clinic that afternoon and saw 30 people! That's one tenth of the entire Phortse population. I guess everyone wanted to come along and have a look at the new place. Unlike the recent down-valley clinic when I inserted 32 Norplant devices, no one wanted Norplant. However, we did see some very interesting cases, including one woman who had had five stillbirths and three newborn babies die, until finally she produced a live baby boy, who is now 6 months old. We were shocked to discover that this precious child had been left with fever and diarrhoea for two weeks before the mother brought him to the clinic for treatment! Another, a 46-year-old woman, was very unhappy at being six months pregnant. She has five live children, five babies who died under the age of one year, and a stillbirth. Despite this being her twelfth pregnancy, she does not want contraception after this baby is born.

The next day we wandered up to Pangboche. We waited for three hours, but only one patient turned up, and she only had a sore back from digging riggis. This was very disappointing since the main reason I had set up the Norplant clinics was because of my concern that the Pangboche area was not receiving adequate family planning. A few months ago a woman and her new-born died, after her thirteenth pregnancy. Several of the villagers had complained to us that because our health worker in that area does not provide contraception, it is not readily available for the women. This health worker refuses to provide family planning on "moral grounds". My own personal feeling is that it is entirely *immoral* to deny local families the right to limit their families to the size they want and can cope with. I guess we will never agree about that one!

We had advertised the clinic about a month ahead of time, and had stuck notices up at Deboche, Pangboche, Pheriche and Khunde Hospital. It was disappointing to have such a poor turnout.

Shortly after we returned from Pangboche, Di and I went down to Lukla. I'd advertised that we would do a medical clinic and spent two very busy days seeing 67 people at Lukla and 70 at Chaurikharka! Neither Mingma nor Kami came down with us, and the Lukla health worker kindly translated for both of the clinics. I really am impressed by him, and even more so to discover that he only went to Class Five, and is mostly self-taught. He is becoming a real asset to the Trust.

After a couple of days at Khunde, we shot off to Thami. Again, advertising the clinics made a big difference. We saw 36 people. No one wanted Norplant, because everyone is busy digging riggis and cutting their grass, and are worried about having a sore arm for a couple of days. Obviously my timing was out, and we may have more interest when the local women are not working quite so hard.

We were delighted to discover that Kami's wife, Da Doma, is six months pregnant. They have two live children, but their last baby developed neonatal tetanus at a few days of age, and died about four years ago. They have been trying hard to have another baby ever since.

Twenty-eight years ago, Professor Ibbertson found that 92 per cent of the Khumbu inhabitants had a goitre, and 17 per cent of the people who lived in Phorste suffered from cretinism. This is the result of a lack of iodine in the area. Since then there have been a number of iodine supplementation programmes, and people have started using iodised salt.

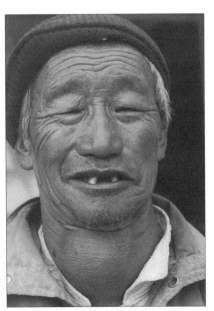

LOCAL MAN WITH A GOITRE.

During our clinic visits we managed to collect 120 urine samples from randomly selected Sherpas; some we had met on the trail and others had sampled in their houses or at the clinics. We would give the person a clean laboratory container to take away and fill with urine. This was then poured into two separate test-tubes, and coded with their demographic data. It created great hilarity throughout the villages, and we collected a following of interested locals, who would congregate outside each of the houses we visited chortling away at the crazy memsahib and her odd requests. Some of the oldies we asked just shook with laughter at first, thinking that this was some weird practical joke I was pulling on them. But once we convinced them that, yes, we really did want to collect a little sample of their urine to put in a bottle and send on to America, they would return with their contribution, cackling away to themselves. I'd then carry the samples back home and they were all stored in the darkroom.

One day I'd been showing some trekkers around the hospital, and happened to mention that I was doing a small study about iodine and goitres in the area. One of the men said that he was a doctor and had an interest in this area. He turned out to be Professor John Dunn, one of the great gurus in iodine-deficiency disorders, and he very kindly offered to analyse the iodine content of our urine samples for free in his laboratory. It was a real performance getting the samples to America, since neither the Nepali nor American customs officials were happy about bodily fluids being sent around the world. One set was eventually posted off to America while the other was kept, in case the first set didn't get through. It took a long time to hear from Professor Dunn, and we were very concerned that the samples had been lost. We tried to get several American trekkers to "smuggle" our samples in, but — very wisely — no one would play. I'd examined about 700 Sherpas and found only 21 per cent to have goitres. Forty-four per cent of people use iodised salt.

I also conducted a disability survey of the entire Khumbu region as part of the iodine study. That also caused some excitement around the village. We would find a group of residents, point to each house in the village, and get them to tell us how many adults and children lived there. Were any of them disabled, and in what way? Had anyone died in the past 28 years (since Professor Ibbertson's iodine supplementation program)? As you can imagine, soon everyone joined in and each enthusiastically had their own opinions. It took a while to get some consistent results. We then visited each house where a person with a disability lived, and I examined them or got full descriptions of those who had died, to gauge what the disability was.

Sherpas call anyone with a disability either kur (male cretin) or kumar (female cretin). Of the 2262 Khumbu Sherpas surveyed, 61 (2.7 per cent) were described as having a disability. Thirty-one suffered from deaf-mutism (one of the consequences of intra-uterine lack of iodine). Twelve had cretinism. Five were intellectually disabled but not cretins. Three had spina bifida. Three had a speech impediment. Two had cerebral palsy. One case each of hearing impairment alone, spinal tuberculosis, below-knee amputation secondary to gangrene, late-onset neurological disorder (possibly motor neurone disease), and adult-onset mutism (cause unknown) were seen. Despite its bad reputation, Phortse's disability figures were no higher than the other areas. I was shocked by the large number (almost a quarter) of families who have lost one or more children.

I was also horrified to hear that one of the deaf-mute men of normal intelligence in Khunde was murdered just a few years ago by his brother in a drunken rage. Because the man was a kur, no one ever bothered the police about it, and the brother got off scot-free. He died recently in a climbing accident on Everest. I guess what goes around, comes around.

One of our friends is a very pleasant local man, about 55 years old, who has been married and divorced four times! He had a stroke two years ago, and had recovered enough to be able to walk with the aid of a stick. We noticed that his gums were enlarged and inflamed. I couldn't think why and took a photo of his mouth and sent it to my father. Dad showed my uncle, who is a gastroenterologist, who very cleverly found that this was a rare side-effect of the antihypertensive medication he was on. We changed drugs, and over the next year his gums improved, and he was delighted to be able to eat fruit and meat again.

One day his brother appeared saying that the antihypertensive medication had run out three weeks ago. We gave him a week's supply and insisted that the patient come up for a blood-pressure check before getting any more. We saw him a few times over the next few weeks while out on walks and repeatedly asked him to come up to the clinic. Each time he would say, "tomorrow", but never turn up.

About a month later we were called to visit him in his house. He was lying on the bed unable to speak or move, having had a severe brain-stem stroke. The family wanted to know if he would get better, or whether they should call the lamas in to do their "last rites". I was terribly upset, and explained to our friend and his family that his prognosis was very poor indeed. He died later that day. If only I'd gone to visit him and checked his blood pressure, or even just given him more pills, he might still be alive today. I wish I could turn back time and do it differently. The family were devastated by his death, but not once did they imply any blame to me. Once his brother said, "He should have gone to the clinic." All I could say was that it might have helped, or maybe it was just his time to die. Fatalism should never be an excuse for negligent care, but has a lot to offer compared to the growing medico-legal environment of the Western world, where someone must always be to blame. I envy and respect the way many Sherpas just accept the bad things that life can throw at them.

The snow leopard is still about. The woman who runs the lodge in front of the hospital has just lost another zupchok. This one was grazing just above Deboche when a snow leopard attacked its throat and drank the blood out of it (as is its apparent habit). The animal survived long enough to stagger back to its caretaker, then died. The owner spent a couple of frantic days trying to sell the meat before it went off in the monsoon heat.

We have had a thief at the hospital! Over the past few weeks, we have realised that about $NZ80 has slowly been disappearing from the patient fees we collect. This has been very upsetting, and we suspect one of the local children, who has a history of theft. This poor girl seems unable to stop the habit and is well known throughout the area. We have been unable to catch her at it. Even if we did, we are not sure what we would do. Her father is very embarrassed by her actions. He says, "I beat her and beat her but nothing changes. Last year I asked the Namche police to put her in jail to frighten her — but it did no good." We didn't want her just to get another hiding.

In the end we had a special box made with a padlock on it. Kami put the word around the village that it has a camera inside it that automatically photographs the person who opens it. Completely untrue, but we haven't lost any money since. As for the girl, she continues to rob her friends and neighbours. I doubt that there are any child therapists in Nepal.

Last week I developed the flu and lay miserably in bed reading trashy novels. I had refused to do a house call to an old man in Namche who sounded as if he had urinary obstruction, since even getting up to go to the loo made me feel dizzy. The family refused to carry him up to me, as they thought he was probably going to die, and it's very bad luck for someone to die on the trail. I agonised over the situation until I received a very welcome message from a trekking doctor who was in Namche and had heard of this man's plight. I immediately sent down a urinary catheter and some other medicines, and asked him to catheterise the old man. Just as well. He took three litres of urine from the poor man's bladder. Just imagine the agony he must have been in! Soon after he was catheterised his breathing improved remarkably. Maybe his bladder was so distended that it was pushing on his diaphragm and interfering with his breathing!

Di was away, and I was feeling very lonely and particularly sorry for myself. Kami called me to talk to "some trekkers". "Are they sick?" I snapped. He found out that no, they were all fine. "Well, if they only want to look around the hospital, tell them I'm sick and show them around the place yourself." He returned saying that they particularly wanted to see the doctor. "Do I know them?" Kami returned with the answer that we were complete strangers. I was thoroughly hacked off. We do get a lot of trekkers who arrive and insist on the doctor showing them around the place. These ones tend to be the more arrogant and confrontational types and seem to feel that we should be eternally grateful that they have deigned to brighten our day in this way.

I climbed out of bed, threw a jacket over my pyjamas, and stormed angrily out of the flat, only to find a young man leaning against the surgery door smoking! I saw red and bellowed, "OY, DON'T SMOKE!", more aggressively than I'd meant to. Instead of the expected surly arrogant reply, I was greeted very charmingly by the young man, who is researching a documentary for television about the Tibetans who come across the NangPa La to see the Dalai Lama in Dharamsala.

He had brought letters for us from the group of Tibetan refugees I had done the amputations on. It was wonderful to hear how they had got on, and most were very happy in various parts of India. Sadly the lama and one of the young monks were still stuck in Kathmandu, but are due to be transferred to Dharamsala very shortly. This was the third time the lama had written to us, but the other letters did not get through. The letters were lovely, and full of thanks and good wishes for our future. Of course they were written in Tibetan, but we were able to get them translated. We both wept at hearing from our friends again, and I was able to send a letter back to them.

What was upsetting for us was being told that the Tibetan camps in India are no paradise, and that often these people, who have risked and lost so much, are disappointed when they arrive. The Tibetans have also changed their policy and are trying to get people to stay in their own country. The fear is that so many people are leaving Tibet that soon it will be completely overrun by the Chinese, and this will strengthen their hold there. So these poor refugees are finally arriving in India after often traumatic and arduous journeys to find that they are not welcome, and are being asked to go back! Most of these people have given away all their land and belongings, have no family left, and really have nothing to go back to. It is a real tragedy.

I have been asked to appear in the documentary, but have insisted that Ed Hillary be contacted first for his permission for Khunde Hospital to be named. This kind of publicity could damage the Himalayan Trust's relationship with the Nepali Government, especially if the Chinese decide to put pressure on them, and could conceivably jeopardise our work here. If Ed says no, then I could just give a professional medical opinion on the refugees I saw without mentioning where they were treated. I have a couple of weeks to think it over before the film crew arrives.

We mentioned a young Tibetan woman who is stuck in Phurte (about one and a half hours walk from Khunde). She is 19 and became pregnant to her boyfriend, a Tibetan member of the Chinese police. They decided to run away to India, and left without even telling her parents, who have never met the boyfriend. As their group got to Phurte, the woman collapsed on the trail, in great pain, and rapidly delivered a stillborn baby. The group went on and left her with her boyfriend. As soon as he saw that the baby was dead he ran off, telling her that he would go and get a doctor and medicine. But he didn't return. She was taken in by a Tibetan butcher family, and has been working as their unpaid servant ever since. She has no money, and they keep pretending that they will get her to Kathmandu soon, as long as she keeps working hard for them.

The reporter dressed the woman up as a Sherpa and booked her on the helicopter to fly to Kathmandu with them. We all waited in the lodge at the airfield. The woman had to remain silent since she could only speak Tibetan, and everything was going well until one of our Sherpa friends unthinkingly commented to the chap sitting next to him that she was the Tibetan woman who had had her baby on the trail a few months ago.

Unfortunately, he happened to be sitting next to the airfield policeman, who suddenly leapt up and demanded that she go outside with him. We all imagined that she'd be dragged off to jail, or even shot, and were really worried about her. The reporters talked to the policeman for a long time. He initially said that there was no way she could fly to Kathmandu, but did not mention arrest. After a while he said his price was $NZ160 (over a month's wages) for him to turn a blind eye and let her fly to Kathmandu. This discussion of the bribe was done quite openly in front of a lot of the locals, and a series of bartering ensued, where the crew said they were happy to pay $NZ40 but not $NZ160.

We advised them that they were crazy to set this kind of precedent. They could fly down to Kathmandu without the Tibetan woman, register her as an official refugee, and then take her back legally in only two weeks, when they were returning anyway. Finally they decided that this was the best way to go — much to the disappointment of the policeman! The woman ended up staying with a good family in Namche, and will wait for their return.

We recently received a very excited letter from one of our Sherpa friends in Kathmandu about how the boy from Khumjung is going to marry the Duchess of York soon, "which will make him the first Nepali member of the British Royal family". In fact, he is living at Fergie's house as a guest/servant only (not as man and wife), and is soon off to America to visit his Sherpa girlfriend who is studying there. Sorry to spoil such a good story.

Last Friday, Saturday and Sunday, Diane and I helped out at the Namche dental clinic, at their request. We anaesthetised some of the local children, using ketamine, allowing the dental therapists to extract a large number of rotten teeth. The procedures all went very well, and we have arranged another visit in the future.

The head of the foreign hydroelectric power station is back in the Khumbu, and assures us that Khunde will have power by November. Now where have I heard that before? He may well be around for the next few years, since the company have now decided that they will build another hydroelectric power station at the bottom of the Namche hill for Lukla! Maybe they should get one to work before they plan the next one.

We spent some time with some members of the British Medical Everest Expedition. As well as the main climbing and research group who passed through about a month ago, there are 70 associated people (60 per cent of whom are doctors) who are trekking up to Base Camp in 10 groups. Some will then climb a few of the trekking peaks in the area. They are all collecting data such as weight, temperature, oxygen saturation, peak flow, intra-ocular pressure for the keen ones, and filling out an altitude sickness assessment form each day as they ascend. We have met some delightful and interesting people amongst them, and also a few who are not. One doctor is a fundamentalist evangelical Christian whose main aim of the trip seems to be "to bring the word of our Lord Jesus Christ to the poor heathens" who live in the Khumbu! And yes, he is about as popular as a bacon sandwich in a synagogue.

Another of the medics decided he would try hashish and bought 500 g in Kathmandu. He is an asthmatic, so instead of smoking it, he ate it mixed in with sultanas and nuts. He tried a little and nothing happened, so tried some more, still with no effect. By the time he started to feel anything, he had polished off the whole half kilo! He then spent the next 48 hours in an acute psychotic state of intense paranoia with extremely unpleasant hallucinations. To make things worse, he had chosen to try this the night before his group was due to fly up to Lukla, and the members of the group had to hold him down in a corner of the helicopter while he screamed in terror, frightening them that he might try to jump out of the aircraft! Anyway, he survived, and now feels perfectly well, apart from a well-deserved acute attack of embarrassment. He had been tossing up between trying hashish or opium. Well, I guess we'd never have met him if he'd taken the latter option!

We don't hear a lot about hash up here. Some of the down-valley porters smoke it, but it doesn't seem very popular with the Sherpas. But the next day I came across it again. I treated a young man — who I suspected of having amoebic dysentery — with metronidazole. This medicine frequently causes nausea so I also gave him some Stemetil to help with that. He came back to me a couple of days later, furious that I had "poisoned him with toxins", and that the metronidazole had made him vomit. His bloody diarrhoea was improving, so I was able to change him to tinidazole — a similar drug with less side effects — and again offered him something to help the nausea. He was not at all happy with this, and announced that he would just smoke hash all day to "numb" the symptoms, since he didn't want me "poisoning his system with unnatural drugs again". He has disappeared up valley to climb Kalla Pattar, and to "just see how it goes". He was annoyed at having to pay the consultation fee, stating that it wasn't really fair, since he didn't have any medical insurance and couldn't claim it back. I really don't think he believed me when I explained that if he did get into trouble up valley, we were the closest source of medical attention and that he would have to be carried down here. He said he'd just organise a helicopter to rescue him. "That's what the Embassy is for." He had not signed up with his embassy, of course, and would not believe me when I explained that even if he could get someone in Kathmandu to guarantee the $NZ4000 for the helicopter, it could take two or more days for the chopper to arrive. He left with each of us holding the view that the other was a complete idiot.

We were also shocked by the number of people we met in Namche who were going up to Kalla Pattar wearing only T-shirts, cotton trousers and a woollen jersey. They seemed to have very little concept of the fact that it gets very cold up there, and it was hard work convincing them to hire a warm jacket, or buy a cheap woollen hat.

Some had seen the notices I put up in the lodges and changed their itinerary, but a few had some outrageous ideas of how far they could travel each day. Interestingly, a number of these people actually held trekking guide books as they spoke to us, but had obviously not browsed through them. I don't really know what the answer is. Maybe there could be a compulsory test about the itinerary, clothing needed, climate, terrain, altitude sickness and conservation requirements of the area before a

PLOUGHING BEFORE
PLANTING RIGGIS.

trekking permit could be issued in Kathmandu. I guess that's a bit idealistic and unrealistic, but I'm sure that it would save a few lives, and make it far more likely that the tourists would enjoy their time up here.

I also met an earnest surgeon, who certainly has an interesting story. He and two friends were trekking together in the Langtang area last year. One morning one of his companions said that he had not slept well, and wanted to go on ahead without breakfast. The other two stayed in camp for about one and a half hours before they headed off after him. They were to meet at the next village, but he never appeared.

The trail is safe and easy, with no cliffs. There is an alternative route to the village, which is not very obvious, and does cross a river. When they searched this trail, they found some trekking-boot footprints and wrapping paper, so decided that he must have taken this path for some reason. They asked all around the area, with no luck, and a week later brought in tracking dogs, who found nothing. It seems unlikely that the man had been attacked by a wild animal or thieves, since the dogs picked up no scent of blood and did not find his body. The river flattens out a little further down, so if he fell or jumped into the river, it seems likely that his body would have been found down-valley.

He did not have his passport or any documents with him, and only had the equivalent of $NZ200 in cash. When I asked the surgeon if there was anything in his friend's personal history that might encourage him to stage his own disappearance or suicide, nothing seemed to come to mind. He appears to be in a stable relationship with a woman whom he had just asked to marry. He has a five-year-old son from a previous relationship, living in another country, whom he has good contact with. His father turns 80 very soon, and the man was apparently looking forward to celebrating this family event.

There is a $NZ2000 reward for any information leading to solving this puzzle. Radio broadcasts and photograph posters have been put out around the country.

The surgeon had visited the lama at Boudanaath (in Kathmandu), who a few years ago foretold where an Australian medical student, who lived in a snow cave for 40 days with only a chocolate bar, would be found. The lama told him he would find his friend working as a doctor in the Solukhumbu. The surgeon said he knew it sounds a bit cranky, but he was having one last attempt to find his friend, and had come to ask me if I knew anything about him. I can't imagine any foreigner doing anything but the usual trekking without the Sherpa grapevine knowing about it.

To me there seem to be a number of possibilities:

1. He could have decided to disappear and start a new life, for some reason. False documents and hidden money are possible, but surely there are more intelligent ways to disappear, such as on a high cliff above a raging river where no one would ever expect to find your body.

2. He could have fallen and sustained some form of amnesia. Very rare, and people probably would have commented on a confused foreigner wandering around not knowing who he was. (Although, considering some of the trekkers we meet, the locals may not have thought this so strange.)

3. He could have tied rocks to his body and thrown himself into the river, so his body would not be washed up.

4. The Yeti could have got him!

CHAPTER

24

*I*n 14 weeks we will be home! We cannot wait for the time to pass. Here is an indication of how exciting our social life is at the moment, and why we're looking forward to a more normal lifestyle when we get home. Two weeks ago we asked our friend, a foreign engineer, around for dinner the night before he was returning home for good. We made a large batch of momos (like steamed dimsims), and waited for him. At 5.30 pm it got dark, and we assumed that he'd forgotten, since most people here try to arrive at their destination before night falls. We had tea on our own at 6 pm, washed up, filled the hot-water bottles, and headed off to bed to read. Later on we were woken by a knocking in the middle of the night, with our friend saying he'd come around for dinner. We muttered away about him as we put on a few more layers of warm clothing. "He must be drunk, how inconsiderate, what does he think he's playing at?"

We unlocked the kitchen and, hiding our irritation, let him in, graciously offering to reheat the momos for him. *It was ten past seven!* We want to be home, and do normal things and stay up late, and go to bed at a normal time.

I have almost finished my study on iodine/goitre/salt-use in the Khumbu. The professor in Virginia has just sent the results of the 120 urine samples. They were surprising. Overall, there is definitely a deficiency of iodine in the Khumbu and an urgent need for supplementation. What surprised us all is that there was very little difference in urinary iodine between those people who take iodised salt and those who don't. Obviously the ones who take iodised salt are not eating enough of it. So now I have the challenging job of searching out the 60 people who provided urine samples, all over the Khumbu, to find out just how much iodised salt they actually consume. It may take me the rest of my time here.

I have also added another component to the study, trying to ascertain people's general knowledge about goitre, cretinism, and the benefits of iodised salt. I am staggered at how little the local people know about an illness that has affected them for centuries. The most common reasons given for why people have a goitre or cretinism are:

- bad karma
- drinking dirty water from a hole
- drinking the sap from a broken join of a berch tree
- eating dirty food
- being dishonest or rude to other people
- not caring about your religion.

Only a small minority know that it has anything to do with salt or iodine.

I am about to be on the telly for the third time since this job started. The first time, I was walking behind Ed Hillary as we arrived at a fancy do in Kathmandu celebrating the fortieth anniversary of him summitting Everest. Then, someone told me that they recognised me from a television documentary on the Everest marathon last year. But now, real true fame! We got the OK to talk, and I was interviewed for an hour by the television crew making the documentary about the Tibetan refugees. It was fun really, and I was pleased that I was able to relax and just ramble on. After taping me for an hour, the reporter said that they'd probably use 40-50 seconds of it. So don't blink, or you might miss me!

We recently received another letter from one of the Tibetans we treated with frostbite earlier in the year. We were very upset to hear that the farmer (from whom I had had to amputate eight fingers) had recently been killed in a bus accident on his way to meet His Holiness the Dalai Lama. It seems so unfair after all he had been through to meet the man. His daughter (who passed the sad news on to us) is settled with her sister in a Youth Education Centre in Dharamsala. One of the young monks is very happily living in a monastery in Southern India. The lama is still having trouble with his feet and is facing a bureaucratic hitch in Kathmandu which may force him to return to Tibet!

The really *big* news is that *we have hydroelectric power*! They have finally done it! We now have electric lights that are bright enough to read by at night, a computer that I can turn on any time, rather than having to go

around the back to start the generator, and a ghetto blaster that doesn't need its batteries recharged every second day. Pure luxury! Soon we may have our electric stove working, although there are one or two snags with the wiring. We have outside lights for patients who turn up in the middle of the night, and even a buzzer they can press, which rings in Kami's bedroom so he can sort them out before they need to wake me up.

Soon we may also have an international satellite telephone. Another group of foreigners have set up a solar-powered satellite phone at Shyangboche. The hydroelectric company have agreed to allow six lines to run along with their underground cables. We have applied to have one of the lines, but competition is stiff. The hydroelectric company has demanded two lines, one for Thami and another for Thamo, in return for allowing their cables to be used. Shyangboche Asian Airlines, the foreign hotel, the Sagamartha Pollution Control Committee, National Park Headquarters, the Namche mayor, and three other rich Namche businessmen and, of course, Khunde Hospital have all put in bids for the four remaining lines. So we'll just have to see how it goes.

I imagine that having a telephone will bring a number of headaches as well as benefits to the hospital. I guess it's progress, but I'm not too disappointed that our time will almost be over if/when we ever get one here.

After an extremely long monsoon, which started three weeks early and persisted well into October, winter has hit us early too! The water in the pipes started freezing almost two weeks ago, and usually we don't have that problem until well into December. It has snowed every day for the past three weeks and the thermometer drops below zero by the afternoon. At the beginning of this year, the Sherpas predicted a very long and extra-cold winter, and I am devastated to have to accept that they may well be right. The kerosene heaters do a pretty good job, but we have given up rationing the coal to once a week (as we did last winter), and are trying to keep the fire going every day, for as long as our dwindling supply of charcoal will last.

We ordered some "brickettes" from a company associated with the National Park, but have ended up with Indian coke, which burns poorly and doesn't give out much heat. Mingma and Kami seem to have sorted out how to keep it going to augment a charcoal-started fire, but it will not stay alight overnight, so every morning the stove has to be carefully relit. It is quite a job for them. We are already too cold, and unless things improve we may have to get some electric heaters to augment the kerosene ones.

One night three Australian climbers turned up. Six of them had climbed Ama Dablam — in two groups. These three men had summitted, and everything had gone well until the weather turned bad on their descent. They holed up at Camp Two during the storm, miserable and cold, all of them with frostbitten hands and feet. After several days, one of their Sherpas fought his way back up to their camp, and found that they had given up, and were just waiting there to die. He managed to drag them all down to Base Camp, carrying them in turns, abusing, pleading, and generally forcing them against their own will to get off the mountain. Six Sherpas took turns to carry the three men from Base Camp to Pangboche in a day. The next day, they made their way to Khunde Hospital on yaks, arriving miserably cold and tired in the late afternoon. We were able to warm them up, feed them, give them antibiotics for their swollen cellulitic feet, adequate pain relief and sleep, before they flew down to Kathmandu the following morning. I'm sure that all of them will end up having some minor amputations. We have been warning the many trekkers who come to visit the hospital that it is a lot colder than usual up-valley, and to hire extra clothes at Namche.

Another hazard that many do not think about is falling off the side of a cliff while engrossed in photographing the magnificent scenery. When the previous doctors were here a young woman was trekking up-valley with friends. They were crossing a glacier and she decided to take a group shot. She arranged the group, then took a tiny step back just to get a better frame. She tripped, fell on to her bottom and slid down the glacier. Initially she laughed at her silliness, but then found she couldn't grab anything to stop her slide and continued off the side of the cliff screaming to her death. Such a terrible accident, but easy to do as you try for that perfect photograph.

Here's the latest mad scheme for the tourists. On one of my walks down to the airfield, I got talking to an Asian woman who was waiting to fly out. The Asian Airlines had flown her whole group straight up to Tengboche

255

from Kathmandu. They then took three days to walk from Tengboche to Shyangboche. When I asked her if any of the group suffered any altitude sickness, she replied pleasantly, "Oh yes, we were all ill." I was relieved to see that they were all able to walk to the chopper, blissfully unaware of the risks that they had been exposed to!

I suppose that they spent their first night down at Phunki Thanka, which is lower than Namche, so possibly is no worse than the increasingly large number of trekkers who are flying straight up to Shyangboche and sleeping down at Namche. We have already treated trekkers with high-altitude sickness who got off the plane at Shyangboche and headed straight up, and quite a few who have not been able to acclimatise even with two nights in Namche. Then there are, of course, the bane of our life, the elderly tourists who arrive in hoards to stay at the foreign hotel.

Quite a lot of people seem able to get away with flying straight up to this altitude, especially if they only spend a few days here, but a significant number spend a miserable holiday feeling nauseated, headachy and washed-out. For some it is just too high too fast, and they become seriously ill with cerebral and/or pulmonary oedema. So far no one has died from this new helicopter service, but this is often thanks to emergency medical care and evacuation, and I believe that it is just a matter of time before we lose someone. I have sent an advisory notice to the Asian Airlines to be handed out to passengers, worded very diplomatically, letting them know that they should spend two nights in Namche before proceeding further, and what to do and where to go if they develop symptoms of altitude sickness, but most people we have asked have never seen a copy. Maybe the Asian Airlines think that it will hurt their business.

Another interesting outcome of the improved helicopter service is that now some of my richer Lukla patients fly up on the chopper to see me! At only $NZ20 each way (local fare), and an $NZ0.33 consultation fee covering all medicine or investigations, we are still a far cheaper option for them than going down to Kathmandu. Some of the Lukla people are amused that the Khunde doctor still walks down to the clinic there!

At other times I have received notes from trekkers asking that "the Khunde doctor jump in his helicopter and fly up" to rescue them. We may be moving into the high-tech world up here, but we're not that far gone yet, thank goodness!

Kami is on holiday anxiously awaiting Da Doma's delivery. She is due any day now.

On the 28th of November, we expected to see Kami back at work. He'd taken a couple of weeks off to help Da Doma with her delivery, and told Mingma at the market that he'd be back in a couple of days. He didn't tell Mingma how he'd got on, and Mingma didn't like to ask, so we were very anxious to see Kami and find out what had happened.

Instead of seeing him, we saw his Tamang servant boy who appeared with a note, saying that Da Doma had not had the baby yet, and that they both planned to walk over that morning and stay at the hospital until the delivery. The note went on, in a shaky scrawl, to say that Da Doma had been having intermittent backaches for two days. She'd had definite contractions since seven o'clock the previous night, and had been passing small amounts of blood throughout the night. Kami was very worried, and could I send some medicine that might help her?

Of course there was no medicine to help. I wasn't sure that I could do much to help in Thami if she was having an antepartum haemorrhage, and, for a fourth delivery, it was very likely to be all over by the time I got there. Kami sounded so distraught, and Diane's intuition said that I should be there, so as a show of support I headed off to see them. I grabbed the obstetric house-call box and threw in a pudendal block needle and the Kiellands forceps almost as an afterthought, hoping that it would be like bringing an umbrella so it wouldn't rain. We gave Kami's servant boy these things, my sleeping bag, warm clothes, and a note telling Kami that I was following and would be there soon, and that if he needed anything, the obstetric equipment was there for him to use. Mingma made sure the boy understood that this was an emergency and that he must go as quickly as he could back to Kami's house.

I headed off and was furious to see the boy just leaving the hospital, ambling along at a very slow pace. I waited for him to catch up, then said encouragingly, "Chito, chito, Thami jaunu hunchha, emergency chha," ("Hurry, hurry. Get to Thami. It's an emergency.") He just smirked and ambled on ahead.

By the time I got to Thamo, I was feeling really tired and cold. It was snowing heavily, and I was just getting over the 'flu. I stopped off for some noodle soup and chiyaa, feeling a bit guilty for not going straight on, but consoled by the thought that Kami's servant boy would already be in Thami, and Kami could send someone running along the trail if he needed me urgently.

After lunch, I arrived at Samde to find the servant boy chatting happily with a friend, without a worry in the world. I was furious. I shouted at him, told him he must hurry, that it was an emergency. He just smirked and ignored me. I called him every bad Nepali name I could think of (fortunately, my vocabulary is quite limited) and came as close to hitting someone as I ever remember.

Diane and I have had quite a lot of trouble lately with down-valley Nepali sexism, where some Nepali men will not show us any respect (but that's another story — well, many of them in fact), and I was very much at the end of my tether. It wasn't until I raised my fist to him and pushed him along that he started moving towards Thami.

Anger got me up the hill to Thami in record time, and the servant boy only just beat me to Kami's lodge.

Everything was closed up and quiet, and I had a sick feeling of premonition as I approached the house. As I entered the kitchen, Kami looked totally miserable, slumped on a bench, while Da Doma crouched over the fire, staring glumly at the wall. I thought, "Oh my God, the baby's dead." It wasn't helped when I quietly asked Kami how things were, and he mumbled, "Oh well, you know," in his typically vague fashion. I started to say how sorry I was, when he finally explained that Da Doma was still in labour, but he thought maybe it was a breech — anyway, something was definitely wrong.

I quickly examined Da Doma and found that the baby's head was well down, and there was a good strong foetal heartrate, but Da Doma was only four centimetres dilated after 20 hours of labour. It just didn't make sense for a fourth pregnancy.

I made reassuring noises, and everyone perked up a bit. Two hours later, her cervix was seven centimetres dilated, and I ruptured the membranes.

258

Within five minutes, she was fully dilated and pushing. At last, I thought, things are going right, and we got ready for the baby, which Da Doma was sure to pop out in just a few minutes.

We waited an hour, and nothing happened. I kept checking and checking, and the head stayed just above the level of the ischial spines. I could feel the posterior fontanelle on baby's scalp, and it was facing the right way. It didn't seem that the baby's head was too large. We tried Da Doma on her back, on her side, on her hands and knees (much to her disgust), but nothing would make the head progress.

Finally, I decided I'd have to try to lift the baby out with forceps. I put in a pudendal block, but after ten minutes had achieved no anaesthesia. I was pretty sure I was putting the local into the right place, but had another go. Half an hour later, there was still no hint of anaesthesia. It seemed that I had missed the pudendal nerve, but it just didn't make any sense.

The second stage of labour had now lasted over two hours, and we were all very anxious about the baby — in fact I wondered if it was already dead. I felt hysterical at the thought of my good friends losing their much-wanted baby. At one point I left the room, and though I would describe myself as an aestheist, murmured "The Lord's Prayer", and even recited "Om Mani Padme Hom" a few times, in an attempt to calm myself down.

Da Doma kept saying that it felt all wrong, nothing like her other deliveries, and that this was the worst pain she had ever had in her life. Yet the baby's position seemed OK to me, and I couldn't work out why it wasn't going well. At last Da Doma became hysterical with the pain, screaming that she didn't want a "kumar" baby, and just to get it out. Kami was also pleading with me to just get the baby out, whatever I had to do to achieve that. Now Da Doma is one of the most stoical women I have ever met. She did not even flinch when I was trying to put the pudendal block in, so I knew we had to do something.

I told Da Doma that she would just have to be incredibly brave. I covered the Kiellands forceps with obstetric cream and, as gently as I could, placed them around the baby's head, without any anaesthesia for the mother. On the next contraction, Da Doma pushed as hard as she could, and I yanked and yanked, to no effect. At this point I was beginning to feel desperate. I just couldn't work out why it was all going so terribly wrong. I tried again, twisting and pulling. I seemed to have a type of out-of-body experience where I felt that some greater being had taken over the use of my arms. Somehow, with a bit of a turn and then a very hard flexion

259

of the head, something sort of popped and suddenly everything felt normal again. I was able to gently ease the head out.

The baby looked very blue, and Kami and I looked heartbroken at its still little face. Then the baby scrunched its eyes, and I shouted, "Come on Da Doma, just one more big push, this baby's *alive!*"

Soon the baby let out a loud healthy bellow, one of the most wonderful sounds I've ever heard. When I checked and told them they had a daughter, Kami's face fell and his whole body slumped, but he recovered himself admirably in response to my very stern and pointed, "Kami, you have a healthy, *live*, beautiful little girl!"

The placenta came out easily, complete and with all its membranes intact, and we were just showing Da Doma her new daughter, when she suddenly said there was something wrong. Blood started pulsing out of her as if someone had turned a tap on full blast. Within seconds, Kami and I were up to our elbows in blood. I grabbed her uterus, and squeezed and squeezed it trying to get it to contract, while Kami injected a number of drugs to try to contract the uterus until finally the bleeding settled. I thought she'd lost well over a litre of blood.

I was able to check out that I hadn't done any internal damage with the forceps, then tried to anaesthetise her perineum to stitch up the large tear I had made pulling the baby out with the forceps. Again the local did not work. It had expired a couple of months ago, but we often use expired local anaesthetic to good effect. Da Doma has had local anaesthetic in the past, and it has worked well, so it just didn't make sense. Da Doma didn't even make a peep as she put up with me suturing her up with no anaesthetic! But the tear was bleeding a lot, and I couldn't think of anything else to do.

We finally got Da Doma cleaned up, changed the bedding, and settled her down. We tried to get the baby to suckle, since the letting down of milk releases hormones that help the uterus to contract, but Da Doma couldn't produce anything. We gave her lots of sweet tea, and were delighted when she announced that she was very hungry. We watched her polish off an omelette and a plate of Sherpa stew with great gusto, and then went off to the kitchen to have some tea ourselves.

Kami insisted that I wet the baby's head with a glass of beer, and we were just congratulating ourselves on a job well done, when we heard a terrible moan from the bedroom. We raced back in to find Da Doma looking pale and shocked. Pulling back the blankets we discovered half the bed floating in blood! Again I grabbed her uterus, while Kami injected her with whatever we could find in the obstetric house-call bag to help stop her bleeding, until we ran out! I had no books with me and had no idea how much was too much, but just knew we had to stop her bleeding. Finally it slowed and then stopped. She had certainly lost at least another litre of blood.

I said that we must carry Da Doma to the hospital. The snow was very thick on the trail, it was well below zero, and we were exhausted. It would take us at least four hours to get there. Kami asked whether another bleed like that without any more medicine could cause her to die, and I had to say that yes, I thought it probably would. They discussed this and decided that if Da Doma was going to die, it was better that she did so at home. It was all terribly upsetting.

Just then Da Doma started vomiting (a reaction from all the medicine we had given her to stop the bleeding). As we were giving her an injection of Stemetil to help stop the vomiting, we found another precious ampoule of the uterus-contracting drug.

Kami and I came to a compromise. We decided that if Da Doma started bleeding again, we would give the last ampoule and a few similar pills we had, and carry her immediately to the hospital. I really didn't think that she would survive the trip, but it was all we could come up with in the middle of the night.

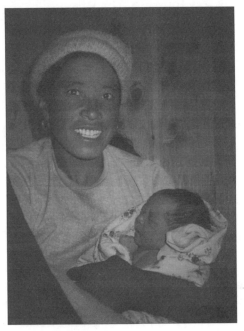

DA DOMA AND HER BABY TWELVE HOURS AFTER DELIVERY.

Da Doma continued to vomit regularly through the night, and Kami was kept very busy cleaning up after her and checking on her bleeding. He insisted that I go to bed and get some sleep! Some chance! I was so worried, I just lay awake for what I think must have been the longest night in my life.

At daybreak, I lept out of bed, all ready to help get Da Doma carried to the hospital. There she was, certainly pale and washed out, but grinning from ear to ear, baby on the breast, announcing that her bleeding had stopped completely. Indeed, everything seemed just fine. She wanted breakfast, so Kami cooked us all some toast and omelette.

THAMI MONASTERY.

Da Doma insisted that Kami go up to see the Thami lama/fortune teller so he could name their new baby. They had done this with all of their children. I was keen to accompany him, to check on the lama's congestive heart failure and arthritis, for which I had recently started treating him.

Kami wrapped up some hipflasks of rum in khaarta, and we wandered up to the monastery. Halfway up the hill, we were met by a Tibetan man who told us that the fortune-telling lama had had an enormous gastric bleed in the night, and was dead! We raced up to see the Rimpoche, but found only his wife. She confirmed that this highly respected and loved man had died, and her husband was at his house performing the appropriate pujas.

I last saw this lama about three months ago, when he'd asked me to visit to help his increasing shortness of breath. He had quite marked congestive heart failure and severe deforming arthritis. He did not have any gastritis but had had a gastric bleed many years ago, so fortunately I had given him paracetamol and heat rub (and not anti-inflammatories or aspirin, which can irritate the stomach) for his aching joints. When I gave him some frusemide and digoxin for his heart failure, he thanked me, but wanted me to know that he had foreseen his death, and that he would not last out the year. In fact, he had arranged for a larger house to be built for him, because this one was too small for everyone to come in and view his body in meditation after he'd died. I told him that I was sure that he would have much more idea than me about when his time to die would come, but that the medicine might make him feel more comfortable until that day arrived. He laughed at that, said he was happy to try my pills, and blessed me with a khaarta. It was a special experience to have had the chance to meet him.

We went back down to the lodge to give Da Doma the bad news about the lama. She seemed well, and I asked Kami to stay an extra week at home, to make sure she was fine. We started her on a few more medications to help with her recovery, and Kami arranged for his sister to move in for a month. He also employed another servant boy, so Da Doma can really take it easy while she gets over the shock and builds up her blood supply.

I was still suffering a bit of shock myself when I headed off home through the snow. I went over and over the delivery in my head, and finally came to the conclusion that baby's head was extended, and must have been a brow presentation. When I thought I was feeling the posterior fontanelle, it must have been the anterior one. I don't remember feeling any supraorbital ridges, but then the head was still high and I couldn't even feel baby's ears. I was rather blown away thinking that I had somehow managed to do a high rotational forceps delivery (only my second use of forceps ever), and realised how incredibly lucky we all were to have come out with a live baby and mother. Later, when I looked it up in the books, I read that a brow presentation is the one of the worst malpresentations because the diameter of the head is so large, and that the *only* course of action is immediate Caesarian section! Ignorance is bliss! The gods must have been smiling on us over that one!

I was still full of thought when I passed a charming old woman from Thami, who delightedly said, "Oh, you're going to Lauder!" I smiled kindly at her, thinking she must be quite confused, until I realised that Thamo was miles down the hillside. I had, in fact, taken the wrong turn at Samde, and was halfway up the hill to Lauder monastery!

I was cold, exhausted and maybe even suffering from a touch of exposure, and in my confused mind I thought of how Kami and Da Doma's last baby had died near Lauder, and that they were going to cremate the fortune-telling lama near Lauder, and maybe I was supposed to go up there. I think I half expected to see a vision, or experience some kind of religious phenomenon.

I puffed and gasped my way up the hill to the monastery, only to find the gates locked and no one about. So much for the great religious experience. It was a steep climb back down to the usual trail, and the walk back to Khunde seemed to take forever, but I made it just before dark.

The next morning, Kami's servant boy arrived with my gear and a letter from Kami saying that baby and mother were very well. When Kami returned to work, he told me that the day after the delivery, Da Doma tried to get up and start working, and couldn't understand why she felt dizzy all the time. He practically had to tie her to the bed to make her rest.

Well, the excitement of having hydroelectric power has been very short-lived. We had power for about a week. On the first day, the X-ray blew a fuse and, despite our cries that we had two patients waiting with fractures and another man with suspected tuberculosis, the Sherpa technicians seemed totally unconcerned about helping to fix it for us. In the end, Diane changed the plugs back to running it off the generator.

The next day, I turned on the computer and saw smoke pouring out of our inverter! It was fortunate that I was there to turn it all off, or we could have had a fire in the office. Apparently the wiring in the inverter is faulty. We have sent this off to Kathmandu to be repaired for the second time in a month, and have changed the plugs back so we can run the computer from the generator.

Later, we turned on the food processor to grate potatoes for riggi couer, and everything blew again! So all we had were good lights (which is still quite an improvement).

The next morning, Di wandered around the back of the hospital to find one of the Sherpa technicians and Gaga Doma's son — very drunk as usual — piggybacking a line from our fuse box up to the gompa. They were using two single phase wires with no earth, stringing it along the pathway at about three feet off the ground!

Diane went berserk, saying that obviously neither of them understood anything about the dangers of electricity, and that she refused to let them continue, since someone could be electrocuted, or the gompa or hospital could be burnt down. Gaga Doma's son got very angry and accused us of being greedy and not wanting to share our power with the gompa for their three-day Nguing Ne (fasting festival). The Sherpa technician was furious with Diane for undermining his expertise, and, I think, came very close to punching her.

We closed down the fuse box, locked the classroom, and refused to let anyone near it until one of the foreign engineers came to check the situation out. We were certainly not popular.

One of the engineers came the next morning, looked a little pale at the work that had been done, said rather patronisingly that he didn't expect much more from the Sherpas, and fixed things to be safe. He assured us there would be no further problems.

I guess there were no problems, as long as we didn't want to use any power ourselves! Every night at about five o'clock, the people in the gompa would turn their lights on and everything at the hospital would blow. So we didn't even have lights! We decided that rather than make ourselves even more unpopular we could just use the solar power and generator for the three days of the festival.

The piggyback line was removed, but still we couldn't get any of our appliances to work. We finally wrote to one of the foreign bosses. He came and just stared open-mouthed at the fuse box. He said rather shakily that he'd never seen anything like it and couldn't believe that one of his technicians had done such a thoroughly shoddy job. He said that he would rewire the whole hospital himself, and that it would take him two or three days.

That night, as we sat under our dim little solar lights, we noticed that the village looked unusually dark. In fact we couldn't see any lights on in Khunde or Khumjung.

The next morning we discovered that one of the pipes from the penstock (which carries water from the holding lake down to the turbines in the power station) had burst. This pipeline consists of about 500 pieces, each 3 m long, welded together apparently very poorly by Nepali contractors. The foreign boss cheerfully told us that this was the fourth time that the pipe had burst, and we were very lucky that they had found the break so early or we would not have had power for another year or so. As it was it would take at least 10 days for them to fix the problem.

He then went on to tell us that he is leaving for good in two weeks, and that his replacement is a mechanical engineer, who doesn't really know much about electrical things. "He has been here for a month, and knows nothing about how the power station works, but refuses to let me teach him. As soon as this pipeline leak occurred, he jumped on a helicopter to Kathmandu, saying he is tired and needs a holiday. I think he is frightened, and will be no use in the next breakdown. But by then I will be gone. I have other work to do at home."

The foreign company has also found another crack in the inlet lake.

BUILDING A CHORTEN ON THE WAY TO THAMI.

The rumour is that the Nepalis who cemented the last one sold half of the concrete mix and used a watered-down lot on it. Who knows? Anyway, he says that we should expect to be without power for a month or so next spring when the snows melt and burst through the leak in the inlet lake!

The good news is that we have received our gas cooker and bottle, and

WASHING CLOTHES.

soon will have it operating. This should improve things in the kitchen considerably without the unpleasant noise and fumes. We also have an electric heater, which, as long as the power lasts, should keep us warm over winter. The electric stove that the foreign company donated to the hospital especially for the project is also up and running, although we can only use either the oven or two of the three elements. If we try to use all three elements, or two elements and the oven, this overloads the system! This cannot be fixed, and we will just have to remember only to use the appliance partially. It is still a great improvement, but does seem an ill-thought-out gift.

Fifteen years ago the foreign company's government provided the equivalent of six million New Zealand dollars of their taxpayers' money to build a wonderful hydroelectric power station for the Khumbu Sherpas. So far it has cost them twenty million dollars!

We have been amazed to discover that we have won our bid for a satellite telephone! The foreign organisation has decided to offer only three lines at present, instead of the original six. One has gone to the Thamo hydroeletric power station, one to the National Park Headquarters in Namche, and we have a lovely red pushbutton phone for our office. It has not been connected yet, but it looks pretty impressive just sitting there.

I am concerned that the local people may make phone calls that they can ill-afford and leave us paying the bill. We will lock up the phone, and only allow it to be used with us timing the call and with money up front. I can also see hassles with trekkers needing emergency evacuation who claim that they have no money on them. After medical treatment we sometimes need to give trekkers a bill for them to pay to the Trust office in Kathmandu. Most people do, though one or two have skipped the country leaving very large unpaid bills.

The autumn Everest expeditions have now all gone home.

The elderly owner of the foreign hotel surprised everyone by getting up to the South Summit. He was apparently going well until he suddenly developed high-altitude cortical blindness. He had to turn back, and fortunately his vision returned completely after a few days.

All we had ever seen of this man was him getting off the plane at Shyangboche and riding a horse around to the hotel (now locally renamed Lower Base Camp). We had significant doubts about his fitness and ability to climb. He and another man were to attempt to summit, accompanied by 21 climbing Sherpas, and I'm afraid we were all guilty of making jokes at their expense, suggesting that possibly the Sherpas could form a chain gang and pass the foreigners up to the top, or that one of them may aspire to being the first man to summit Everest in a doka! But he did very well, and impressed us all.

From the other teams, one man suffered a stroke while on ascent, which fortunately resolved within a day at Base Camp. Another climber from the Tibetan side was unfortunate to have a stroke that looks as if it may leave him permanently disabled. But at least no one was killed on Everest this season.

I do wonder, however, if anyone has records of the number of Sherpas who are killed while working for expeditions. Of the 250 women on Norplant, I have removed the devices from three whose husbands have recently been killed in this way.

Some of the expedition groups have been enormously generous with donations of medicines to the hospital this season. This is particularly gratifying after the disappointing yield in the spring. I was also delighted that a number of groups wrote beforehand, and I was able to send them a list of the medicines most useful to the hospital. We now have a very large supply of the simple antibiotics and pain-relievers that we use regularly. I don't think we'll have to order very much of anything for the next six months.

The only sour note involved the delivery of the supplies from the British Medical Expedition. Although I stressed to many of its members how important it is to deliver the medicines directly to the hospital, they were dropped off at Shyangboche. By the time Mingma had received the message that they were there, and had dashed down to organise porterage to the hospital, all six barrels had been taken. Only the injectable medicines were left sprawled out over a nearby grass field. Some personal gifts to us from the expedition members had also been stolen. It is so important for donations to be handed directly to a member of the hospital staff, or to the Trust office in Kathmandu!

The Pheriche doctors have closed their clinic for the season. They have had a busy time and done an excellent job.

We had really enjoyed having them stay with us on their way up a few months ago. Usually only two doctors are selected for the post, and we were surprised that the two New Zealand women were accompanied by a Japanese anaesthetist. When we asked about this, they laughed and said it was a bit of a botch up and was our fault really.

The two New Zealand doctors are friends and flatmates. When the head of the Himalayan Rescue Association (a Nepali doctor we had made friends with while down in Katmandu) received their applications, he noted their shared address, assumed they were a couple, and thought that only one would be a doctor. He therefore selected another doctor to accompany them.

When they met him in Nepal and voiced surprise that three doctors had been selected for the post which has only two bedrooms, he said, "But I thought you were like Liz and Di. I understand this is a New Zealand thing."

They fortunately could see the humour in the situation, but we realised it would be quite an inconvenience since both of the New Zealand doctors had their boyfriends coming to stay for most of their time up there.

Sadly, in their last week, they had a trekker death. A 45-year-old man had followed all the correct ascent guidelines, until he got to Lobuche. He woke that morning with a mild headache and nausea, but continued on up to Gorak Shep. He had hoped to climb Kalla Pattar, but felt too unwell, and went back down to Lobuche that same afternoon. Although his Sherpa guide asked him to go on down to Pheriche, he refused. He still felt unwell, but was able to eat a large meal that night, and a small breakfast in the morning. He again refused to go down, and stayed the day in Lobuche. By lunchtime, he was drowsy, confused, and coughing up bloody, frothy sputum. He again refused to go down, and asked for a helicopter to be sent for him. He weighed 120 kgs, and no one was prepared to carry him.

One of the Pheriche doctors received the message mid-afternoon, and raced up to Lobuche with a Gamow bag and oxygen in two hours.

When she arrived, he looked dreadful. He was able to let her know that he had had no previous medical problems. The doctor gave him oxygen and put him in the Gamow bag. Fortunately, before she gave him any medications, she discovered that a "helpful" foreign paramedic had given him a 500 mg slow-release Diamox tablet, and 100 mg of intramuscular dexamethasone! This is 25 times the recommended dose, and at first she would not believe that this had been given, until the man brought the packaging to show her, which indeed was one ampoule of 100mg/5mls of dexamethasone! Apparently a doctor at home had given this to the paramedic for him to use in case he found anyone with altitude sickness on his holiday.

Then another doctor wandered over and said, "I know the Himalayan Rescue Association doesn't recomend the use of diuretics in treatment of high-altitude sickness, but I just gave this man 40 mg of frusemide." All the Pheriche doctor could think of to say was weakly, "No, we don't recommend it at all," and he wandered off. Now, it is understandable when medical people who do not understand altitude sickness give a diuretic to treat the pulmonary and cerebral oedema, but this is entirely the wrong thing to do. Although the man's lungs and brain had too much fluid, paradoxically, he was severely dehydrated, and giving him a diuretic (which made him lose more fluid) only worsened his condition.

The Pheriche doctor was finally able to convince the man's companion to pay the porters a large amount of money to carry the patient down to Pheriche. She only kept him in the bag for an hour, wanting to make the most of the dwindling daylight. They had great difficulty with the weight of the load and, finally, at the top of the Dugla hill, the frame of the stretcher snapped and they gave up. This poor, ataxic, almost unconscious man who was remarkably breathless and coughing up copious bloody, frothy sputum, then had to walk down to Dugla himself, supported on each side. It took them two hours to get from the Sherpa memorials at the top of the hill down to Dugla (usually an easy 15-minute stroll).

At Dugla the man collapsed. None of the lodges would let him inside since no one wanted to risk having a dead body in their house! Fortunately, one of the Pheriche health workers arrived. One of the lodge-owners is his sister-in-law, and he convinced her to let them in. They gave the man more oxygen and put him in the Gamow bag, while the porters were fed and talked into trying to carry him on down to Pheriche. These 50 kg men decided that they would each put him on their back and carry him in short relays.

They had just carried him out of the lodge when he suddenly said that he needed some oxygen and promptly died! The Pheriche doctor did cardiopulmonary resuscitation on him for about 20 minutes, with no effect, and she said that he suddenly looked so dead that she didn't feel that they had any chance at all.

The stretcher was able to be mended, and his body was carried down to the Pheriche clinic. The man's companion had previously been given permission to have him cremated up in the Khumbu, should anything happen, but the local police would have none of that, and his body was flown down to Kathmandu the next morning.

Certainly three factors significantly contributed to this man's death. First of all, he had the unreasonable expectation that he could be rescued by helicopter within a few hours and because of this did not descend as he should have. Secondly, his large bulk made it difficult for him to be carried down to an appropriate low altitude. And thirdly, the well-intentioned attempt of other people to help him by giving him entirely inappropriate medication undoubtedly contributed to his demise. It was a sad end to the autumn trekking season.

Another horror story! The Asian trekkers still manage to astound me. Last month I met an English doctor who had seen an Asian woman being carried *up* Kalla Pattar in a Gamow bag. When he asked what the group was doing, they explained that she had bad altitude sickness, but had paid all that money and didn't want to miss out on the view from the top of the hill. They would not listen to his insistence that they must turn back, and he left them to continue on up. We didn't hear of a helicopter going up-valley to collect any dead bodies, so we assume that it wasn't the last thing she ever saw!

We saw a 22-year-old Japanese student the other week, who was extremely lucky (or unlucky, depending on how you look at things). When we saw him at the hospital, he was confused, short of breath, producing copious sputum, and really didn't know what had happened to him. We treated him for pneumonia and high-altitude cerebral oedema and pulmonary oedema. Over the next few days, we were able to fill in the gaps with the help of the Sherpa grapevine.

He had been trekking on his own, without even a porter, and had been attacked. He was found on the trail near Lobuche (4928 m), unconscious, with blood pouring out of his nose. The trekking group who found him organised for some porters to carry him down to Pheriche. However, because the trekking season had officially finished, the clinic was closed.

Finding that the clinic was closed, the porters who brought him down, tried to get him into a lodge. None of the lodge-owners would let him stay because he looked too unwell, and they were frightened that he might die.

So the porters put him inside his sleeping bag and just left him lying unconscious outside, and went on up to join their group! He spent two days and nights sleeping outside at 4272 m, in temperatures well below zero, and, finally, somehow managed to get himself down to Deboche (3750 m). One of the lodges took him in, and he lay dying in one of the back rooms.

Another Japanese man was staying at nearby Tengboche, and heard about his compatriate who was dying in the Deboche lodge. Although he did not know this man, he went to the lodge, aborted his own holiday, and arranged for him to be carried to the hospital. He then spent the next week caring for him, buying food from the lodges, getting him to the toilet and generally making sure he survived.

The student refused to fly to Kathmandu from Shyangboche, and finally made it down to Lukla to catch the cheaper plane. He was still very confused when we saw him. He had no recollection of the assault, and no sense that this very kind man had sacrificed his holiday for him and undoubtedly saved his life. All I could do was put a letter in with his passport, explaining what had happened to him and giving details of his Good Samaritan, in the hope that he or his family might be able to thank his helper in some appropriate way when he gets home.

Bad luck to have been attacked and then refused a bed in Pheriche, but amazingly lucky to have survived.

There were some incredible dust storms yesterday (fortunately not removing any of the monastery roofs this time). We watched in horror and amazement as a mini-tornado whipped across the ridge behind the hospital, picking up trees and throwing them high into the air as it moved along! We were very concerned when we saw a large group of villagers sprinting up the hill, thinking that someone might have been up there and been badly hurt, but it turned out that the mad rush was for people to initial the fallen trees. One man got to claim 20 trees all for himself! A real windfall, you could say!

CHAPTER

26

*T*here's been a lot of snow falling this winter, and it's been much colder than last year. Days rarely get above minus 5°C, and often go down to minus 10 or 15. Real cabin fever stuff, although Di and I have been determined to go for at least one and usually two walks every day, even in one-metre-deep snow. It helps pass the time and keeps us active, and almost every day we end up being asked into someone's home for a cup of tea. I think the locals think we're quite mad walking about in the snow for no particular reason.

One problem with the cold weather is that there's been very little water available. The pipes from the spring freeze up, and we go for days and days without any water supply. Showers or even a basin wash are very rare luxuries. I guess all that dirt gives us another layer to keep warm with, but we can't wait to be able to shower *every* day and wear clean fresh clothes. We are still filling our hot-water bottles at night, but re-use the water the next morning. No unnecessary flushing of the loo or rinsing of hands allowed. Just as well it's too cold for most of the bugs.

We get the water first, so the poor villagers have had to do without water for a lot longer. One day last week we had a lot of sunshine in the morning, and everyone hoped that the pipes would unfreeze. We counted 40 empty jerrycans lined up at the village water tank, with everyone eagerly waiting. Sadly, it clouded over again, and no one was able to get any water. The unpopular alternative is to walk down a very steep hill to the rivers near Phurte or Phunki Thanka and carry the water load back up to the village (about a three-hour round trip). Most families are having to do this several times a day in this weather.

We are burning all five kerosene heaters and two electric ones all day, and keep a couple going at night so that our own pipes won't freeze up and burst. I am so sick of wearing five or six layers of clothing. Getting dressed in the morning is quite a performance. It's a long time since I've seen any skin! However, visiting local friends in their houses during our walks makes us realise how lucky we are. On snowy days most families just spend the day snuggled up together, too cold to do anything else.

One morning we were called to see Gaga Doma's 52-year-old son, who had got drunk and fallen down the stairs of the house. He had lain there all night, probably unconscious, until he was found by a friend the next morning. He had sustained a nasty infraorbital fracture, but was alert and oriented and otherwise well. As is expected with these fractures, his face swelled considerably — to the extent that he could hardly open his eyes. We visited a few times, but each time he was very drunk, so decided not to give him any pain relief, which could react badly with the six bottles of rum he was drinking a day!

He didn't seem to get any worse, but wasn't improving much. We weren't achieving much, so his family called in the lhawa. The lhawa went into a trance and then started abusing Gaga Doma's son. He said that Gaga Doma's god was very angry at him for beating his mother and making her leave her own house. The son was shocked when the lhawa announced things that he felt no one else could know, such as when he broke his mother's special eating bowl and cup many months ago. The lhawa said that the gods were too angry with him, and would not be appeased. The man would die soon.

Gaga Doma's son was terrified, and the family immediately arranged for him to go to Kathmandu to see a specialist.

The next morning, he walked supported by his friends towards Shyangboche, chatting away to them. Suddenly, he threw his head back and collapsed. He tends to be a practical joker and his friends laughed, thinking he was acting the fool. But when they bent down to check him he was dead! It just doesn't make any sense to me. There was no particular reason for him to die.

We were all very shocked, and I felt terrible in that I may have missed something. He was not an altogether good man but we were still distressed by his death. He was cremated on the top of the ridge, near his half-brother's chorten.

There has been a lot of concern around the village about this man's nerpa causing trouble for Khunde people.

It is very bad luck for his family that he died on the trail. At his funeral, his brother got drunk and fell down the same set of stairs. He was not seriously hurt, but the local wisdom is that the man's ghost pushed his brother. Most people believe that the drink killed Gaga Doma's son, but a significant number agree with the lhawa, who said that his mother's god was angry with him for mistreating her, and caused his death. Interestingly, I seem to be the only person who is worried that I could have done more to help him.

Gaga Doma returned, and appears to be devastated at the death of her son. We thought she would be relieved, but, despite the ill-treatment she received from him, she obviously loved him a great deal. The first evening she arrived back, she slipped and fell in the house and sustained a large bruise in exactly the same place as her son's injury. Even I was a little freaked out by that, which seemed too much of a coincidence. The lhawa has been very busy doing exorcisms for many of the villagers, who are frightened that the man's ghost will move from Gaga Doma's house to their own.

In the end, the entire village got together and organised a huge good-luck puja. Each Khunde household contributed $NZ10 to pay for the highly respected lama from Pangboche to come down and bless the village.

It was a very impressive puja, culminating in the entire village making a procession through Khunde, with the monks blowing horns and clarinets and banging drums, carrying a large zinshung (two-metre-high woven web, like a nenga) and many flags. Many of the villagers carried an item of old clothing, and these were all piled in a heap near to the zinshung. The monks did an interesting puja, with everyone joining in, throwing rice, clapping hands, and shouting "woo-woo" in all the right places. Then kerosene was thrown over the pile and a very impressive fire was lit. People got very excited, and some ripped clothing off their backs and added it to the good-luck fire. It seemed such a pity to see the zinshung engulfed by flames too, after all the hard work involved in making it. It was a very happy good-luck puja, and everyone seemed delighted with the day. Hopefully the ghost will have moved on.

It is great to have Gaga Doma back home. She says that she will stay here now, and we are enjoying dropping around every day for a cup of tea and a sign-language chat. We both love her.

Kami went to see a 70-year-old lama from near Lauder. He has named their daughter, Dawa Phutti (Monday — bring a boy next time). Di and I are disgusted, and even Kami is embarrassed. They have wisely decided not to have any more children, and I have already inserted a Norplant device. For a while they thought about naming their daughter themselves. Because their last baby died, Da Doma wanted to name her Kami or Serki (a low-caste name, so the gods would not bother to take this baby from them) but Kami was very much against this. Da Doma is quite a traditional woman and feels strongly that if the lama chose this name, then that's what it should be. We have imposed our own cultural values, and call the baby Ang Dawa (Young Monday). Kami quite likes that and only calls her Dawa Phutti when he is with his wife.

The Christmas party went well again this year. All of the staff's families turned up, with Temba, Ang Doolie and Tsumje's brother making a total of 17. It was lovely to see the 27-day-old Dawa looking so alert and well. Da Doma also appears to be completely recovered. Everyone seemed to enjoy their presents, and the chicken curry I made went down a lot better than the hamburgers and chips of last year.

Losar (Sherpa New Year) was late this year, starting on the 31st of January. Kami advised us not to have our usual hospital party, in deference to Gaga Doma's son's recent death. However, we did attend a number of the local parties, and had a great time. People are beginning to realise that we will be going soon, and are making a bit of a fuss of us.

Three more trekkers have died of altitude sickness in the last month! On the 28th of December, a 27-year-old Hong Kong man died at Na (in the Gokyo Valley). A week later a Japanese man died at Macchermo. Two days later another elderly Japanese man became unwell in the Thami Valley, and died as he was being carried down from Shyangboche. The most frustrating thing is that, once again, the first we heard about any of these people was when the helicopters flew up to collect their bodies!

There really is a need for a health clinic in the Gokyo Valley. It should be run by someone who speaks good English, and has training and the

MAKING TIBETAN TEA.

equipment to start treatment for altitude sickness. However, finding someone this capable who is happy to live in Macchermo or Gokyo is a real problem.

We were sad to hear of a young Thamo Kami woman who committed suicide three weeks ago. She was only 19, and married to a Manang man who spent all of his meagre income from chopping firewood and breaking rocks on chang and rakshi. He would come home and beat her and their one-year-old son. She had a miserable life, not having any money to buy food or clothing for herself or her child, and finally decided to end their lives by throwing herself and her son into the river.

We are experiencing another measles epidemic. Last year it was in Pangboche, the year before, Phortse, and now closer to home. A 30-year-old man and a 14-year-old girl have died of measles in Thami this last week. An old Tibetan nun is very ill down in Namche, and is expected to die. We are desperately vaccinating everyone we can, but keep running out of the vaccine.

We have had our first death at the hospital. A 20-year old servant from Namche was admitted with bronchopneumonia and mesenteric lymphadenitis (stomach pain) secondary to measles. We tried everything we could, but by the third night here his oxygen saturations were down to 31 per cent (and then to an unbelievably low 11 per cent) when he was off supplementary oxygen. Because people were frightened to stay in the ward in which he died, we paid a local lama to come and do a good-luck puja to clear out the teep from the ward. It seems to have worked and new admissions are happy to move into the boy's old room.

Because he was only a servant, it took a while for his owners to organise the disposal of his body. When the Tibetan butcher (whose other roles in life are cleaning out toilets and carrying the dead) arrived, rigor mortis had set in, and they were unable to straighten the boy out. It was very ghoulish as the butcher borrowed a hammer and tried to break the boy's bones to bend him into a sitting position. He was unable to set one leg, and in the end carried the boy on his back through the village, with one ungainly leg stuck out into mid-air. The group didn't know what to do with the leg so tied a khaarta around it. In this undignified position, the poor boy was carried through the village and buried by the yak fields.

Five Sherpas have been jailed for a number years for smuggling heroin into the States. One from Khumjung, a Thami man, and three Solu Sherpas. At first we heard that the husband of one of our health workers had been caught. He usually goes to the States for three months each year, courtesy of a sponsor. This year he decided not to go, and sold his passport and visa to the Thami drug smuggler for a little over $NZ8000. It took a while for the US officials to realise that the Thami man was using a false passport and visa. Now our health worker's husband has no passport, and his sponsor will have to explain to the US officials why he has been recommending this man for a visa each year! I guess there'll be no more trips to the States for him.

A couple of families in the village who used to be friends had a fight at the end of last year, and are now feuding. The first family had arranged for some foreigners to sponsor the other family, saying that they were very poor. (Not entirely true, but I guess they're not rich either.) So, for the past few years, the hospital passes on $NZ25 every month for this family.

After the fight, the first family wrote to the sponsors and told them that these people no longer needed the sponsorship, and that it should be stopped. They did in fact stop it, but one of our workers found out about it and wrote to Ed Hillary saying that it wasn't fair. He agreed, and has decided the Trust will pay this family $NZ33 every month instead!

When the Trust people wrote to the family telling them what had happened, we tried to make a joke of it, saying that they should ask the other family to write again, and maybe they'd get a bigger sponsorship raise.

But, oh no! The feud is really on now. The family who is getting the sponsorship have spent their first payment getting the now very famous Namche lhawa to do a bad-luck puja for the other family! They are praying every day that their sons will be killed in a motorcycle accident in Kathmandu, or their helicopter will crash when they next fly up here!

I was very shocked, thinking that this was hardly the Buddhist way, and that the people who had paid for the curse would be terribly upset if, by chance, something did happen to the other family's sons. Kami explained that, no, they would be very pleased, and feel that it was the gods' justice and the other family's karma if they came to harm.

It's interesting that I have come to feel that most of the Sherpas I know are very gentle, caring people. In general, if someone harms you, the Buddhist way is to leave any retribution to the gods. People who do bad things have their own bad karma to face in the future. Apart from the occasional drunken man who gets a bit pushy, I don't think I've ever felt so physically safe from harm by other humans. I think nothing of walking around at night, or not locking up the flat when we retire for the evening. So seeing this side of things has been rather a shock.

The hydroelectric engineer explained to us before he left that we shouldn't expect to have the telephone connected before we leave. The Nepali telephone "experts" had a meeting with the company, deciding that they would get together a couple of days later, and the foreigners would show them how to connect the line. The next day, the Nepali telephone people dug up the line on their own, tried to connect the phone, pronounced it "broken", decided that it was too cold to stay up here, and flew immediately back to Kathmandu, saying they would return after winter! The engineer had tried the lines and said they worked perfectly well, but suggests that the Nepali contractors found the temperature too low to bother staying the few extra days it would have taken to set the service up. We weren't too concerned about having a telephone anyway. Despite his prediction, a couple of weeks later another team of Nepalis turned up and set the thing up.

We now have an international phone at the hospital! It's all a bit of a shock to the system. One evening the phone rang in the office. We all sat there a bit stunned — not quite knowing what to do. Finally I hesitantly picked up the phone and heard from Lynley and David, the previous Khunde doctors, who had rung from Christchurch just to see how we were all getting on and to talk to Kami and Mingma again. It was all a bit too much for us to comprehend. After almost two years of isolation it seemed so odd to be talking so easily to someone on the other side of the world.

We have had to pay a $NZ420 deposit, then will be charged $NZ40 every month. For this, we can make one hundred local calls (Lukla and above) each month. After that, we are charged $NZ0.04 per local call (however long). Phoning home will cost $NZ10 a minute, which is still well above our budget — so sorry Mum and Dad, no phone call home. If we want a fax machine at the hospital, this would cost $NZ20 per month. We can also set up a modem for the computer if we want. I don't think we can cope with that much technology just yet. We'll leave it up to our replacements.

The place is really changing. There are now four television satellites in Namche. One Khunde family is just about to set theirs up and already have a video. The water-driven flour mills will soon be redundant. One family in Khumjung has bought an electric flour mill. And . . . wait for it . . . another family is building a bakery in Khumjung. They will also have a shop in Namche. Anyone for cream buns with shakpa? It's all a bit much for me. About time we went home, I think!

It has been a very long two years for us, but amongst all the loneliness, boredom and isolation we have achieved a few things. I'm sure that in years to come we will look back on this time as a very special life experience.

Di and I have trekked up to Everest Base Camp, and across the Cho La Pass into Gokyo. We've also been to the Thami Valley a number of times. I, of course, went to Bung (well, enough said about that!). I also completed the Everest Marathon, which was a real thrill for me, definitely a once-in-a-lifetime experience!

Medically, it hasn't been as challenging as I had hoped for. However, I have still been able to deal firsthand with cases that in New Zealand would be referred to a specialist before I could blink. Dealing with and getting to know our Tibetan refugees with frostbite was a very intense experience that I am never likely to forget. We are delighted to find that we are still writing to each other after almost a year.

I was able to set quite a few fractures with varying success. The obstetrics load was very quiet, but I was extremely lucky with three difficult deliveries.

We seem to have got a grip on altitude sickness, but it is still heartbreaking to have several people die of this condition unnecessarily every year.

It has been fascinating to practise amongst a population where traditional attitudes about health and religious beliefs are so much part of their normal daily lives.

We have been very fortunate to have been included in a number of religious events, such as the Gen Lama's 22-day meditation after his death, and his cremation. We have also attended funerals, weddings and baby-naming ceremonies (not usually open to foreigners).

In general, the local people have been very kind and welcoming. We have enjoyed being "big fish in a small pond", and doubt that we will ever experience such a privileged and respected role again. We've met some wonderful people, and some not-so-wonderful but certainly memorable! I can't say that we've made any really deep meaningful friendships (language and culture are larger barriers than you'd think), but we've made a few friends who we'll miss when we've gone.

We have made some very good friendships with some of the trekkers/foreigners we've met up here, and hope to continue those ties. We have also been delighted by the many friends who have written, keeping us up with what's been going on at home. We've really missed our friends and family, and have come to realise how lucky we are to know so many really good people. I've found it very difficult to be away from my dog, Matt, and just can't wait to see him.

Academically, I've been able to use our abundance of free time to good use. I've written a few soft articles about the job here, frostbite/amputation, traditional Sherpa medical beliefs and altitude sickness. The iodine study looking at iodised salt use, goitre rates and disability, especially cretinism, around the Khumbu has kept us all busy, and has produced some interesting results. I'm looking forward to being able to publish an article about it.

I've also read 130 books (Di has read many more!), which has rekindled my almost forgotten love of reading (replaced by a lifetime of television and videos). Television and video are still great forms of entertainment and information, but more alternative and thought-provoking issues and more depth of description can be produced on the written page. Until I started reading books again, I don't think I'd realised how much of what I watch on television is a watered-down, middle-of-the-road portrayal of life. Rather an insidious form of propaganda and social control really. I hope that I'll keep reading when I get home.

It has been wonderful for Diane and I to discover that we get on very well, even under difficult circumstances. At times we've had to depend on each other an awful lot, and have come across very few problems. We have enjoyed working together, and have both been impressed and delighted to realise each other's particular work and coping skills. We make a good team that, I think, will last out the distance very nicely.

But the experience has not been entirely positive. I do not think that living in an isolated and often very boring situation has been emotionally healthy for either of us. It is very hard not to become a little paranoid and petty about small day-to-day things which, in a busy, stimulating lifestyle, we would barely notice. In general, the Sherpa hospital staff are good people, but there have been considerable difficulties living in such close proximity with people who have quite different standards of acceptable and unacceptable behaviour. Let's just say that it's been a growing, learning experience. I'm not sure that it's made me a more tolerant or better person though!

Overall, I guess you don't have to have thoroughly enjoyed an experience for it to have been worthwhile!

*T*he replacement doctors have arrived. They seem to be lovely people —
a husband and wife, both doctors, and their two daughters aged four and
six. We have handed the hospital over to them and they seem to be very
competent. Maybe it is the North American style of medicine, but they
both seem to do things a lot more thoroughly than me. I am worried that
I have been negligent or lax in what I've done. I had been concerned that
I would be jealous of their arrival, wanting to possessively cling to my
hospital, but I am ready to go, and have the utmost confidence in their
ability to do an excellent job.

On the night that they arrived we put on a
coming-going party in the hospital kitchen. We were
packed in like sardines as the villagers had a chance
to see the new doctors and especially their blonde-

THE COMING-GOING
PARTY, WITH THE 5.2
KG BABY I DELIVERED,
BY SYMPHYSIOTOMY,
DANCING ON THE
TABLE.

haired little girls. The party went well into the night and was enjoyed by all.

The next morning Diane and I visited Gaga Doma. We walked in and signed that we were flying off soon. She immediately burst into tears, which started us off, and we all huddled together and sobbed against each other's faces. It was more emotional than I'd expected and when we walked away it physically hurt to realise that we will never see her again.

During our last two days people just kept coming and coming. They brought chiyaa and chang and khaarta. We would sit together, hold hands and say our goodbyes. Some were quite formal and controlled. We were told that for the rest of our lives we would have Sherpa good luck, and things would go well.

At other times it was very hard to say goodbye. Temba and Ang Doolie brought presents, and both cried and hugged us. Ang Doolie started shaking uncontrollably and keening, and Di and I howled our eyes out with her. I am not used to such public displays of emotion and struggled to control myself, but each time I would calm down another good friend would turn up and the convulsions of tears would start again. I was embarrassed for the new doctors, who must have wondered what they'd come across. This went on for almost two days and was exhausting, though certainly an experience never to be forgotten. At the end of the second day Tsumje just went home without a goodbye, and we were surprised and hurt by the sudden departure. An hour later she came back with her entire family, all dressed up in their best clothes. The crying and hugging started all over again, and it was particularly sad to kiss Tsumje's daughter goodbye. She didn't know what all the emotion was about and was quite upset by the scene.

On the morning our flight was due, we burnt a juniper branch in front of the hospital to give us good luck in our travels. Kami and Mingma walked with us to the airport and insisted on carrying our bags for us. We had been disappointed not to see Gaga Passang before we left, but as we walked past her house she ran out with khaarta for us and we hugged and cried again. At the pass just coming out of the village we stopped and tied a khaarta each to one of the prayer flags. This is covered with khaarta and is said to ensure that we have a safe return to the village one day.

At the airport we said goodbye to a few other people and waited for the helicopter. Mingma hugged us both and headed back. We didn't know what to say to Kami. We had been through so much together. He had been such a friend we had grown to love. When the helicopter arrived, everything happened so quickly. Kami also didn't seem to know what to do. He gave us a quick hug and ran off. All the thankyous and things I'd meant to say to him were left unsaid as we scrambled on to the helicopter and rapidly disappeared down the valley.

I wondered if we would ever come back. We were so happy to be going home finally yet we didn't know how things would go for us. We had no money, no jobs, and would start off living with my parents. As much as we wanted to leave I knew that we would miss this place, and that it would become a more and more special experience as time went on.

POSTSCRIPT

Since the writing of this book we have been very sad to hear of the death of Rob Hall. While performing his duties as a guide, having summitted Everest for the fifth time, he found himself unable to get off the mountain. He was a great man with a good soul and will be sadly missed. Our hearts go out to his wife Jan Arnold and daughter Sarah.

Glossary

aachhu	sorrow / sadness / cold temperature
acetazolamide (Diamox)	a carbonic anhydrase inhibitor used for altitude sickness
allergic rhinitis	constantly dripping nose
amjik	Tibetan doctor
amoxycillin	pencillin based antibotic, eg, Amoxil
ang	young
ataxic	walking as if drunk
bandh	strike
BaDaasahib	big boss; Ed Hillary
bideshi	foreigner
Bier block	a method of providing anasthesia to the forearm and hand
bonbon	lolly; sweet
Burr hole	hole drilled into the skull to let blood out
Caesarian section	operation where the baby is surgically delivered through the mother's abdomen
catheter	tube generally passed along a vessel to control the flow of fluid, eg, urine / blood
cellulitic	infected, red, swollen tissue
cerebral oedema	swollen brain
chang	rice wine
chiyaa	tea
chorten; stupa	religious statue with eyes, usually at village entrance
chronic obstructive airways disease	long-term damage to lungs
congestive heart failure	weakened heart muscle producing an overload of fluid especially in the lungs and ankles
Cheyne-Stokes	abnormal breathing pattern — usually a sign that death is imminent
co-trimoxazole	antibiotic, eg. Bactrim, Septrin
cretinism	low intelligence, short stature, deaf-mute condition, caused by the pregnant mother being hypothyroid due to lack of iodine
Clostridium	anaerobic bacteria
Clostridium perfringens	causes gas gangrene
CT scan	computed tomography, which provides a cross-sectional view
Damai	tailor; untouchable caste
Darsain	major Nepali holiday
dental dam	a square of latex rubber used by dentists to isolate a tooth / protection when performing oral sex
"Das klickers"	colloquial term for European trekkers who walk quickly using a ski pole in each hand
Depo Provera	progesterone contraceptive injection lasting three months
dexamethasone	steroid used to reduce brain swelling
dhaal bhaat	rice with bean curd or vegetables

digoxin	a drug to regulate the heart beat and help congestive heart failure
doka	pack carried with a band around the forehead
Dumje	religious festival in June
emphysema	long-term collections of blocked air in lung tissue
episiotomy	cut made between the vagina and anus to help delivery
fontanelle	soft area between scalp bones in a baby
frusemide	a drug which expels excess fluid from the body — a diuretic or water pill
Gaga	old person — a term of respect
Gamow bag	portable recompression chamber
Gen	Tibetan term of respect for older people
ghee	clarified butter
gompa	temple; chapel
hardtal	a type of poison
infraorbital	below the eye
ingi	Sherpani dress
inguinal hernia	lump of bowel pushed through a gap in the groin muscle
ischaemic	lacking blood supply
Kami	blacksmith / untouchable caste; Sherpa name for first son after a boy has died
ischial spines	part of the bones making up the pelvic outlet
kani peyo	"Where are you going?" (Sherpa)
ketamine	An LSD derivative used as a general anaesthetic
khaadeina	"I don't want to eat / drink" (Sherpa)
khaarta	silk scarf given as a farewell, thankyou or blessing
khukuri	large Nepali knife / machete
Khumbila	god of the area; mountain next to the hospital
Kielland forceps	instrument similar to salad tongs used to lift the baby's head out during a delivery
kumar	female "cretin" / person with a disability
kur	male "cretin" / person with a disability
lhawa	traditional healer / spiritual medium
longin	beggar; also the hospital dog's name
loong	Tibetan word for depression
losar	Sherpa New Year
lu	water spirit
Manang	one of the Nepali races
mani	prayer
Mani-Rhimbdu	religious festival in April and November
memsahib	madam
menarche	first menstrual period
mendung	junior lhawa (spirit medium)
metronidazole	an antibiotic, eg, Flagyl
Mingma	Tuesday
momos	Tibetan steamed meat in pastry jackets
Monteggia fracture	fracture / dislocation of the elbow
motor neuron disease	degenerative neurological disorder mainly affecting the periphery

moxibustion	a form of acupuncture involving burning herbs
myocardial infarction	heart attack
nak	female yak
Namaskar	more respectful Nepali greeting to someone of higher status
Namaste	Nepal / Sherpa greeting with hands in prayer position meaning literally, "I bow to the god in you."
nawa	person responsible for keeping stock out of the village
nebuliser	asthma machine which converts liquid medicine into a gas to be inhaled
nenga	cross with bright cotton webbing to exorcise bad spirits
nerpa	ghost
nifedipine	calcium antagonist used for pulmonary oedema at altitude / antihypertensive medication
Nirvana	heaven
Norplant	five-year contraceptive device placed under the skin
O-Sho	procession to bless the crops before monsoon
oedema	swelling due to excess fluid
oesophageal varices	engorged veins in gullet often secondary to alcoholism
Om Mani Padme Hom	Buddhist prayer — "Hail to the Jewel of the Lotus"
paraphimosis	retraction of the foreskin causing painful swelling of the glans
Passang	Friday
pem	bad spirit
perineum	the pelvic floor/region between the thighs
Phangi	monsoon parties — everything eaten will go to fat!
phogmar	herbal root believed to cure poisoning
Phu	Thursday
Phutti	"bring a boy next time" (a Sherpa girls' name)
pre-auricular	in front of the ear lobe
pudendal block	a local anaesthetic which numbs the skin between the vagina and anus
puja	blessing
pulmonary oedema	fluid in the lungs
pung	Sherpa word for depression — usually post-partum
queeri	derogatory term for a foreigner
rakshi	alcoholic spirit similar to schnapps
riggi	potato
riggi couer	potato or buckwheat pancake
rilu	herbal pill
Rimpoche	reincarnate lama
Rs	rupees (25Rs = NZ$1)
Sagamartha	Nepali name for Mount Everest
sahib ·	sir
sciatica	lumbago / back pain radiating to buttock or leg
Serki	shoemaker / untouchable caste
shakpa	meat and vegetable stew / Sherpa stew
sharman	spirit medium / healer / lhawa
Sherpa stew	meat and vegetable stew / shakpa
sheto	funeral blessing

shey	"eat / drink" (Sherpa)
sirdar	Sherpa expedition organiser / leader
somma	rancid cottage cheese
soongtaak	lama's diagnosis obtained by throwing dice and reading books
Stemetil	anti-nausea medication
Stonewall riots	major event in Gay Liberation movement where New York gays refused to allow police to expel them from the Stonewall club
stupa	religious statue
subclavian	below the clavicle/collar bone
supraorbital ridges	prominent bones above eyes
subcutaneous emphysema	the presence of air or gas under the skin
subdural haematoma	bleeding between the brain and the skull
supracondylar fracture	fracture above the elbow joint
sur	hot coal with nak butter used to exorcise bad spirits
symphisiotomy	separation of the symphysis pubis / pubic bone to widen the pelvic outlet
takhari	curry
Tashi Delek	Tibetan greeting meaning good luck
teep	pollution
tempo	a three-wheeled motorbike / taxi
Thok	bad age
tika	dot, usually in middle of forehead, worn by Hindu women
touche	"thank you" (Sherpa)
toxaemia	high blood pressure and oedema in late pregnancy
tsengi	blessed herbs from the lama
Tsumje	"no more boys" / a Sherpa girls' name
Ventouse extractor	suction cup that fits on to a baby's head to help pull the baby out during delivery
zee	precious black and white stone, possibly originally Viennese
zendi	Sherpa wedding
zinshung	large religious statue made of wooden and cotton web
zum	female cross-breed between yak and cow
zupchok	male cross-breed between yak and cow

REFERENCES

Gauri Pradhan, *Misery Behind the Looms*, Child Workers in Nepal Concerned Center, Kathmandu, 1993.

Omar Sattaur, *Child Labour in Nepal* — A report by Anti-Slavery International and Child Workers in Nepal Concerned Centre, 1993.

Prativa Subedi, *Nepali Women Rising*, Women Awareness Centre, Nepal, 1993.

Priscilla Annamanthodo (ed), *Red Light Traffic* — *The Trade in Nepali Girls*, produced by ABC/Nepal, 1993.

BHAKTAPUR.